Praise for
Corrie and the Rose Accordion

"A crafted, inspirational true-life story at the level of Angela's Ashes, that comes only once in a generation; an unyielding emotional and living reminder for us to appreciate all that we have, and how - in the end - what matters most is family and helping those in need. Corrie and the Rose Accordion is a literary beacon showing us how the pure heart of a little girl can conquer the staggering adversity of history's most evil event. This book is a keeper, a must-read for all - a biography that flows like a masterfully depicted epic."

—Vic Schukov, long-standing author/journalist/ biographer; interviewer of thousands of everyday heroes.

"A truly notable recant of [Corrie's] experience throughout this time...As I read, my heart was heavy with sadness...[Corrie] is a true heroine."

—Cheryl Langevin, Sick & Visiting Representative, Brighton Legion, Branch 100. Formerly Chair of Raise the Roof Committee.

Corrie and the Rose Accordion

Dutch Girl
Hitler's War
A Symbol of Hope

By Liesje Wagner
with
Corrie Gelauf Wagner

TINA ASSANTI
Stories of the Human Spirit

Tina Assanti Books

This book is inspired by actual events in Corrie Gelauf Wagner's life
and is told as truthfully as her recollection permits and verified by research.
Other events corroborate with historical facts, where possible.
Events depicted at Birkenau, Auschwitz are based on stories
passed through the family from great-uncle Frans Riep.
Events grandfather, Henk Gelauf, played a role in after taken as slave labor
are fictionalized but are within historical records where possible.

Library of Congress Control Number: 2020908403
Library of Congress
US Programs, Law, and Literature Division
Cataloging in Publication Program
101 Independence Avenue, S.E.
Washington, DC 20540-4283

Paperback ISBN: 978-1-7771774-0-9
Cover designed by Rade Rokvic

www.tinaassantibooks.com

I thank my mother, Corrie Gelauf, for her strength and love and for sharing her story so bravely. Rudy Wagner, my dear father, I am grateful for his drive and wisdom, and for always being there. I also want to express my endless gratitude to my partner, Andy Smith, for all the abundant good he brings into each day. And my thanks to cousin Jacob van Rijswijk for all his help in gathering family details together, as well as for photos and information generously shared by cousins Karel Gelauf and Janny Gelauf. Vic Schukov, I thank you, our friend, neighbor, and editor, for your expertise and humor. A hug for Sam.

Above all, our gratitude to *Oom* (Uncle) Piet, who as a child became the 'man of the family' in our grandfather's absence and did all he could to ensure the survival of the family through one of history's most horrific and challenging times. He is a hero in the most real sense of the word.

Bedankt, Oom Piet.

Liesje Wagner

This book is dedicated to all brave Canadians
who fought on behalf of the
impoverished Dutch during World War ll.
Lest We Forget.

TABLE OF CONTENTS

Introduction xi

Prelude xv

Chapter 1: March 1938 1

Chapter 2: March 1939 13

Chapter 3: April 1939 21

Chapter 4: May 1940 27

Chapter 5: May 1940 38

Chapter 6: June 1940 57

Chapter 7: September 1940 66

Chapter 8: November 1940 80

Chapter 9: June 1941 95

Chapter 10: September 1941 109

Chapter 11: September 1942 123

Chapter 12: March 1943 142

Chapter 13: April 1943 163

Chapter 14: July 1943. 172

Chapter 15: September 1943. 186

Chapter 16: October 1943. 203

Chapter 17: April 1944. 218

Chapter 18: June 1944 237

Chapter 19: November 1944. 252

Chapter 20: December 1944 276

Chapter 21: January 1945. 287

Chapter 22: March 1945. 296

Chapter 23: April 1945. 312

Chapter 24: May 1945 325

Chapter 25: September 1945. 332

Epilogue. 341

Glossary of Dutch, German and Russian Terms 347

INTRODUCTION

Apart from a few embellishments where memory may have failed or died with long-gone relatives, this book is a memoir for my mother, Cornelia Hendrika Alwina Gelauf Wagner (Corrie).

Her experience of World War ll in The Hague, Netherlands—one of the worst-hit cities during the war—left her suffering a lifetime of PTSD (Post-Traumatic Stress Disorder). She was five when Nazi Germany suddenly invaded the neutral country. By the time the war ended in May 1945, she had spent half her life living in fear, hunger, loss, horror and death; she knew nothing else.

Seventy-five years later, she and my father, Jan Rudolf Wagner, were invited as Guest Speakers for Remembrance Day at the Brighton Canadian Legion to share what it was like for both of them living under five years of Nazi Occupation. My mother fearfully shied away. Her own memories were too painful and horrific. Instead, we created and showed a video in which my father carried the weight of the story, sharing a portion of my mother's story as well.

However, during the taping of the video itself, something shifted. My mother, who didn't want to say anything at all, wished to expound on a point my father made. While she was still off camera, we kept rolling until, suddenly, courage left her and she was unable to continue. As she hurried away with heart-wrenching tears, there was a long pause, and my father turned from watching her go and looked at the camera. He sighed and sadly said, "You think the war is over, but the war is never over for people."

When we showed the video that Remembance Day dinner, there wasn't a dry eye in the Hall. Many expressed their surprise at learning to what extent people suffered under the Nazi Occupation. We realized, then, not everyone lived as we did, with almost daily reminders and references to the war.

My mother realized, then, she had to share her story. People needed reminding as to why their uncle, grandfather, or father bravely fought and died in some of the worst physical conditions of the entire war to save a people they didn't know. She survived as a direct result of Canadian soldiers liberating—at great cost—a starving Dutch population from Hitler's brutal war machine. The Dutch hailed them as heroes—which indeed they were. To this day, every generation of Dutch children is taught anew how these soldiers' selfless courage and love freed their country from tyranny.

Research helped clarify and confirm my mother's recollections. It also helped fill in what may have happened to her father—my grandfather—after he was taken as slave labor by the Nazis. I have him written as ultimately ending up working at ever-expanding Birkenau—the largest part of the Auschwitz complex, where my mother's late Uncle Frans was forced to work, doing jobs that ultimately drove him to suicide in later years. The remainder of their story I placed within the historical arena of Birkenau, their details intermixed with events recorded at the time.

It goes without saying that my grandfather's departure from home suddenly put my mother's family at greater risk. In his absence, my mother's older brother, Piet Gelauf, just a child, stepped in as the 'man' of the family. It was largely through his unending scrounging and encouragement that the family was kept safe and alive throughout the worst part of the war.

My grandfather's red-rose accordion was indeed an underlying thread throughout the trauma and horrors of my mother's war. As a child, her love for his playing and watching the rose pattern appear and disappear in the bellows was a form of magic she never forgot. After he was taken, they believed that so long as they kept that accordion safe, her father would magically return; and this they did, even in the face of starving to death. Better to

CORRIE AND THE ROSE ACCORDION

die of starvation than to give up any kind of hope. For without hope, there is absolutely nothing.

Here is my mother's story, Corrie and the Rose Accordion.

Lest we forget.

Liesje Wagner
Weston, Florida

PRELUDE

NOVEMBER 2019

Corrie leaned back exhausted, wishing more than anything she could get up without being noticed and leave the long, sumptuous banquet table. Her fragile heart's wings beat with fear against her chest as she forced herself to stay. She and her 88-year-old husband Rudy were featured guests at the Remembrance Day Event, and they were about to play a video depicting some of their wartime experiences as children in The Hague, Holland. She had no desire to relive them again, but she had to stay for her husband, daughters, and the other 150 people who had come to meet them on such a solemn occasion in the decorated hall.

The lights dimmed in the Brighton Legion Hall. She watched the guests lean toward the drop-down screen at the far end of the hall. A hush fell as she looked away. She stared at the place card in front of her, "Corrie Wagner, Guest Speaker."

The video soundtrack started off with a World War II German marching band—with heavy tuba, crashing drums, trombones, and French horns. She heard jackboots marching in rhythm on the cobblestones of her memories. The once so familiar and frightening sound of hundreds of thousands of voices cheering the Nazi salute echoed in the hall.

"Sieg Heil! Sieg Heil!"

She shook, and quickly wiped away a tear trickling down her cheek. It was gut-wrenching having to even consider regurgitating stories for the taping of the video, but for the hundredth time she had to remind herself that it wasn't for her she was sharing her story; it was an opportunity to explain, albeit just a little, what it was like as a child fighting to survive the horrors of Hitler's War. She needed people to understand what drove young and old to cross the ocean to fight a war that was not theirs to fight. These brave strangers came from an exotic land called Canada. They were superheroes facing death and destruction. They could have looked away, but didn't. Corrie and her family were on the verge of dying of starvation when tens of thousands had already succumbed during the Hunger Winter of 1944/45. She was alive because Canadian soldiers fought with all their might against the Nazi hordes. The Canadians fought in the streets, along the dikes and in the flooded polders of southwest Holland. So many of these heroes died so that so many more may live.

Corrie peeked at the screen. She saw the image of a whirling prop on a Luftwaffe fighter plane and quickly looked away again. Bombs exploded, and fires roared and crackled.

Her husband, Rudy, leaned toward her and put a reassuring hand on the clenched fists she hid under the table. She looked over at him.

He leaned over and whispered in her ear. "Corrie, think positive, happy thoughts, if you can. From before the war."

She looked at him blankly, blinked, and nodded. She bowed her head and closed her eyes.

She remembered the happy days before the war; her mother putting a massive pink satin bow in her hair, visiting her father's family at the big house over the pub on the canal. Her father had 15 siblings who had their own families, so there seemed to always be birthdays to celebrate at the big house. There were endless streams of mouth-watering food, and drinks, and happy music.

She took a deep breath and let it out slowly. She could see herself sitting cross-legged in front of her father as he played his rose red accordion—his pride and joy. It was a brightly-polished cherry red instrument with a beautiful rose pattern on the bellows. She remembered sitting watching those roses expand, dance, and hide as they came to life with every movement of his hands. Everyone danced and sang into the night and the floor bounced under the weight of so many bodies in one room. No one seemed to care. They were more carefree before the war.

She thought back how that accordion became a coveted possession in her family after her father was swept away as slave labor in factories, eventually at Auschwitz. He was taken just when living conditions became unbearable for her mother and siblings. They eventually believed he would never come back. That accordion became Corrie's sacred symbol of her father's life and potential death in a horrific existence where hope was a precious commodity.

She called that hope the Rose Accordion.

Chapter 1
MARCH 1938

Corrie's grandfather's home vibrated with the beautiful sounds and rhythmic beat of the delightful music emanating from her father's accordion. Voices cheered and sang as the music wafted from the second floor of the grand building, above a corner pub. On this particular night, three Gelauf generations ranging from six months to 65 years old were packed into the upper rooms to celebrate the 65th birthday of the clan's patriarch, *De Heer* Gelauf. People cycling along the canal below rang their bells in support. Others walked by laughing and did short polkas in the middle of the quiet street before moving on.

Above the heads of these gentle passersby, the second floor was a grand space of large, high-ceilinged rooms. Most of the windows overlooked the canal below; they were magnificent and tall through which long lace curtains softly billowed in the North Sea's evening breeze. That night, the sashes were thrown wide open and, here and there, a hand stuck out to flick ash off a cigarette onto the swept pavement below. The odd little child poked his or her head out before being pulled back to safety. A woman sat on a window sill, her ample buttocks swaying to the beat.

Little four-year-old Corrie's young father, Henk, and all of his 15 siblings were born there, including the very last sibling, now 14, whose birth sadly marked the end of their mother's life. The older children raised the young, keeping the family together.

Some had left home, married, and had children. But tonight, they were all together making a raucous noise.

It was a fabulous party. Loud talking, happy laughter, babies screaming and crying. Henk had played all evening. The dancers were showing polka fatigue. Henk looked like he could use a break and a drink. Someone had already stuck a cigarette into his mouth and lit it. As he wound up his bouncy rendition of their favorite, "Roll Out the Barrel" beer polka, Henk tipped his face back so as not to get smoke in his aqua blue eyes.

Little Corrie sat cross-legged on the floor in front of him. She was surrounded by some of her young cousins, all gaily jostling and pushing each other. She ignored them as she clapped softly along with the music, while a big fat satin pink ribbon jiggled in her hair to the rhythmic bounce of the floor. She sat as close as she could and intently watched the bellows of the accordion. They squeezed shut and reopened again, over and over, exposing bits and pieces - and sometimes all - of the beautiful rose pattern within its thick paper folds.

To little Corrie, it was called the Rose Accordion. It had gleaming white and black piano keys on the one side and shiny small round black buttons on the other. Corrie watched her father's fingers play and dance over both sides. Click-click they went, performing magic.

Henk finally held the accordion up in the air with the last chords of the polka. Everyone whooped and hollered and cheered, and collapsed, panting and sweating. A couple of Henk's brothers slapped him on the back while a third handed him a small shot glass of Dutch *Jenever*.

"Ah," said Henk before he threw his head back to down his drink. He smacked his lips, wiped them with his sleeve, then he stood up and let the broad shoulder straps slip off his shoulders. "That's it for now," he said grinning as he pushed back a lock of blonde hair from his forehead.

As he gently lowered the accordion into its heavy wooden case, someone turned on the ultra-modern and handsome *Van der Heem Erres* radio set sitting in the far corner of the main room. This radio took no time to warm its inner workings. Quite suddenly, Tommy Dorsey and his swinging band reflected the evening's need for a slower but still happy swing. "*Music, Maestro Please,*" calmed the quickened pulses. This was the newest music from America. It marked a turn in the evening. As if as one, everyone refreshed themselves with the food laid out on every flat surface in the home: *Loempias*, beef croquettes, gouda cheese squares, and bits of pickle and ham. *Spekulaasjes, Tom Poesjes*, smoked eel, fresh raw herring with finely-chopped onions on the dining room table. A massive pot of Dutch vegetable soup with tiny meatballs sat surrounded by ample potato and beet salads, and little Corrie's mother's liverwurst on crackers with smoked mussels and oysters.

Some of the children shuffled to the new radio. They leaned toward the shiny gold screens over the speakers. Eight-year-old Pietje, little Corrie's brother, sauntered over close enough to see his breath on the radio's finely-polished wooden frame.

"Pietje, get away from that radio," yelled Henk, as he moved the accordion case against the wall behind his chair.

Pietje dutifully stepped back, flicked his blond hair from out of his face, and stuck his hands in his pockets.

"And stop putting your hands in your pockets," added Henk.

Most of the people in the room looked over at Pietje. He withered under all that attention and blushed. Pietje took his hands out of his pockets and disappeared into the adjoining grand room, out of his father's sight.

"You should give that boy some slack," said *De Heer* Gelauf from under his heavy eyebrows. He eyed his handsome, blonde son. "He's just a boy. He wasn't doing any harm."

Henk straightened up and looked at his father. "I know, Pap," perusing the room, "but he can do the stupidest things. Whatever he touches, breaks. He has no sense of— I don't know." Henk put his hands in his pockets, saw that his father smiled, and raised his eyebrows. Henk looked down at his hands and withdrew them.

"He's your love child, Henk. Not a symbol of shame. You should get over that guilt thing. That's life, after all." *De Heer*

Gelauf bent over his ample stomach and reached for a cigar from a tray on the table next to him. "Just wait. He's a good boy." *De Heer* Gelauf struck a match, lit his cigar and sucked at it, puffing and pulling at the tobacco until there was a nice bit of ash on the tip.

Little Corrie suddenly came over and held her arms out to *De Heer* Gelauf.

"*Opa.*"

"*Ja, schatje,*" he said, as he bent down and pulled Corrie up on his lap. He bounced her on his knee, and she giggled. "You just watch, Henk," he continued. "That boy will surprise you one day."

"Who, *Opa*?" asked Corrie, playing with the gold chain of his pocket watch.

"Your brother, Pietje," he said. He then put her down, patted Corrie on the head, and turned her around. "Go play with your cousins, *schatje*. *Opa* will smoke his cigar."

Little Corrie looked around the room and then skipped back to join a few of the children still on the floor listening to the radio.

With a doting smile Henk watched his daughter. She was his little angel. He looked over to where his other daughter, six-year-old Beppie, sat with a few of his older sisters on chairs along the wall. As it was her nature, Beppie sat pouting. The women around her swayed from side to side smiling, nudging her in fun. Every single one of them held a cigarette in their hand, seemingly without a care in the world. He noticed everyone did their best not to show any concern. There was trouble brewing, but no one knew what to do about it. Yet.

He looked past them to the next grand room. There he could just see the beautiful, delft-blue tiled backing behind the wrought-iron coal stove. He saw some of the younger women in the cramped kitchen, rushing out with desserts and beverages, keeping up with mouths that needed filling.

Henk patted his father on the shoulder before moving over to the mantle where a few of the men stood smoking cigars. Here, he knew he'd find conversations addressing everyone's deepest fears.

"Jansje is terrified that a war will come here," someone said.

Henk listened attentively. His other brother, Piet Junior, spoke about his wife who had Jewish relatives and friends.

"She's afraid for them. She thinks they should all dye their hair blond and pretend to be Christian."

"Impossible," said Philip, their brother-in-law, the shortest of all the men. "How can you hide a whole lifetime of the person you are by simply dying your hair? You'd have to move away to where no one knows you. Otherwise, it wouldn't work."

"Why even worry? Nothing's going to happen to us. You're wasting your breath." Louis was married to one of the sisters. Henk watched Louis tap the ashes off his cigar before he went on. "If I were you, I wouldn't do a damn thing. Why bother?"

"Did it ever occur to you, that by being a neutral country, we are standing by and allowing the bloodshed? By default, we are approving it!" Lately, the naiveté in his younger siblings and spouses rubbed him the wrong way.

"What do you mean?"

Henk looked at Louis. "You were very young when the Great War finished. We still see men with missing arms and legs. God knows how many came back crazy. War's not nice on anyone, even for those who stand by watching. The guilt can be too heavy to bear. Besides, I can't help but think we were only lucky the last time."

Louis squinted at his brother-in-law, while offering him a cigar from his breast pocket. "You mean our luck will run out?"

Henk put out his cigarette and took the cigar. He leaned toward a match Louis struck. "I mean, this Hitler seems to be casting a spell on the Germans. And I don't like hate." Henk's handsome uni-brow squished together as he frowned.

The men looked at each other.

"Henk, what do the other reserves think?"

Henk thought for a moment and raised his shoulders. "First of all, we're not a big army. That's one concern."

"How many divisions?" asked Louis.

"Officially? Only ten." Henk puffed at his cigar. "And then we have ten smaller divisions. A total of about 400,000 men."

"That's a heck of a lot more than I thought," offered the older Piet Junior. "A lot more than during the first war."

"And you guys in the Reserves?" pressed Louis.

Henk shrugged. "I'm not sure, but it's not enough." He leaned in conspiratorially. "If Germany really wanted to, they'd go right through our borders and straight to our harbors. We could try to stop them, but we would have to destroy our bridges, maybe a dike or two to flood the land. Hopefully, that might slow them down."

The men quietly contemplated such extreme measures.

"Never thought of that." Piet Junior rocked on his heels, ponderously.

"Also, our border is long, irregular, and we have very few tanks. We're still practicing with guns from the First World War. We have no experience in modern warfare. I doubt my horse will do well against one of those German tanks we've heard so much about." Henk turned and flicked his ash into a brown glass ashtray they all shared on the mantle. "War is too close. You've heard of the refugees already pouring in from Germany."

"Mostly Jews," offered Piet Junior. "My wife's relatives from Berlin stayed for a while before finding a home in Amsterdam. The pressure on the Jews is like nothing we've ever known here."

Suddenly, Henk's legs started to cramp. Every evening this happened around the same time. It sometimes drove him bonkers. "Sorry, *jongens*, my legs are cramping again. I have to keep moving." The others nodded as they witnessed his problem every time they got together. He shuffled his feet, kicking his right leg a little before finally turning his back to the men. He moved to look out the closest window down on the waters of the canal. The surface shimmered and reflected the lights from across its narrow width. Over the cacophony of noise in the rooms behind him, he heard bicycle bells and the odd horse clomping along the cobblestones somewhere outside. It rained slightly, and the freshness of the night's mist curled indoors, caressing the heat built up over the evening. He leaned out further and gazed straight down. He saw his obedient black Lab Poekie, patiently waiting, curled up against the wall. He whistled softly. Poekie jumped up and looked around, ears cocked. "Poekie!" Poekie looked up. His tail wagged happily as he looked from the door of the building and back up at the window. He whined softly at Henk.

Henk turned back to see his heavy-set father stand up from where he sat between the two middle windows. He pulled out his gold pocket-watch and squinted at it. He looked across the room at Henk.

"Henk!" *De heer* Gelauf deftly swung his gold watch back into his vest pocket.

Henk straightened up and shot his one sleeve while stretching his left leg. "*Ja!*"

"Play some more accordion for us before it gets any later!"

Many in the room cheered.

"Ja, Henk. Play again!"

"Henk, play another polka!"

"Do an Oompapa, Henk!"

"No, do something that Ella Fitzgerald sings to."

Someone laughed. "Ella Fitzgerald can't sing to an accordion."

"She can sing to anything…"

"*Hou je mond!*" *De Heer* Gelauf raised his hand, and almost everyone quieted down. He nodded at Henk. "*Speel iets leuks*, Henk. Something nice."

At that moment, Henk's wife, Cornelia, stepped into the room, carrying the gangly Corrie on her hip. Cornelia looked at Henk curiously. She had her dark hair styled recently in the latest fashion, cut just below her ears, the new look accented by a new dress with a dropped waist. Suddenly, Pietje stood beside her, still looking humiliated. Henk watched her turn to their son.

"Pietje, get your father's accordion for him," Cornelia said.

Henk frowned. Cornelia was the Mother Bear. She always encouraged Henk to be gentle with their son. But Henk couldn't help it. His son aggravated him. The guilt it generated in Henk was an inconvenient distraction in life.

Pietje looked at him sheepishly from where they stood across the room, then over at the accordion. Henk didn't usually allow anyone to touch it, but nodded approval anyway. He watched Pietje walk over and pick up the case by its handle. He moved to take it to his father, but Henk forgot he hadn't snapped the clips closed, and the accordion case opened suddenly. With a groan and a scream, the accordion fell out against the sharp corner of one of the side tables' legs before tumbling with another long metallic cry onto the old Persian carpet.

Everyone fell quiet. The radio played the Mills Brothers' "Georgia." Some dishes clattered in the kitchen.

"Pietje! Can't you do anything right?" yelled Henk as he turned to quickly rest his cigar in the groove of the brown glass ashtray.

Pietje turned crimson red, quickly bent over, and picked up the accordion, causing more moans and groans from its baffles.

Henk lunged at his accordion, grabbing it from Pietje. Pietje humiliated, turned and disappeared into the adjoining room, once again. Cornelia watched him scurry past. She reached out to him, but he was too fast. She turned to look accusingly at Henk.

Henk pretended not to notice. Instead, he carefully examined the accordion, fingering a fresh dent in the polished surface at the middle edge of the right half just over the piano keys. He took a deep breath and let it go in disgust, shaking his head.

De Heer Gelauf raised a pudgy hand. "Henk, it's only an accordion. Don't be so childish. Play for us."

Henk looked at his father and blinked. He was aware his entire family was watching. Deep inside, he knew he was being petty. It was an accident. Someone pulled a chair to him and tucked it against the back of his legs.

"The boy tried to help, Hendricus," said one of his many sisters.

Henk nodded. Then he feigned a smile, sat in the chair, and settled down. He hooked the leather shoulder straps around his shoulders, once again.

Little Corrie struggled to get down from her mother's arms, to get to her father. She ran over leaning toward him until he bent down for her to kiss him on the cheek.

He looked at his wife, Cornelia, slipping into the adjoining room. He knew it was to comfort Pietje.

"Come on, Henk. A few more songs and we'll all go home."

"What? The night is still young, old man!" said another.

"Okay, stop with this rabble!" Henk replied in jest. "Shut up and let me play."

"Come," motioned little Corrie to her cousins. The younger children scrambled forward and sat in a row on the carpet in front of Henk.

Henk ran his fingers over the piano keys to limber up. The radio blared Mary Martin singing "My Heart Belongs to Daddy."

"Turn that radio off," yelled *De Heer* at no one in particular.

Little Corrie jumped up and ran over the other children to get to the radio.

Henk frowned. "Corrie, *voorzichtig*! Someone help her turn that off."

Suddenly, the radio crackled, and everyone heard a harsh and hateful voice bark over the airwaves.

"Hitler," said someone. An angry murmur spread through the room.

"What's he saying now?" asked one of the women.

Everyone listened to his harsh version of German.

"He's saying they're taking Austria!" said Philip, standing frozen by the mantle.

"Austria?"

People were aghast.

"What do you mean?" someone else asked. "Isn't Austria part of Germany already?"

They listened carefully.

"He claims they're taking it for *Lebensraum*. He's calling it the *Anschluss*. It's now part of the German Reich. He's saying they belong together."

The voice ripped through the airwaves as the family craned their necks to hear more. Suddenly, their father raised his heavy, burly arms for everyone's attention.

"We're not going to let that Hun ruin this evening. Agnes, turn that radio off so your father can play."

"It's Corrie," yelled little Corrie from the radio.

Everyone laughed.

"Okay. Little Corrie! There's so many of you. How can I forget? My little angel. I can't remember all of your names. Turn that stupid thing off!"

Corrie couldn't reach the knob, so one of her older cousins lifted her. She searched for the right shiny knob and turned it off. Instead of returning to sit down in front, Corrie ran back to her *Opa*.

She leaned against him with her right shoulder and put her finger in her mouth as he patted her bob-cut white-blonde hair, flattening the large ribbon sitting on top of her head.

Henk noticed Hitler's voice frightened little Corrie. He often agonized over how he could protect his children from the realities of a complicated world. He lived through the First World War, as well as the Depression. Talks and fears of another World War was deja-vu. But he took his father's cue and started to play. As his fingers danced over the keys and buttons, his arms and hands deftly opened and closed the rose-patterned bellows.

Comforted by her father and the music, little Corrie made her way back through the aunts and uncles who stood up to dance. She deftly, fearlessly, squeezed past legs and skirts and struggled through to sit with the children on the floor.

Henk watched her every move as he played. His gaze fell on her as she plunked down on one of her cousin's crossed legs in front of him. She leaned back and watched the roses on the bellows mysteriously appear and disappear between the folds of his accordion. He stole a glance at the nick into the polished surface and shook his head. He closed his eyes as he felt the habitual disappointment in his son. When he opened his eyes again, he saw the light of his life, little Corrie, deeply asleep despite the loud music, shouting, and the floor bouncing under the dancers' feet.

Little Corrie's eyes opened. Her head rested on her father's strong shoulder as he carried her along the quiet, dark street. The gentle rain had lifted, and the night sky cleared enough for the full moon to outshine the soft street lights along the canal, helping to light their way home.

Her eyes focused on the moon, but its brightness hurt them. Then she lifted her head and looked around. She saw houses and storefronts, and rows and rows of parked bicycles along the canal. But that moon curiously still hung in the same place, looking down at her. She looked to where they were heading.

Her brother, Pietje, and her sister, Beppie, were ahead of them, pushing, arguing, and shoving each other. Poekie jumped around them, his pink tongue out and his tail wagging. Her mother walked behind them, carrying the accordion case.

Little Corrie looked at her father's face. She saw her father's dark blond five-o'clock shadow in the light of the moon and passing street lamps. Corrie loved his angular cheekbones, the flush in his cheeks. She saw how moist his skin was. Then she looked at the mist floating above the waters of the canal. She felt the soft and humid air in her lungs.

Corrie touched her father's face.

"Pappa?"

He looked over at her wide aqua eyes. His eyes. "*Ja*, my little Corrie."

"Why does the moon follow us?"

Henk turned to look behind them. "The moon is following us? Where?" He smiled.

Little Corrie pointed up at the moon. "No, up there."

He looked up. "What do you mean?"

"It's walking with us. It won't go away."

Henk laughed. He adjusted her weight in his arms. "Corrie, the moon never goes away. It's either above us or hiding on the other side of the earth."

"But why doesn't it move away?"

"Because it's very far away, and it only looks like it follows us."

"But it's right there over the houses. It's not far away."

"It is thousands and thousands of kilometers away up in the sky."

"Oh," she said, trying to understand. She felt sleepy again, so she put her head back on her father's shoulder and continued watching the man in the moon until finally, her eyes heavy, they closed once again. Before she floated away, although she'd never really known the words, she knew in her heart this was as good as it got.

Chapter 2
March 1939

Five-year-old Corrie felt dry heat emanating from the sun-drenched, crumbling, and weathered plaster of the prickly wall she leaned against. She shifted slightly and focused intently on an ant crawling up and down between the deep, dusty manure and straw-strewn crevices of the hot cobblestones directly in front of her. She leaned further over her gangly-crossed legs and grunted as her white summer dress bunched up against her diaphragm. She let a drop of water drip from her finger on the little creature. Then she carefully traced the meandering and quickly-drying trail left behind by the insect.

Her other hand clutched the handle of a buckled tin cup of water given to her by Henk just moments before. She spent forever in this plane of wondrous discoveries of insects and water. The tip of her pink tongue poked out from between her little pursed lips. She dipped the same little finger once again into the water and carefully dropped another sparkling mini-bomb onto the insect and watched it flail.

"What are you doing, Corrie? You have a new pet?" Her father looked down, smiling, while brushing and untangling the ratty mane of his stately chestnut steed. Henk stood with his feet spread apart and leaned against the half-door of the stall for balance as he reached up to the beautiful head.

Corrie's massive pink ribbon trembled as she looked up, captured by that voice she loved most. Her father's voice felt like 'home.' She pointed up at him and then down at the ant.

"Wet ant. It's swimming in the horsey poop."

Henk chuckled. "Is it now? Don't you think you've made it suffer enough?"

Corrie's ribbon once again trembled as she swung her gaze back to the ant. She frowned and stuck a puzzled dirty finger in her mouth as she wondered what the word 'suffer' meant. She bent over and peered at the bug for any tell-tale clue.

Henk noted, as he always did, that little Corrie's curiosity was particularly sharp. He anticipated her next question.

"It is *suffer*?" She looked up again, inquisitively.

"Is it suffer*ing*? Yes, it suffers. It means when someone or something is making you feel bad. If you cut yourself and it hurts for a long time, you are suffering for that time. You are dropping big, globs of water on his tiny body, and he is trying to protect himself. So, he suffers."

"It's only water."

"Corrie, if you were that small, how big would the drop seem to you?"

Corrie pursed her lips and pondered for a bit.

Henk turned back to his steed and caressed the horse's strong jawline.

Corrie struggled to her feet, tipping the cup of water.

"Oh, no!" Startled, she looked down at the water pooling between the stones. She saw the ant floating, swimming, struggling. She began to cry.

Henk bent down and tossed her against his shoulder, nestling her into his arm. She stopped crying, but still sad, rubbing her eyes.

"Shhhh. It's only water, Corrie. We have lots of water."

"But I make him suffer."

Henk squeezed her. "You are correct. But look now," he said, pointing down.

She saw the ant crawl onto dry cobblestone. She looked at her father, happy and surprised.

He pointed at the ant. "See? He survived. He fought and fought and survived." He smiled, reached out to the steed, caressing him along the proud nose to distract Corrie. He took her dirty hand and led it gently to the horse's forehead. Large, dewy intelligent eyes watched their every move. Then the steed shook his head and neighed gently. Corrie quickly pulled her hand away.

Horses elsewhere on the farm neighed in response.

Henk grinned. "Hear that? They are all happy." He reached up and patted the horse's forehead. "Good, *Joop*. Good boy." Henk waved a few flies away from the friendly eyes.

Corrie felt good. She had watched her father clean the stall and walk his steed around. He even let her sit straddled on top. She had no fear of the animal nor its height. She, of course, screamed bloody murder the first time he plunked her on top of Joop, but she soon acquired a love for it. They'd done this many times. It was their *thing*.

Henk looked at his watch and lowered Corrie to the cobblestones. "Corrie, you play some more. Pappa has to finish brushing Joop, okay?"

Corrie kept her hand on his tie and pulled it out from beneath his woolen vest, separating the starched collar from the shirt. He gently pulled his tie from her hand and straightened up, adjusting his tie and collar.

They were running late. Cycling to the army stables just outside of The Hague took twenty minutes longer than usual because she asked her father to stop at the corner where a portable puppet theater performed. Corrie wanted to see the puppets, so they stayed for one of the skits. It was to be a beautiful day because they were off to her *Opa*'s grand house for another celebration supper, this time for one of her aunts. The usual music, singing, and dancing was something to look forward to. As usual, her father was going to play his accordion.

Henk had tried to fix the dent that Pietje caused, but no matter what he did, he couldn't push the cut outward. He couldn't access the dent. Henk wondered why, of all places, it had to be right at the top where he couldn't help but see it everytime he played. He knew it would forever aggravate him. Surely, its worth was acutely diminished by the damage. *Ach, Pietje,* he said to himself. He shook his head.

He quickly brushed Joop's mane. The horse did not belong to him. As a reserve in the Royal Dutch Army, he was responsible for the horse's care and for the antiquated weapons and tools he had in his possession. Queen Wilhelmina allowed only 4% of her nation's budget to be spent on the military, consequently, the army was outdated. Some of the weapons were even pre-World War One. But she reminded the country that The Netherlands was neutral and they would never have to prepare for war. Henk knew the state took precautions by hunting and arresting Nazi sympathizers and spies as quickly as they could. The Dutch also opened their doors to waves of refugees running from Nazi Germany. Though they kept a wary eye on Hitler's doings, everyone believed war was the very last thing that would happen to them.

Yes, the First World War had affected the Dutch economy despite their neutrality. And there were continuous hordes of biplanes crossing overhead between England, France, and Germany. However, these were minor inconveniences compared to the millions of soldiers from other countries massacred in the muddy trenches of Europe.

The compulsory army service which Henk and every young man had to give to the Dutch Crown was no hardship, almost a gesture. Nonetheless, he took great pride in his service. And Henk received a tremendous amount of pleasure in taking care of his beautiful steed. He believed there would never be any fighting in any war.

His thoughts went back to supper as he worked another knot out of the horse's mane of hair. The day before, Cornelia bought liverwurst at the *markt* to take along, and he looked forward to his traditional sharpening of the knife against the sharpening stone while everyone watched expectantly. Of course, you didn't need a sharp knife for liverwurst. It was all show on his part.

"Pappa! Guess what?"

Henk looked away from the steed to see nine-year-old Pietje storm into the square. His sudden entrance into the enclave startled the horses, who neighed and stomped their hooves in protest.

"Pietje, look what you've done! You've frightened the horses." Henk looked at his son's one woolen knee-sock sagging, both knees scratched and dirty as usual. His shirttail stuck out from under his woolen vest, and he had lost a button on one of his sleeves. His wide eyes were just like his, and he had the same white-blonde hair, which now stood up like stalks of dead wheat. "And what are you doing here? You should be getting ready for the *feest*. Look at you. You look like a rag. A clown."

"Mamma sent me. You're late!"

Henk quickly opened the bottom half door to the dark stall. "Help me finish here then, Pietje."

Pietje grinned as little Corrie yanked at his shorts to give her a piggyback. Pietje gently pulled her arms away. "I have to help Pappa."

Corrie whined. Pietje quickly went down on his knees and looked into her beautiful face. "Don't worry. I will never leave you. Pappa, too. Right, Pappa?" Pietje looked hopefully at his father.

"Don't be silly. Of course, I won't. I will never let that happen. You let Pietje go, Corrie, we have to finish here with Joop."

Corrie let go, and Henk glanced at her. She stood with her finger in her mouth, watching her brother and father finish brushing down the steed. Smiling, Henk turned back to the horse.

The joy Henk felt for the coming evening festivities waned halfway home. As they quickly walked the bicycle home with Corrie in the child seat, Henk noticed new announcements plastered on the general information board. The last time men gathered like that around billboards was when Hitler walked into Austria and, without a single shot, claimed it for Germany. Things developed in very unsettling ways at their neighbors' in Germany. Lately, he had gotten in the habit of listening to the old radio his father passed on, hoping for positive news.

"Pietje, hold the *fiets* and watch Corrie. I have to see what this is about."

Pietje held the bike with little Corrie on the back even though it towered over him. Henk waited a moment to make sure Pietje was able to keep it from tilting before he moved into the outer edge of the crowd, craning his neck to read as best he could. Suddenly, he heard little Corrie's cries. He swung around.

Henk lunged at Pietje and grabbed the bicycle, at a precarious angle. Little Corrie's foot had somehow lodged between the small rungs of the seat, and it hurt her thigh. She also had her foot caught in the spokes of the back wheel.

Pietje looked helplessly from Corrie to his father as he strained to keep the bike from falling on top of him altogether.

Henk straightened the bicycle and rolled it back enough to take the pressure off Corrie's foot. He pulled Corrie out of the back seat. She tried to reach her foot, crying. Henk lifted the foot slightly and saw the red welt just above the ankle sock. Henk became upset at himself. He should have known better, but he felt it was such a simple chore for Pietje.

"How could you always be so *stom*, Pietje?"

Pietje looked down at his feet.

"How many times do I have to tell you, think before you do anything? You don't *think*."

"I was taking good care of her," argued Pietje on the verge of tears.

"It's not in you to take care of anything. Sometimes you're useless."

Pietje, overwhelmed with remorse, looked at the people around them and then took off running.

Henk looked on as he shook his head. He closed his eyes and sighed. He opened them and looked around. Some of the men were watching him. Suddenly, behind them, he caught sight of his younger brother-in-law, Frans, who stood, myopic and edgy, right at the front, peering up at the notices through his thick glasses.

"Frans!"

Frans turned his head and peered back. Seeing Henk, he nodded and pushed people aside as he made his way back to Henk and little Corrie. He adjusted his glasses and, smiling, patted little Corrie on the head. She was still sniffling, but as soon as Frans was close enough, she grabbed his glasses and put them on her nose. She giggled and grinned. Both men laughed as did the bystanders nearby.

"So, what's up now?" Henk motioned to the board with his square chin.

"The Allies, with the British Prime Minister Neville Chamberlain, agreed that Hitler could have the Sudetenland region of Czechoslovakia," Frans retrieved his glasses and readjusted them on his nose. "In return, Hitler can't ever proclaim war against them and their colonies."

"It wasn't enough for Hitler to take Austria?"

The two men shook their heads at the disturbing news in the afternoon sun. Birds chirped gaily in the thick branches of the trees that lined the street. As if nothing untoward was happening in another part of the world.

"He's also got Hungary to pass his anti-Jewish laws officially."

"My God," whispered Henk.

"What?" asked little Corrie.

Henk looked over at her cherubic face and wide eyes. He thought of the mounting drama in Germany and Britain; it gripped Henk's heart. He started to sweat, a chill crawled up his legs and back. What if war did happen? How would he protect his children, his wife? *But we are neutral and will never be affected,* he argued with himself. He thought about Cornelia's relatives in Germany. How her family suffered during the first great war. Born in Heidelberg, they fled to Holland, starving and stripped of everything but a glimmer of hope. It really wasn't that long ago.

He thought of his Jewish friends and neighbors and the stories their relatives shared as they started trickling in from Germany. Jews were not allowed to participate in public activities. Hordes ransacked Jewish merchants' stores. There were ugly rumors that

Jews were picked on by swarms of hateful people. There were even deaths.

He cast his eyes across the crowd of men and saw that some of his Jewish friends and neighbors were there, reading intently with worry creasing their foreheads. Something extremely distasteful was brewing around that crazed man with the ridiculously small mustache and shock of black hair.

"May God keep us safe," he whispered.

Frans heard him. "Don't worry, Henk. Nothing will ever happen to us. Our families are safe."

"*Ja*," said Henk thoughtfully. "We are all safe, God willing.

Chapter 3
April 1939

"Stop it!"
"Leave it. It's my turn."
"Pappa!"

Henk was reading the latest edition of the *Haagsche Courant* in his corner chair close to the window in the front room, with Poekie sleeping on the old Persian carpet at his feet. It was getting dark, but he needed to read on. Russia and Germany had taken Poland and split it between them. He wanted to see if England would finally declare war against Germany. That Chamberlain was frustrating. He was basically befriending Hitler. Henk knew England, like any country, needed to do everything possible to prevent a war. Still, he saw that Prime Minister Chamberlain—along with the United States which wanted absolutely nothing to do with the whole nightmare—only postponed the inevitable. In the meantime, Hitler continued walking into countries, taking them over. Henk was disgusted. And horrified.

He irritably dropped the paper and looked at his quibbling son and daughter before leaning over to turn on the lamp next to him on the side table.

"Pappa," continued Beppie. "It's my turn to listen to the radio. Pietje's been on the radio every day."

"Pappa, there's so much going on in the world. I am listening to important things, Beppie's only listening to garbage on the radio."

"It's not garbage!"

Pietje, out of frustration, yanked at one of Beppie's blond braids.

"Ow! Stop it!" Beppie slapped Pietje on the head.

Pietje hit back in frustration. The blow pushed Beppie back behind the oil stove and almost toppled Henk's beautiful accordion perched on the mantle above. Henk kept it there as he loved to admire its color and sheen. It was the most beautiful object he owned. Beppie gasped, turned, and steadied the accordion. Alarmed, she quickly looked back at Henk.

"Stop! Just stop. BOTH OF YOU," Henk yelled and raised a hand, pointing a finger at Pietje. "Don't you ever hit a woman."

"She's not a woman!"

Henk fought against reacting to his son's insubordination. Lately, he had gotten into the habit of slapping Pietje across the ears, at times causing his son to go to bed with a swollen red ear. He had to control himself. "What did *Opa* tell you when he gave us his old radio?"

Beppie and Pietje stood side by side near the grand old hand-me-down radio and gave each other a sharp glance before looking back at their father.

"Pietje, what did *Opa* say?"

Pietje stuck his hands in the pockets of his short pants.

"Take your hands out of your pockets."

Pietje pulled out his hands.

Beppie smirked.

"Beppie, stop smirking. What did *Opa* say?"

Seven-year-old Beppie, wearing a sweater that was far too big for her, scrunched the side of her skirt with her left hand before answering. "We mustn't waste time listening to garbage and you control what we listen to."

Henk shook the newspaper into its former shape and folded it flat on his lap. He folded it one more time and slapped the folded paper onto the side table as he stood up. He pointed to the dining room table. Pietje and Beppie looked and saw little Corrie sitting quietly in the deepening dusk. She was focusing on knitting with two small needles and some pink yarn. She was oblivious to the mayhem.

"*Kleine* Corrie is keeping busy with something productive. Why can't you two? Beppie, go help your mother."

"Ah, Pappa…"

"Where is your mother?"

"In the kitchen."

"Then go."

Beppie knocked Pietje sideways with her hip before dragging her feet to the kitchen. As she passed Corrie, she hit her chair with her hip as well.

"Ow!"

"Beppie, apologize. And turn the light on for Corrie."

Beppie stomped toward the kitchen out back. Seeming to think twice about not obeying at least one thing her father demanded, she stepped back and pushed in the button switch for the light over the dining room table. Then disappeared into the back, entirely.

Henk shook his head and looked at Pietje. "You go upstairs."

"But why?"

Henk suddenly stood up, startling Poekie, who had been asleep. The dog's ears perked up as he looked at Henk's hand, pointing to the narrow opening to the stairs.

"Get up there."

Poekie lowered his head and sulkily crept to the stairs. Henk quickly bent down and yanked Poekie's collar back until Poekie sat down. No one laughed as they usually did when Poekie did cute things like that. These days everything made Henk severe and miserable, and Henk knew it.

Pietje waited before responding to his father's command. He looked over at the radio, then, in a huff, he ran to the stairs. Henk listened to his stomping up the creaky steps into the attic where Pietje and the girls slept.

Henk looked over and saw little Corrie looking up at the ceiling in response to the noise. Her mother suddenly appeared, wiping her hands on her shift. "What happened?"

"The boy is insubordinate."

"He likes listening to the BBC."

Henk looked at his watch. "I just read that the BBC is off the air until 2116 hours tonight."

"What's that mean?"

"It means the BBC is off the air until precisely sixteen minutes after nine." He knew he was terse. He felt he was going to explode. He briefly thought of going to the pub. Henk looked over at the radio. "They've taken BBC off the air while they set up mobile transmitters. They're planning to keep moving them around so that the Germans can't pinpoint the transmitter and bomb it."

Cornelia gasped. "Are the Germans at war with England now?!"

"No," he muttered, "but the Germans certainly are not as stupid as the British Prime Minister!"

"Who?"

"Chamberlain!" He picked up the paper and unfolded it quickly to read to her what he had read earlier. "Foreign language service starts at 1492 kHz."

Cornelia tolerated his snappy retort and pulled out a chair beside little Corrie at the table. "So, why do you think there will be a war between Germany and England?" Cornelia asked.

"Russia and Germany together attacked Poland. Now Britain, along with France, India, Australia, and New Zealand, are in tough spots, and they *have* to declare war! They *have* to stop him somehow! Because they're allies to Poland."

"What does that mean for us?" Cornelia's face tightened.

"Nothing." He wiped his forehead with a handkerchief from his woolen vest pocket. "Hopefully."

"But if Germany bombs England, and England bombs Germany, don't they have to …" Cornelia turned pale as she motioned a plane flying through the air above her head. "Right over us?"

"That's right."

"What if a plane should fall to the ground? What if one falls on the house?"

"What do you mean fall on the house?" Little Corrie, who up until then seemed oblivious to adults talking, sat bolt upright in her chair. Her eyes were so large that Henk thought they would bulge.

Oh, dear.

Both father and mother looked at little Corrie. They had briefly forgotten about her.

"I'm sure that won't happen," comforted Cornelia.

Little Corrie looked from her mother to her father. "Can you promise, Pappa?"

"Shouldn't you be in bed?" Henk wanted nothing to do with explaining the ugliness of war to his little daughter.

"It's Friday night, Pappa."

Henk sunk slowly back into his armchair and looked at little Corrie thoughtfully. Then he looked at his wife, then at his watch, then over at the kitchen. He picked up his newspaper again, and stuck it under his arm. He checked his pocket and pulled out some *guldens*. "I'm going to the pub. If you need me, send Pietje for me." With that, he walked to the front door, checked that his tie was straight in the small mirror by the coat hooks, and put on his cap at an elegant, rakish angle. Without a goodbye, he opened the door, let Poekie out, and left.

He knew as he passed by the front windows, that both his wife and little daughter were watching him go past. But he couldn't stand them looking at him anymore.

Too many things were brewing. In anticipation of trouble, the Reserves were to report the next day for a briefing. He did not know what to expect. But worse, today was the last day at work. He was sacked and didn't have the heart to tell them. And the Reserves paid practically nothing. Suddenly, he needed some comfort in his misery. He knew he wasn't the only one. In anticipation of trouble with Germany, the company closed its doors to move to Indonesia in fear of war.

Practically the whole neighborhood was out of work, including his brother-in-law, Frans.

LIESJE WAGNER WITH CORRIE GELAUF WAGNER

Not a very good beginning to the beginning of a war brewing over them any day now. And a war that had absolutely nothing to do with them.

Chapter 4
May 1940

Little Corrie's heart seemed to skip backward. An unusual sensation. She dreamt she was in a field, green, grasses waving slowly, bending and swirling around yellow daisies. She bent over to pick one but, as she did, the ground beneath her trembled. She was breathing backward, and the grasses stopped moving momentarily before going in reverse. She looked up into the sky, squinting against the sun's intense light.

Suddenly, a heavy droning noise came from the sky — making the sun shudder in her dream. Then, an explosion around her shattered the world to nothing.

Corrie's eyes flew open. She saw a strange light show playing on the old plaster ceiling. A spider web in the corner danced and pulsated with light. Then another massive explosion and rumble threw her sitting up in fear. She shook her sister Beppie.

"Beppie, Beppie! *Onweer!* It's thunder and lightning!"

Beppie stirred. "Don't," she muttered. She reached back and pushed Corrie away. The next explosion shook the bed, and Beppie sat up immediately. She looked at Corrie's wide eyes. Then she threw the blankets back and jumped out of bed. Corrie watched as Beppie lunged at the window. "Look!"

Corrie, frightened because she was alone in the bed now, slid out and scurried over to her older sister. She looked out the window and saw moving pillars of light, slashing the clouds in the dark sky. It was still night, surely. But there were large objects up in the air, and the beams were spotlights shining on exploding planes. Some fell to large angry red glows beyond the rooftops. Corrie thought it was somewhere between night and day. Perhaps she was still dreaming.

"Am I dreaming?" she asked her sister.

Beppie looked down and frowned. "No, silly. This is real."

Corrie saw a number of large planes chasing smaller ones. She noticed when one burst into a fireball in the sky and fell to the ground, you didn't hear the noise until a few seconds later. Then the glass in the window rattled, and the house shook.

Corrie's heart skipped. The world had stopped and changed somehow. She looked down at her nightgown and her heavy woolen socks. As she did, she was aware of Beppie suddenly disappearing, and although she would rather die than be left alone in the attic at that moment, the dreamlike aspects of the moment transported her to a safe spot within herself. It was all very mesmerizing and weirdly entertaining, like reading a book. You follow the story, but you know it's just a book all along.

The world rumbled again beneath her feet. Plaster dust sifted down from the top frame of the window. She heard Beppie waking up their brother on the other side of the thin wall.

"Pietje, Pietje! Wake Up!"

Corrie could hardly make out anything else as the droning noise in the sky intensified. Planes flew directly overhead. They screamed and swooshed and appeared so close. Guns fired somewhere in the streets. A movement in the pillars of light exposed white floating objects floating down to the ground. Angels?

Piet suddenly joined her at the window, Corrie turned and clung to her ten-year-old brother. He patted her on the back.

"That's okay, Corrie. They're planes! They're fighting in the sky!" He opened the sash as wide as he could, which made Corrie step back in fear. The noise was now deafening.

She watched him as he bent out of the window as far as he could, looking up and around. The wind blew at his hair. "Pappa's out there somewhere. They're shooting down the Germans!"

"What are those?" asked Beppie, pointing at the white objects in the sky.

Now both Beppie and Pietje filled the window.

"Angels?" asked Corrie. But they didn't hear her. The noise was deafening.

"Parachutes," said Pietje excitedly. "The Germans are dropping out of the skies!"

Little Corrie covered her mouth. She gasped. Forgetting her fear, Corrie turned and ran into the small dark hallway and, as carefully as she could, placed both hands on the rough plaster walls on either side of her for balance as she scurried down the narrow winding stairs. She ran past Poekie, where he lay whenever her father was away. Poekie's head rose, and his ears perked up. She ignored him.

"Mama! Mama!" she cried. She ran into the dining room, where her parents had a Murphy bed. She could just make out her mother's sleeping form under the covers. Street lights filtered through the living room lace curtains, but they were faint compared to the flashes of light that exploded and reflected off the walls around her. As she ran past the front windows that rattled a few seconds later, she could see neighbors running out of the houses across the narrow street to look up to the sky. She sprung onto the bed and shook her mother. "Mama, wake up!"

Her mother opened her eyes suddenly and shot up. She grabbed Corrie tightly. "What's going on?" Her eyes searched the room. Through the lace curtains, she saw movement. Suddenly another explosion rattled cups, glasses, plates, lamps. "What's happening?"

"The Germans are falling from the skies!" cried Corrie.

Suddenly, an unfamiliar sound echoed through the sky outside. Sirens.

Her mother swiveled out of bed and grabbed Corrie's hand. She ran to the bottom of the stairs and screamed for Beppie and Pietje. Then she ran to her bed and pulled the blankets off the mattress.

Corrie watched as her mother grunted and yanked at the mattress. By then, Pietje and Beppie had stumbled down the staircase and joined them.

"Help me, Pietje! We have to put this against the wall in the center of the house. Move the table!"

Pietje yanked at the heavy oak table. Beppie helped as much as she could. The table was cumbersome, and the rug beneath bunched up. Eventually, between Corrie's mother yanking at the mattress and her brother and sister pushing at the table, they were able to mount it against the dining room wall in the middle of the house.

Another explosion created a shattering sound.

"Get underneath," yelled their mother.

Corrie yanked at Pietje, but Pietje pushed her hand away.

"I'm going to look. Everyone's outside watching." He ran to the front door and threw it open. Corrie, wide-eyed, watched him slow down once he was through the door and onto the sidewalk. She saw him lift his face to the lightening skies. "They're coming down from everywhere!" he yelled back.

Cornelia, Beppie, and Corrie followed him out. Little Corrie craned her neck and saw that the day was beginning to dawn. Above her were hundreds of parachutes dotting the skies around which planes were still fighting. She heard a clattering above them.

"Look! A German landed on the rooftop over there!" yelled Pietje as he pointed behind them. They swiveled their heads, and Corrie saw a parachute billow and collapse onto a rooftop. A form stood up and pulled at the long parachute.

"Everyone! In the house!" Cornelia grabbed Corrie and lifted her. Corrie's heart beat fast as she looked over her mother's shoulder and saw people scurrying back into their houses. As her mother slammed the door shut, they heard more menacing sounds. Machine guns. And not far away from their home.

Cornelia threw Corrie under the mattress, and Beppie crawled in on one side, as her mother crawled in on the other. Pietje scrambled beside Beppie. Pietje held out his arm and tried to pull Poekie's head under the mattress. Even in the dark, little

Corrie could see the whites of Poekie's eyes. It occurred to her that animals also felt when it was the end of the world.

The mattress muffled the noise somewhat. The air felt heavy with the smell of the old spring-coiled mattress and Poekie's foul breath, but it felt safer crouching under protection. Explosions rocked the house around them.

Corrie cried. Beppie's body shook violently beside her. Corrie felt her mother free one arm to put across all their shoulders.

"What about Pappa?" asked Pietje. Corrie could barely hear him.

"Pappa will be fine."

Little Corrie wondered how on earth he could be okay with so much exploding and shooting going on. The concept of ever losing him had never occurred to her until then. And now that she was aware of it, she couldn't see how this fear of loss would ever go away. Somehow, she sensed she was quickly growing older than her five years. Whether she liked it or not.

"Tonight, we go to bed in our clothes, just in case," announced Cornelia. The radio had informed them their soldiers were still bravely fighting the Germans on the streets, bridges, and airfields. Sometimes the announcer said they were winning, and sometimes they were not. But the final tally was more Germans and German planes had gone down than those of the Dutch.

During the third day of fighting, a note dropped through their brass letter slot. It was from their father.

"Will Pappa come home soon?" Little Corrie asked as her mother read the note.

Her mother shook her head. "No, your father will be busy for a while." She folded the letter and put it in the front pocket of her work shift.

"What does it say?" asked Pietje.

"Just that he's alive. He is not in combat. He helps with rubble and communications."

"What's for dinner?" asked Beppie suddenly. "I'm hungry."

Little Corrie looked at her sister. Food never even entered her mind. Not since worrying about her father.

"We're talking about Pappa," reminded Pietje.

Beppie looked at him blankly. She had dark circles under her eyes like everyone else Corrie noticed. Corrie looked at her mother, and then at Pietje. They were all tired-looking.

Her mother sighed and nodded. "Pietje, go ask *Mevrouw* van Der Horst if she has any extra potatoes. Maybe we can trade. Tell her I have enough carrots if she should need any."

Pietje nodded at his mother.

"But look before you go out! And when you get back, I'll make supper, and we will all sit by the radio."

Pietje smiled. He flicked his blonde hair out of his eyes and unlocked the door. Slowly he looked out—first one way and then another. There was distant gunfire. One explosion lightly rattled the windows. He quietly slipped out and shut the door behind him.

> *"Today we have to admit that no happiness can be expected in this world if those who are solely responsible for the present situation are not definitely checked in their force of unscrupulous destruction and utter disregard of law and the most elemental principles of morality. I pray God that our allied force be blessed and that the dawn of the day when freedom would be restored for the Netherlands and to all other victims of German aggression would be near..."*[1]

Little Corrie watched her mother wipe tears from her eyes and then cover them with her right hand. Little Corrie, spread out on her mother's lap, fiddled with her mother's necklace.

---

[1] May 1940. Queen Wilhelmina spoke to her people through the BBC from England.

Impatiently, her mother pulled it out of her hand. Little Corrie sat up. She looked over at her brother, Pietje, who sat with Beppie on the floor in front of the radio. Poekie was there, too. All of them were listening to what Queen Wilhelmina had to say over the BBC. She looked at the roughly boarded-up windows of the living room, then at the large radio. To her horror, Corrie saw a hole splintered in the large casing. She looked over at the living room wall and saw where a stray bullet had sliced through. Then she looked at her mother's necklace again, for distraction, resting on one of her mother's collarbones. Its pendant held tiny photos of a world that lived before this Hell. Whatever Hell this was.

"Mama." Corrie needed comforting.

Beppie turned to her and raised a finger to her lips. "Shhhh! It's the *Koningin* speaking!"

"I'm not talking to you," whispered Corrie loudly.

Beppie gave her a dirty look.

Corrie played with the pendant some more, "Mama."

Corrie's mother lowered her hand and looked down at her. She had a bandage across her eyebrow. Small shrapnel. Some plaster from somewhere.

"Why is everyone so sad."

Pietje looked back at her. Queen Wilhelmina had finished her speech, and the radio announcer returned reiterating what the Queen had said.

"Turn it off, Pietje. We've heard enough for now." Cornelia shifted in the armchair and shook her head.

Pietje crawled to the radio and turned it off. He sat back and leaned against the radio cabinet and pulled out a little Indian rubber ball. He bounced it in front of him on the carpet, catching it quickly.

Corrie's eyes stayed glued on the ball.

Pietje met her gaze. He stopped bouncing the ball and blinked as if he suddenly remembered Corrie's question. His eyes looked unusually large. His face was drawn, and dark circles ringed the eyes. "Because the Germans are here. Many people died, Corrie. And we don't know if Pappa is safe."

"Who was that lady speaking? Does she know where Pappa is? Maybe she knows."

"Well, Corrie, that was the Queen. The Queen is the mother of all of The Netherlands and the colonies. She ran away to go to England to be safe." Her mother hesitated to try to find the right words.

She could sense that her mother was struggling to be positive. What would they do if their Pappa…

"The Queen has to take care of the colonies from England because the Nazis won't let her do it from here. They promised there would be no more killing if the Queen gave up everything, but she refused. And everyone is glad she refused to give in. Otherwise, Hitler would be in control of everything."

"That bad man who yells on the radio?" asked Corrie.

Pietje snorted. "*Ja*, now she's safe in England, and we aren't."

Cornelia looked at her son. "Sometimes, it's very complicated."

"Mama."

"*Ja*, Corrie."

"Did it hurt when that scapel hit you?"

"Shrapnel!" corrected Pietje.

Corrie gave him a hurt expression.

"No, it didn't *liefje*."

"She is in England now?" asked Beppie.

"Yes, she's just across the channel of the North Sea. Remember how I pointed to you where England was from the beach in Scheveningen?"

Suddenly, a loud explosion rattled the windows. Then almost immediately another, and then another rocked their room. The sirens went off for the umpteenth time.

"Pietje!" their mother exclaimed. "What is that now?" Explosions drummed against their house, their roof, their eardrums. "Not again!"

Pietje got up and ran to put his shoes on, then opened the door.

Beppie shot up. "I'm coming, too!"

Pietje looked back as he closed the door. "No, stay." But the door opened again almost immediately as Pietje instantly returned. He kicked off his shoes and picked them up. "Mama, I'm going up to the roof. The Germans are bombing somewhere again, but I can't see where. I want to get a better look."

The loud, sad wail still cut through the heavy rumble of the distant bombing.

Pietje scrambled up the rickety stairs. Beppie, Cornelia, and Corrie got up and quickly ran to the front hallway to look up the stairs. Suddenly, there was a frantic knock on their door. Cornelia turned and opened it. *Mevrouw* Van der Horst from across the road stood crying, holding her little boy.

"*Mevrouw* Van der Horst. Come in!"

"I'm all alone in the house with little Robbie. Gerhardt is fighting. I don't know where Leo went and the sirens are going. My nerves are so rattled. Would Pietje know where Leo is? And what is happening?"

"Just one moment," Cornelia said, then turned to the stairway. "Pietje? Piet!"

"*Ja*!" Little Corrie could barely hear him over the bomb explosions and the siren.

"Do you know where Leo is?"

"No!"

"*Mevrouw* Van der Horst, come in. We should put the radio back on!" Her mother pulled Corrie closer to her. Corrie responded by tightly holding onto her mother's hand.

Pietje's face appeared at the top of the stairs. "*Ja*, the radio!"

Her mother let go of Corrie and ran to the radio. The tubes were still warm, so it didn't take long to get a signal.

> "*...bombing continues on the impoverished city of Rotterdam. It's a glimpse at burning Hell, the bombs just keep coming, and the country is terrified at the sight of such a blatant show of destruction and lack of respect for human life. Let us pray not too many people are caught in this blaze of a killing machine...*"

"What do we do, Mama?" Beppie cried from the hallway.

Their mother stood, wringing her hands. Then she pointed at the mattress leaning sluggishly against the wall. "There! We have to go back under the mattress! That's all we can do!"

Suddenly, over the noise, they could hear Pietje stomping down the stairs. He appeared excitedly, waving his hands. "You should see this, Mama. Come see!" He turned and disappeared up the stairs again.

Mevrouw Van der Horst grabbed her little boy and scrambled into the dining room, pushing her little boy underneath the mattress. With a huff, she got down on her knees and yanked it back enough to make room for herself.

Corrie saw her mother look back at the mattress and then down at her. Corrie on impulse turned and ran to the stairs. She passed Beppie and steadied herself with both hands on the rough plaster walls as she climbed up the steep stairs to the attic. She could feel Beppie following her in the dark.

Up in the top room, Corrie stopped at the doorway. She saw that the cover to the access hatch to the roof was taken away and tossed onto the bed she shared with Beppie. She saw shafts of glowing faint light pouring through the opening.

"Pietje!"

Corrie turned around and saw that their mother had followed her up the stairs. Her mother hurried past her and climbed up on the bed. She stood looking up through the hatch. Corrie scrambled on top of the bed and stood beside her.

"Pietje? Pietje! Be careful!" her mother yelled.

Corrie saw her brother's head come into view. He looked down and yelled, "I don't know, but I think it's Rotterdam. They're bombing the harbor!"

"Mama, can I go up, too?"

Cornelia looked down at Corrie and shook her head. "No. It's too dangerous." Her mother grunted as she hoisted herself up onto the ledge of the opening, then clumsily shifted her body out onto the roof. Corrie had to duck out of the way of her mother's legs.

Beppie came over and climbed up on the bed beside her, making Corrie lose her balance. She fell on her hands and knees and struggled against the jiggling mattress to stand straight again.

Suddenly, her mother's hand reached down through the hole. Little Corrie reached up and let her mother lift her onto the roof, where she immediately sat down on her behind. Seeing the rooftops all around them gave her vertigo. She started to cry and was only barely aware that her mother helped Beppie up onto the roof, as well. When she realized she wasn't going to slip off the tiled roof, Corrie relaxed a little and was able to look at the glowing horizon. Surely it was Hell she was looking at. It was just as the priest described it in church—hail, brimstone, fire, and death. How many people die in those raging fires and explosions?

Corrie innocently reacted as only a child could. "*Okay.*" She thought to herself, "*That's bad. But it's not happening here, so we're okay.*" She felt disjointed from the grisly scene, watching it as if it was one of those news reels one watched before a Disney film at the cinema.

Perhaps because she was still sitting on the roof and lower than everyone else, or maybe because she was right next to the opening that led down into the attic, she could hear *Mevrouw* Van der Horst screaming with fear below.

The overwhelming unfamiliarity of the activities around her suddenly made Corrie focus on the little mundane thoughts she could understand. There's no way she had anything left to give others, even the time of day.

Mevrouw Van der Horst would have to take care of herself.

Chapter 5
May 1940

"The Nazi's are almost here. They're coming here!"

Little Corrie sat under the kitchen table, drawing airplanes on the wood above her head. Her arm felt heavy as she'd been drawing in that position for a while. She hoped no adult would ever find them. It was her secret.

"What do you mean, Pietje?"

Little Corrie peeked at her mother from under the table. Her mother stood, open-mouthed, holding a hammer aloft and looking around absently. "Where are the girls?" She stepped forward and grabbed Pietje's vest. "Where are the girls? Are they still in bed?"

"I don't know."

Little Corrie thought it was an excellent time to play Hide and Seek. She said nothing.

Her mother ran out of the kitchen. "Beppie! Corrie!"

"*Ja?*" Little Corrie could hear Beppie from upstairs.

"Is that you, Beppie?"

"*Ja?* I'm getting dressed!"

"Is Corrie with you?"

"*Nee?*"

Corrie could hear her mother throw the front door open. She heard her call in the street. "Corrie! Corrie!"

Suddenly, Corrie heard something else in the distance. Engines roared, their sound wafting in from outside. But there was something else. Drums clashing. Music.

"They are coming in tanks, with motorbikes, with trucks, on bikes, on foot. Some of them are on horses! And they have a military band."

Little Corrie could hear *Mevrouw* van der Horst from across the road. She must have her baby with her because Corrie heard it cry loudly. "What's this I hear about the Nazis coming?"

"They're spilling over the border."

Mevrouw van der Horst sounded like she was getting upset. "But aren't we still neutral?" Corrie heard her voice crack.

"I think we're way past that now, *Mevrouw*."

"Well, what are we going to do? With no husbands to defend us? Will they kill us? Will they shoot my baby?" Corrie heard her wail. "Leo! Come quick. Something terrible is happening!"

Little Corrie couldn't take the suspense any longer. She crawled out from under the table and slowly, carefully, crawled across the next room to peer out the front door. She lay on her tummy and leaned her chin in her hand.

A slightly older boy in a heavy undershirt stood beside his mother. Corrie could not remember him from before. But he was smart because his glassy blue eyes looked straight through the door at her on the floor. Leo was the only one who could see her. He blinked.

She blinked, still resting her chin in her hand.

"Leo, they've come over the border!" *Mevrouw* Van der Horst clasped at her loose top.

"Who?" he asked, still looking at little Corrie.

"The Germans, Leo, the Nazis!"

Corrie watched as the boy's face dropped. "Seriously?" he asked his mother. Then he looked at Pietje beside him.

Pieje cocked an ear. "I can hear them!" He quickly tucked his shirt into his corduroy pants and disappeared through the door. "Come on, Leo, let's get on my bike and see!"

Cornelia bent through the door. "*Nee*, Pietje!"

"Aw, Mam!" Pietje kicked at paper garbage, spread by the wind from nearby bombed houses.

Mevrouw Van der Horst also got into the act. She yanked at her son's collar. "*Jij blijft hier!*" she screamed.

Suddenly, a noise of a different caliber echoed through the street. Little Corrie, not caring about hiding any longer, got on all fours and quickly stood slightly behind Beppie who was watching her mother. Little Corrie saw her mother and *Mevrouw* Van der Horst standing outside, looking to the end of their street. Corrie stepped past Beppie and looked out. Hordes of people were passing on foot and with bikes.

Pietje turned to look pleadingly at his mother. Suddenly he eyed his little sister. He pointed at her wordlessly.

Cornelia turned and saw her little daughter in the doorway, and sighed. "For crying out loud." She walked to the door. "I'm going to turn on the radio and see if I can get some news." She grunted as she picked up Corrie. "Where have you been?"

"I was playing Hide and Seek," Corrie answered uncertainly.

"I was so worried. Don't do that again. You come when I call."

Little Corrie bit her lip.

"*Mevrouw* Gelauf, may I come and listen to the radio, too?" *Mevrouw* Van der Horst looked sick and pale.

"Yes, of course, *Mevrouw* Van der Horst. Please, come in."

Corrie struggled out of her mother's arms and stepped back as her mother led her neighbor into the house to the radio.

Corrie saw *Mevrouw* Van der Horst motion to Leo, who immediately followed his mother into the living room. Corrie turned her head just as her mother turned on the radio. It took a while for the tubes to warm up, but eventually, slowly, static grated from the speakers. Her mother gingerly twisted the tuning knob until she zeroed in on a talking voice.

> "*Dames en Heeren*, we have been informed that
> Hitler had this planned for a long while.
> Tens of thousands of their soldiers have been trained
> just for this moment and have crossed the border."

"My goodness. We must have lost," whispered *Mevrouw* Van der Horst.

Corrie's mother frowned and silently nodded her head as she held her ear to the radio. As if on cue, a rumble filled the sky. As the thunder mounted, the ground beneath them shook. The windows rattled. They all scrambled out of the house into the street. They stopped and looked up at a flying hoard covering the sky.

"They look like flying grasshoppers," said Pietje.

Corrie, frightened, craned her neck to peer into the sky.

"Like in the Bible," yelled Beppie over the din.

Mevrouw Van der Horst raised her voice over the roar and recited, "And when it was morning, the east wind brought the locusts." She tightened her hold on her toddler.

Little Corrie looked at *Mevrouw* Van der Horst before looking up once again.

What remained of the early morning's expanse of blue sky was now completely filled with thousands of planes. The sky darkened as the sunlight couldn't get through.

As if on cue, a marching band was passing the end of their road. Pietje and Leo bolted down the street. Corrie watched until they disappeared into the gathering crowd at the end of the street.

Mevrouw Van der Horst shrugged her shoulders at Cornelia. Then together—she, her mother Cornelia, Beppie, *Mevrouw* Van der Horst and her baby—all made their way to the end of the street.

Along the way, *Mevrouw* Van der Horst's baby began to cry. Soon her cries were muffled by the marching band and the sound of engines. The mass of people at the end of the street had increased in numbers. As her mother lifted Corrie to get a view of things, Corrie saw Pietje and Leo shimmy up a street light and cling to the bottom of the cast iron shades. She watched their eyes squinting into the air at the planes, then down at the passing band. She looked over at the band. There were trumpets, tubas, trombones and French horns.

She saw the big drum player bang the beat with large sticks. Behind the band, an endless mass of soldiers. Thousands upon thousands of soldiers stomping stiffly in their highly polished boots, marched past with their guns and packs. The odd Dutchman or teenager cheered and shot out their hands in a salute to Hitler.

"Dirty Nazi sympathizers," yelled *Mevrouw* Van der Horst. She spat in their direction, but the spit landed on a person next to her. That person, fortunately, didn't notice, and Corrie looked at the glob of spit on the back of their coat and wondered if she should laugh.

She looked questioningly at her mother who was too engrossed in the frightening scene before them to share in the funny secret of the spit not going where it should.

Little Corrie sensed a strange mixture of fear and curiosity in people around them. Some of them were as solemn as if watching a death march go by. She saw some of the older on-lookers cry.

The whole world was upside down, and little Corrie intuitively realized that nothing would be the same anymore. It was a different world. And she had no idea what to expect.

Corrie sat behind her mother's elegant tea trolley. She knew she had to be very careful. Corrie wanted to trace the elegant carvings in the wood with her finger. She traced the edge of the upper tray, and followed it to the floor, by going around and down the wooden wheels. Then Corrie traced the other end and followed the other wooden wheel to the floor. She was getting quite bright at it, she felt.

However, she got bored as it was far too easy to just follow the carved pattern with a finger. So, she wondered if she traced the design with a pencil, she might learn how to re-trace it later on a piece of paper. She could impress her father when he came back with how talented she was, creating such beautiful designs. She reasoned she would make lovely home-made *Kerstmis* cards for the coming year because there certainly wasn't enough money to buy them the year before. She was going to be the hero of the day and make them. She remembered her mother saying how embarrassed she was that she couldn't send a single card to her relatives who were under so much stress in Germany and could use a little lift.

She bit her tongue as she followed the carved patterns with the lead point. After a few moments, she sat back and eyed her work. With quiet horror, she realized that one could easily see the squiggly lead marks she had made. She didn't mean to push so hard. They didn't at all look like the patterns they were supposed to copy. Frustrated, she retraced it all again. Then she licked her palm and rubbed at the pencil markings. Her stomach turned—she realized that the pencil had ruined the soft wood carving. She leaned back against the wall. She slapped her cheeks with both her hands, as she saw Shirley Temple do once in a magazine picture. "Oh," she whispered to herself. Corrie shrugged. "Oh well," she whispered down to her little doll beside her on the floor. She picked it up and showed it what she had done.

"*It's not that bad*," comforted the doll as it pointedly looked at Corrie.

Corrie opened her eyes wide and said, "No?"

"*No*," said the doll. "*Forget about it. No one will see it. Now, what about me and my bed?*"

Corrie had knitted a new little outfit for her doll, and had promised it a beautiful bed. Earlier that morning, she found her mother's lipstick and, though the end result was quite smudged, she managed to put some on its little mouth. She also found her mother's old handkerchief she thought would make a beautiful blanket.

"*Now I want to play with the tea trolley*," demanded the doll.

So, Corrie helped the doll sit and then slide off the beautiful wheels. Finally, her doll decided she wanted to sleep after all, but insisted on sleeping on the top tray with the cups and saucers.

"No touching the cups and saucers," Corrie reminded the doll in a whisper. But maybe, just maybe, she could perhaps carefully lay it down for a moment's rest between the delicate items without having to move them.

Corrie looked through the spokes of the large wheel at the rest of the room to make sure the coast was clear. No one was around.

She knew her mother was in the kitchen, plucking feathers off a chicken. She was guaranteed to be busy for a while.

With a grand gesture, she held up the doll as if in a royal pose. Then it slowly made its way up the wooden wheel. Somehow, she miraculously hopped from the large wooden wheel to the overhanging edge of the tray. Poof! She finally stood on the glass platform amongst all the beautiful cups and saucers. Carefully, she meandered between them, and past a teapot and sugar bowl. Then the little milk jug. Hooray, she made it to her royal bedroom.

Almost.

She couldn't easily reach that spot from where she was sitting on the floor against the wall, so Corrie got up on her knees to give herself a more extended reach. As she did, her doll swiped at a cup, and it teetered off the saucer and onto the tray's glass top. It made enough of a clatter that it shocked Corrie. And the doll.

In her surprise, she fell back on her behind, shoving the elegant tea trolley sideways with her knee.

The cup fell off the tea trolley, and before it reached the Persian carpet below, Corrie had already covered her ears and screwed her eyes shut.

Her innocent and childlike version of, *'If the tree falls in the forest and no one is there to hear, does it still make a sound?'* She took it a little further: *'If she doesn't hear it fall and she doesn't see it fall, did it actually fall? And more importantly: Would it keep from breaking?'*

Corrie's little heart jumped up into her throat. She couldn't breathe. Suddenly, under her behind, she felt a strange vibration in the floor. Despite her commitment to not allow the reality of a broken cup happen, she dropped her hands and opened her eyes wide. She could hear Poekie barking from the back of the house.

The front door rattled again under the weight of a heavy sharp object. Corrie heard her mother hurry from the back of the house to the front door. The door creaked open. *"Ja, Meneer?"* Her mother sounded strange.

Little Corrie got on her hands and knees and peered around the corner of the room into the narrow hallway. She saw two

German soldiers standing menacingly in the doorway. Behind them, she could hear the rumble of jeeps and car doors slamming. German instructions barked through their street. One soldier held out a white sheet of paper to her mother.

"*Mevrouw*," he began in stiff Dutch, "You are ordered to leave this house immediately on behalf of the Reich. We require this place to house a German officer."

Corrie noticed her mother's legs start to tremble.

"You can speak German to me. I was born in Heidelberg," her mother briefly announced.

The soldier softened his tone and continued to speak in German, and her mother replied likewise.

Corrie rarely heard her mother converse in German. Intuitively, she hoped it would help their case. But to no avail. After a few moments of intense conversation, the soldier spoke stiffly and clicked his heels. In Dutch, he announced loudly. "*Mevrouw*, you have exactly fifteen minutes to gather your things."

Corrie choked. And as she sat crouched on the floor with her doll, the soldiers stepped into the front room. They looked down on her, then stepped past her. She scrambled up, clutching her doll.

She watched as they touched the Persian rug on the dining room table and nodded. They spoke in German, but she could sense they were looking to see what they can use. Then the one soldier stepped over to the tea caddy. He picked up one of the coffee cups with the delicate gold trim. She could only understand the word "*kaffee*." As they stood there, admiring the teacups, Cornelia rounded the bend with a quickly thrown-together blanket roll and clothing. She was crying.

"Pietje! Get the wagon in the alley."

Pietje, who had been upstairs, was right behind her. He froze when he looked into the dining room. He saw the soldiers at the mantle where the Rose Accordion was perched and looking magnificent. One of them fingered it appreciatively.

"*Schon.*"

Her mother froze when she saw the soldier touching the accordion.

Corrie looked at Pietje, who looked quite frightened. She saw her mother look back at him and motion to him to get to the kitchen.

Pietje passed his mother and little Corrie and disappeared into the back of the house. Corrie could still hear Poekie barking. Suddenly, Poekie stopped. A moment later, Pietje came back holding Poekie, who strained against his collar and snarled. Pietje pulled him back hard.

One soldier drew his pistol and aimed it at Poekie.

Cornelia screamed. "*Nein!*"

The other soldier put a reassuring gloved hand on his companion's arm. The pistol was lowered.

"That's okay. Here, come, boy," said the soldier softly, motioning to Poekie.

Pietje pulled back on the collar again, staring at the soldier. Poekie bared his teeth and growled.

"*Ach*, I have one just like him at home. I miss him! He's a good boy! He's just doing his job well!"

Pietje remained standing, staring at the soldier.

The second soldier blinked and nodded. "You better take him in back. Tie him up."

Pietje didn't move.

"Why don't you leave him with the house. We will take care of him. Train him." The other soldier grinned.

Little Corrie felt a shiver up her spine. She didn't know precisely why, but it was the coolness, the feigned friendliness, that she sensed. *Don't leave Poekie here*, she thought.

"We're not going to leave him with you, Nazis!" Pietje sneered.

"Pietje, don't show them disrespect! Don't say anything. Just take Poekie to the back until we're ready to go!" Their mother turned to the soldier and, in Dutch, said, "We must take him with us. He is my husband's dog."

"Oh? Where is your husband now?"

"Probably cleaning up your mess," she said, trembling. She turned and slowly moved forward, placing her hands on the handlebar of the tea caddy, and started to maneuver it out of the corner.

The soldier lunged closer and put his gloved hand over hers. "*Nein. Das bleibt.*"

Corrie watched as her mother gasped. Tears that had welled up in her eyes rolled loose and dripped off her cheeks. Her mother begged in German to let her take her beloved tea caddy, but the soldier simply stared at her. Finally, a third soldier showed up in the doorway.

"*Geh raus!*"

The first soldier grabbed Pietje by the collar and, together with Poekie, threw them out the front door. Immediately, he drew out his pistol and aimed it at Poekie, who had snarled and nipped at him.

"Stop! Stop! We're going!" screamed Cornelia. "Pietje, take Poekie to *Mevrouw* Van der Horst and come back for the little wagon! And the old baby carriage! Beppie, help me with the kitchenware."

Corrie hadn't seen Beppie standing around the corner up the stairs. Suddenly Beppie ran past her through the dining room into the kitchen. Her mother followed but made a quick detour to the mantle to collect the beautiful Rose Accordion. She placed her hands on it and glanced back to see if the soldiers saw, but they were back to admiring the coffee cups. Her mother bent over and grabbed the accordion case, as well. Deftly, quietly, she moved the accordion into the case. Then she slipped the blanket that was on the side armchair, over it. She picked it up and cradled it against her chest as she hurried back to Corrie. She grabbed Corrie's hand and led her to the kitchen.

"*Kom, schatje.* Help Mamma in the kitchen."

"What about Pappa?"

"What about Pappa?" her mother whispered.

"How will Pappa know where we went?"

"Pappa will find us."

"Where are we going?"

"To *Opa*'s. I know there's not much room, but we have no choice."

Little Corrie felt better, knowing they will be safe with her *Opa*. Beautiful, lovable *Opa*. And she can play with her cousins, Sientje and Rieky, who lived nearby. Then an awful thought occurred to her. "My dolls!" cried Corrie. *The big one is upstairs*!

"No time, but you can take this one." Her mother motioned to the doll on the floor behind the tea caddy. She bent over to retrieve it.

Little Corrie wailed. "I want both my dolls. I can't leave them. They need me!"

Her mother bent down to face Corrie. She wiped Corrie's tears away. "Okay, you go upstairs and get your bigger doll. I'm sure they can wait a few seconds. I'm sure they won't shoot us if we go upstairs one more time." Her mother quickly glanced up at the soldiers. One slightly nodded and then looked up at the ceiling.

Corrie looked back at the soldier who had drawn the pistol. She eyed his holster and noticed he was still holding the gun, slightly behind his leg. She wasn't too sure about whether they minded or not, but her mother dragged her upstairs before she thought any further of what awful outcome would come if she dared hold them back a minute longer than allowed.

Corrie struggled with her two dolls. It was raining, and their ceramic faces had smudges all over their hand-painted pink cheeks and lips. Dirt even showed within the depths of the eyes. Alarmingly, she noted that one of the eyes on the smaller one lost its eyelashes. She frowned at the unsettling sight as she continued sauntering along. She quickly looked behind her to see if there were eyelashes on the ground, but she only saw Poekie ambling behind at a distance. She held onto the dolls by their clothing, desperately trying to keep up with the rest of the family. Then something in the corner of her eye caught her attention, and she looked down at the now muddy dragging hem of the long dress that was on the largest of the two dolls. It was a lavender lacy Victorian dress, best described to her as an old-style dress from a country called *Engeland.*

It was then she realized it was England, and that's where the Queen was. She wanted to run away to England, too. Take her dolls with her and keep them safe.

She thought of those terrible German soldiers at the door who wanted their house. They didn't even wait for her mother to invite them in, when they banged at the door. They handed her mother a piece of paper, which was enough to make her mother cry.

It was all too confusing.

It didn't matter.

What did matter was that her dolls needed a bath, and she needed to wash their clothes. "Mama, I need to give my dolls a bath. Soon."

Her mother, eyes swollen with tears, looked at her wearily. She was pushing Corrie's old baby carriage with all the kitchen wares piled into it.

"Come on, Corrie. You're slowing down. Try and keep up." Cornelia stopped to adjust her scarf around her head, against the cold early summer rain, and pulled up her gloves before grabbing the handrail of the carriage anew to push it further.

Corrie squinted up through the rain in a grey sky as she walked along. She looked at the surrounding trees. Having left their neighborhood, slowly the scenery looked different but still familiar. It looked grey and sad. She thought they were on their way to *Opa*'s grand house over the pub by the canal. But it usually felt happier than this.

Unfortunately, she didn't watch where she was going and stepped into a pile of horse manure. Pietje, who struggled ahead of his mother, looked back. He pulled the wagon stacked high with chairs and a table they had taken apart. All were on top of the old radio which they managed to lug out while the soldiers were out on the street overseeing the unloading of a truck.

"Keep walking, Corrie," Pietje said as he kept walking backward against the weight of the wagon. He motioned to her feet.

"I stepped in poop," she yelled, standing and looking down at the caked mess around her shoes.

"Wipe it off against the edge of the curb."

She shuffled over to the curb and scraped off as much of the pungent-smelling mess as she could.

"Next time, don't follow us on the road. Walk along the sidewalk."

She hurried, this time along the sidewalk, and eyed the dirty waters of the canal on her left. Much debris floated in its dark waters. She looked up and watched her mother's back as she huffed and puffed ahead of her.

Pietje dropped his load and walked back to her. "Here, Corrie. Just a moment." He bent over and, with an old rag from his pocket, wiped her shoes as best he could. He straightened up, holding the soiled cloth and looked around. He went to the side of the canal and dropped it into its dark depths. Then he stepped back to Corrie, walked her to the wagon, and picked her up. As he raised her into the air, her insides seemed to flip. She gripped at her dolls even harder so they wouldn't fall.

"Oomph!" The air was knocked out of her when she landed on top of the load Pietje had been pushing. As Pietje pushed forward, she almost rolled backward. She didn't know how to tell her brother she was afraid of falling off. She let go of one of the dolls and grabbed at the handle of the accordion case beneath her. To her horror, the doll slipped off her lap and disappeared over the edge of the pile.

"Pietje!" she screamed from her mountain top. She cried in desperation.

"Beppie, get the doll!" yelled her mother.

Beppie, already overburdened with massive blanket rolls of clothes and sundries, looked back, irritated by yet another distasteful chore.

Corrie beseeched her with her eyes before looking back, spotting her doll on the wet cobblestones. She cried. "Beppie!"

Beppie shifted the rolls to the upper part of her ribcage against her shoulders. She looked around for a reasonably clean spot on the sidewalk to drop them but found none. There were either pools of rainwater or dog poop.

"Beppie, get the doll!" demanded her mother, who sounded close to tears again.

Corrie, crying, saw her mother gritting her teeth. Now was not the time to test her patience.

Beppie gave up, dropped the two heavy rolls, and lumbered back, retracing her steps along where they walked.

Corrie watched through tears, her eyes glued to her sister. She saw Beppie reach the doll and pick it up as if it was a tree branch. No gentleness, no mindfulness. She reached out her arms in Beppie's direction.

Beppie ran and caught up to Pietje, who hadn't stopped, and she slapped the doll onto Corrie's lap. "Here. Here's your stupid doll."

Corrie, heart-broken, cradled the doll against the other and felt heated agitation coming out of her pores. "She's not a stupid doll, you stupid!"

"Pietje."

Pietje and Beppie stopped and looked back at their mother. They were worried because their mother's voice cracked, sounding like an older woman's.

Corrie also looked at her mother. She noticed her eyes were dead with shame and hopelessness. It started to rain heavily.

"Let's get under this tree, here," she weakly suggested.

"It's about time," complained Beppie, who had just finished balancing the two large bedrolls again. "These are getting heavier with the rain."

Wagon loads, and baby carriage were carted under the leafy boughs of the nearest tree. Though rain still filtered down through the branches, standing right against the trunk helped somewhat. There was nothing they could do about everything they were lugging. Wet will have to remain wet for now.

Corrie watched Pietje slide down the trunk to the ground. He sat on top of one of the protruding roots and swung his legs over the edge of the canal wall. Pietje picked up a dry branch and started breaking it into little pieces, chucking them into the dirty water below. When Corrie pressed herself against him on the ground, he opened his coat and wrapped one side around Corrie's shoulders, feebly protecting her clothes from getting any wetter.

Beppie decided to do the same and slid down next to them on the other side of Pietje. He opened the other side of his coat and tried to get it around Beppie.

Little Corrie lifted the large doll and held her over her head against the plopping raindrops but then decided against it. So, she stuffed the toy as much as she could under her woolen sweater. She looked over and watched two ducks paddling in the dirty waters. They were cackling and talking to each other. Then Corrie watched Poekie drink from a dirty puddle.

People hurried by on their bicycles, both ways. An old Model A Ford came rumbling around the bend. It honked its horn loudly as warning to the slower cyclists ahead. It chugged past them. Suddenly it stopped and went in reverse. A couple of cyclists rang their bells in protest.

Everyone under the tree squinted at the car. Corrie saw that it was *Oom* Frans. She watched him roll down the driver's side window.

"What the hell are you doing there? What's going on?" he yelled.

Cornelia pulled out the soggy summons from her coat pocket, and it flapped wetly in her hands as she gestured. "The Nazis took our home! We had to get out right away."

Frans got out of the Ford and looked at the things under the tree. "I'm astounded," he bleated. "They're kicking us out of our homes? You're not serious!"

Cornelia sadly motioned her arms to her children before her face collapsed in renewed grief.

"What about the rest of your stuff?"

Cornelia shook her head. "Not allowed to take all our things. We had fifteen minutes to pack!" She cried.

"Come! You guys are getting wet. Get in!"

Everyone struggled to get to the car.

"Everything can't fit in," said Pietje. That was evident to everyone.

Frans went to the back of the Ford and opened the small boot trunk. "Put the blanket rolls in here. We'll stay in the car and keep an eye on the stuff under the tree until it stops raining. Cornelia, you and the kids, get in and stay dry."

Little Corrie had never been in a car before, and she didn't like them. They went too fast on the road. Even the sound of them frightened her. They sounded like sick, roaring animals.

Pietje picked her up and carted her to the car.

Cornelia shivered in her wet, thin coat. "When do you start at the mattress factory?"

"Not soon enough," replied a grim Frans. He looked over at the pile left under the tree and spied the top of the accordion case. "Pietje, you better get that accordion case and take it out of the wet. Keep it on your lap for now."

"*Oh, natuurlijk!*" Pietje bolted out of the car, unearthed the case from the wagon, and ran back with it, covering his head from the rain. He settled into the back of the car and wiped at the wet surface of the case.

Poekie lumbered to the door and whined, getting up on its hind legs, panting, looking in through the window. Pietje shook his head at him.

"Oh, dear," muttered Cornelia. She tore her sad eyes away from Poekie and the wet accordion case.

Little Corrie craned her neck around Pietje to look up at the sky out the window. The rain lessened just as quickly as it began.

"It looks like the rain will stop soon. Where are you heading to?" Frans wiped at his wet forehead.

"To Pap's."

Frans looked thoughtfully at Cornelia.

"I don't know where else to go. It seems the best option until the Nazis summon us with a notice as to where we're going." Cornelia lowered her sad gaze.

"Have you heard from Henk?" Frans knew most of the soldiers, including the reserves, had not come home as yet. They were still employed in emergency clean-up, building bomb shelters, or were dead. Thankfully, they knew for certain Henk was okay. But they hadn't heard from him since that one letter had arrived.

Corrie watched her mother shake her head.

"Listen, when the rain stops completely, Pietje, you stay with everything under the tree while I take your mother and sisters to *Opa*'s. Then I'll come back and help cart the rest of the stuff with the car."

"Okay," nodded Pietje.

Little Corrie got on her knees and put her arms around Pietje's neck. She rested her head on top of his shoulder. Corrie felt bigger because her legs were getting in the way. Now she just didn't fit into Pietje as she used to. She was, after all, almost grown-up.

"I hope we get to *Opa*'s soon. I need to listen to the radio. I want to know what's happening," muttered Pietje.

"I have to give my dolls a bath," added Corrie.

Frans whispered, "Did you hear what happened this morning?"

Pietje leaned forward. "*Nee. Wat?*"

"Germany defeated Norway. And France looks like it's not going to be able to hold on much longer."

Corrie saw her mother's face turn white. She could see her body suddenly slump.

"Norway was also a neutral country," whispered her mother.

Slowly in the distance, Corrie heard a slight humming sound. She looked over through the fogged window.

Suddenly, Beppie jumped out of the passenger seat and looked in the direction of the coast. "What's that, *Oom* Frans?"

The hum intensified to a ground-shaking roar.

Pietje also got out of the car. The rain had subsided. He pointed in the direction of the North Sea, just a kilometer away. Corrie scrambled out and clung to Pietje. She followed his gaze.

Up in the clearing sky, over the ocean and amongst the tall upper clouds, there was a dark mass. She could see twinkling stars.

"They twinkle Pietje. Like stars."

"Those aren't stars. That's the sun bouncing off planes. And they're not German." He sounded as if he was mesmerized. "That must be an RAF Bomber squadron from England. They're heading Northeast. They must be going to Germany."

Oom Frans got out and looked. "Or they're going to Denmark." He rubbed his chin as he pondered the distant sight. "It's the weather. They seem to be going around the weather front. The bombers are heading for Denmark."

Pietje was excited. Not as sad. He ran and climbed up onto the top of the Model A Ford to get a better look over the surrounding buildings.

Wide-eyed, little Corrie looked over at her brother. He was always getting into trouble. She saw her mother get out of the driver's seat and motion for him to get down. She even hissed at him. He went down on all fours and slipped back off.

Suddenly, *Oom* Frans dropped his hand. "*Ja*, well. We better get on our way. We have to get you settled into Pap's house for the night. Tomorrow I'm off to work, and the children are off to school."

"School's open again?" Cornelia asked, looking over at Beppie and Pietje.

"Yup. Life does go on." *Oom* Frans took off his glasses and wiped them with his fingers.

"I don't want to go to school tomorrow," piped up little Corrie.

"Silly, you don't go to school yet," smirked Beppie. There was a two-year gap between the three children.

Pietje laughed.

"You go after this summer," her mother explained. "Well, Frans, shall we head off to Pap's then?"

Frans turned to his sister-in-law and hugged her. "Okay, you get back in. Beppie, you squeeze in with your mother. Corrie, you get in and try to sit or lie on top of the blanket rolls."

Pietje helped Corrie climb up into the back seat and then crawl over the blanket rolls. Her mother squeezed into the passenger seat with Beppie. Frans got behind the wheel.

"Frans, *bedankt*." Cornelia smiled.

"*Graag gedaan*." Frans smiled. He turned to look out his window. "Pietje, I'll be back as soon as I can." He started the engine. As they slowly rumbled off over the cobblestones, the Ford almost hit a horse and buggy.

Little Corrie heard the buggy driver over the rumble of the Ford.

"*Ouwe loren, ouwe loren!*" cried the driver. She saw the driver look over at Pietje and all their possessions under the tree.

"Oh, no, Mama! The *Ouwe Loren* man will take our things and sell them at the flea market!"

"Not to worry. Not if Pietje has anything to do with it," laughed *Oom* Frans.

They watched as the *Ouwe Loren* man raised his arm and pointed at Pietje. At that moment, his horse raised its tail and dumped a healthy pile of pungent horse manure onto the street.

"Well, that's a good omen," Cornelia muttered. She looked back at Corrie, who looked back at her mother wide-eyed, her finger in her mouth.

"*Ja*, the horse is wise. It's telling us we have to put a big *stront* on it all and not to let the Huns upset us," cracked Frans.

Cornelia burst out laughing.

Then Beppie laughed.

And not to be outdone, Corrie laughed gaily as did her two dolls.

Chapter 6
June 1940

Henk turned down his street and allowed the bicycle to crawl to a slow ponderous stop. He kept an iron grip on the handlebars until he was able to control his shaking while he stood in the warmth of the sun, so very relieved to be home. He was tired, weary. Henk hadn't slept properly for weeks and spent well over a week helping to cart away the dead and wounded. He was physically exhausted from clearing bombed debris from roads and canals. Henk and his fellow reserves and soldiers had also frantically destroyed oil refineries and bridges, hoping to hamper the Nazis' onslaught of Holland.

It was all for nothing.

After the humiliating surrender, streets needed to be swept and cleared. Even Rotterdam, poor Rotterdam, had its debris organized into tidy massive piles. The dead were removed, stored, and properly buried.

Images of broken, torn bodies burned in the forefront of his brain. He craved Cornelia's soft arms around him. He wanted the pleasure and comfort of having his dog Poekie at his feet. He needed to get drunk with the guys and wash away the stench that seemed to ooze out of his pores.

Henk had little time to worry about Cornelia and the children while the nightmare unfolded around him. But as Holland's brave resistance against the Huns came to a fatal close with its final surrender, his nerves and heart were shattered. Suddenly, he did nothing but worry. Were Cornelia and the children victims of the bombing raids? Did Pietje get too curious and get shot in the cross-fire on some street? Panic had him in its soul-sucking grip, and he couldn't think straight. He shook, couldn't sleep, couldn't eat. Terrifying images of their torn and burned bodies waltzed and taunted him. His brain was overloaded and exhausted. In Rotterdam, he recovered dead women and children, and he saw his own children in their faces. He could swear a little one was a clone of little Corrie.

To remain functional, he forced himself to trust that his wife and children were safe and well in The Hague. Thank goodness, he survived the initial onslaught and was set free with other surviving soldiers and reserves, and not imprisoned. That, in itself, was a minor miracle. Everyone was anxious to return to their homes, their loved ones, their own beds.

The Nazis told them to go back home and go on with their lives as if nothing had changed. As fellow "Aryan" brothers and fellow members of the "Master Race," there was no need for panic. Adolf Hitler would simply repackage the Dutch soul with black, red, and gold stripes, after stripping them of their proud red, white and blue and, for the final effect, stamp massive swastikas right on top. Painless. Logical. Convenient.

Just like Austria and Poland.

How could one lead a normal life under Hitler?

How could they pick up where they left off as if all that death and destruction did not happen?

Hitler had put one of his ministers in charge of every aspect of the running of The Netherlands. The puppet's name was Arthur Seyss-Inquart—soon to be dubbed "Six and a quarter." Seyss-Inquart became the *Reich Commissariaat* for the Occupied Dutch Territories, a government totally run by a civil administration made up of Nazis and Dutch Nazi sympathizers.

Those dirty sympathizers! He felt sick to his stomach.

Carefully, Henk leaned his bike against the stone sill of one of his living room windows and tapped gently on the windowpane. He leaned into the glass to look for life through the lace curtains, but he saw nothing. No little Corrie at the table. No Beppie or Pietje.

But something was amiss. Henk couldn't put his finger on it. Poekie.

Poekie wasn't barking.

Henk quickly loosened the leather straps of his bundle in the front basket. Perhaps Poekie's asleep in the back courtyard. He was, after all, getting to be an old dog.

Henk whistled for Poekie as he reached his door and turned the handle to step inside. He hit his forehead against the thickly painted wood and bounced back. He frowned. The door was locked. He reached for his skeleton key in his pocket and tried to put it in the lock. His nerves were far from settled, and his hand shook too much. He couldn't get it in. He peered at the lock—it was a freshly-polished brass lock.

Not his lock.

He frowned and knocked at the door. It flung open.

"Who the hell are you?" demanded the gentleman in a thick German accent.

Henk, surprised, looked up at the brass number over the door. It was his address, his house. "And who the hell are you?" he yelled back, shocked.

A German officer stepped in view behind the gentleman at the door. "What do you want?"

Henk craned his neck to look into the house behind the gentleman. He saw the carpet, the tea caddy, and part of the dining room table. Fear gripped his heart. "I'm Hendricus Gelauf. I want to enter my house, that's what I want! This is my home. I live here." He motioned broadly with his arms. He pointed to the windows, the roof, the threshold of the doorway. "This, all this! Mine! I demand to know what happened to my wife and children! That is my furniture in there. What have you done to them?" His anger gave way to fear.

"We have done nothing with them. This is the home of a Wehrmacht Officer now. Me. If you don't leave, I will have you arrested." The officer eyed the bundle in Henk's arms. Henk knew he recognized his Dutch soldier's woolen uniform. Henk suddenly became aware of the potential danger of his predicament. He cast his eye over the officer. Henk saw his gun holster. Whatever they were told, Henk still considered himself at war with these intruders. People still are going to get shot or arrested for subordination. He desired neither at the moment. He stepped back wordlessly, put the bundle back into the front basket, and shakily tipped his cap.

The door slammed shut.

Henk looked up and down the street. He saw Swastikas in a couple of windows. No tricycles in front of doors. No wayward doll or ball. No sign of children playing. Out of one open window near the end of the street, he heard operatic voices singing Richard Wagner's *"Der Vliegende Hollander."* One of Hitler's favorite compositions, he heard. None of his neighbors could afford a gramaphone. So, the street had to be riddled with Nazis.

"Normal living, huh? While you Nazis are in my home," he muttered angrily to himself. "And where the hell is my dog?" He turned and punched the air with his fist. Of course, he waited until he knew nobody saw and it was safe to do so.

Bile waited to fly at the back of his throat, and slowly, stiffly, he swung a leg over the center bar and got on his bike. His street was Nazified. What was next? Change the national language to German? So much for life going on as usual.

So, where did Cornelia and the children go? He pedaled along the road, not really knowing where to start. Henk stopped and let the bike lean slightly against his inner thigh as he looked up and down the street. If he was Cornelia, where would he go?

Suddenly, he relaxed. He sighed and shook his head. He got back on the pedals and did a u-turn on the quiet street. If he was Cornelia, there was no doubt about it. He'd go to his father's place over the pub. He prayed that it was so.

Dusk was settling in by the time Henk finally arrived at his father's grand house. German soldiers stood by the edge of the canal, smoking and laughing.

"Normal life," he muttered, as he eyed them. At least they weren't the SS. But to see German soldiers right in front of his father's house was, well, as bad as having German soldiers living in his own home.

Music wafted out the front door of the pub. He lowered his head to hide his face from the soldiers. He chose the back of the building instead of the front door next to the pub's entranceway. As he carefully walked his bike through a narrow passageway between cold, moist brick walls, he heard one of the most beautiful sounds: Poekie barked a welcome! He had to place the bike against the high wooden fence near piles of empty beer barrels before he could turn and enjoy the hefty welcome he received from an ecstatic Poekie. Poekie pounced at him over and over again, desperately trying to lick his face.

Henk's heart warmed as he wrestled with the lovable canine. He pretended to growl back at the dog, and felt his nerves settling. He gave Poekie a tight squeeze while the dog stretched up on his hind legs. He gently pushed him back on his all fours. Henk said sweet little nothings to Poekie as he took out his army bundle. He gave his dog a final rub on his black snout, then turned to take the wooden stairs, two at a time, to the back doorway. As he reached the top landing, he felt vibrations from the music below. *How can there be music at a time like this?* he wondered.

His nostrils twitched, reminding him he hadn't eaten since the day before. The aroma emanating from the pub made his mouth water. Curry, beef, the sweet smell of carrots and potatoes mashed together. Croquettes, *patates frites*. His stomach churned as he momentarily leaned his forehead against the door jam. He could hear the radio inside the apartment, and he heard a familiar voice speak.

Koningen Wilhelmina!

The Queen had escaped to England before Hitler's men could capture her. Henk suddenly needed to hear her voice and what comforting words she may have to give but, more than that, he needed to hear from the proverbial horse's mouth where the Dutch stood.

He quickly opened the door and stepped into the little hallway. He saw the back of some of his siblings sitting stiffly at the long, cleared dining room table. Evidently, they had gathered together for mutual comfort. There was a red and white checkered tablecloth on top and here and there a coffee cup. He silently leaned over and saw Cornelia. His head drooped, and he covered his eyes. He fought back tears of relief. Henk pulled out his handkerchief and wiped at his nose. Then he walked a little closer into the kitchen and leaned against the wallpaper of the old plaster wall to listen to the radio along with everyone else, cap in hand.

> *"What is at stake in this war is the liberty*
> *of those all over the world who wish*
> *to work for the good of mankind, and to do so*
> *without being frustrated by the evildoers…"*

Henk turned and continued listening as he hung his cap on a hook by the door. He quietly took off his shoes, and walked into the dining room. His father's new radio had been moved to the dining room and sat at the end of the table by his father's elbows. Little Corrie sat next to him, her *Opa*, and was the only one not looking down in deep concentration. Her bright blue eyes clamped onto his face, and she jumped in her seat with gleeful surprise.

"Pappa!"

Everyone swiveled around to look and quickly stood up, pushing their chairs back, and cheered with joy. Cornelia jumped over and grabbed him. She clung to his neck while one or two of his family reached over to rub his shoulder or back.

"Shhhh," came from somewhere at the table.

Henk gave Cornelia a big squeeze, and they stood together at the door to continue listening to the Queen. He looked down at her and kissed his wife on the cheek. Her arm held him tightly to her side, and she placed her left hand on his chest. His heartbeat was fast and hard as he looked around the table. He smiled at little Corrie, who was grinning at him with a newly-developed gap in her teeth. She'd grown so long-legged and dangly. He wondered how she could change so quickly in just a space of a few weeks.

He looked at his father. *De Heer* Gelauf's hand rested on the silver top of his cane, and his moist eyes were watching him. His father nodded and winked.

Henk could feel his face flush with emotion. He let go of Cornelia and walked around to his father. Everyone who could reach Henk gave him a good pat on his back along the way. He held out his hand.

"*Ja, jonge. Welkom terug.*" His father returned the handshake. "I knew you'd be back. No news was good news, *ja*?"

Henk laughed and nodded. He turned to face the length of the table. Not everyone in his family was there, but it was a healthy showing. Those who were able gathered together, sharing their shock and misery at this latest tragic development. His brother-in-law, Frans, was there with Henk's sister, Antonia, and their two little daughters, Sientje and Rieky. He could see the legs of their youngest child, Philip, sticking out from under the table where he was playing quietly on his own. His sister Wilhelmina sat with her husband Herman and their boys. His older sister Anna was there as well as his younger brother Herman. Of course, Pietje was there, sitting on a chair by the mantle with Beppie. Pietje scrambled around the table to his father.

Henk held out his hand.

Pietje looked at it and shook it.

"*Ja, Pietje. Pappa's terug,*" smiled Henk.

Pietje let go of his hand and clung to him. As did Beppie.

Henk patted Pietje on his back while he messed up Beppie's blonde hair a little. He looked over at his father and motioned to the radio. "The enemy is right below us. Could they not hear?" he asked, pointing down at the floor.

"Are you kidding?" offered Frans. "With all that Nazi celebration going on downstairs? If they do this every time *Radio Oranje* comes on the BBC, we're sailing."

Antonia straightened up in her chair and whispered quietly, "The Queen is going to try and make this an ongoing program so long as the *moffen* are here."

That was the cue for everyone to continue listening to the Queen. Henk moved back to Cornelia's side and bent down to whisper in her ear. "I wonder, did we lose the old radio to the *moffen*?" She looked up, tired, weary. "Did we save anything at all when they made you leave?" He wondered about his accordion. His clothes. His Sunday hat. His favorite chair.

"Yes, but we could only take so much," she said sadly. "And we only had about fifteen minutes to pack." She looked over at Pietje. "We were able to take some blankets, a thin mattress, some clothes, and kitchenware." Cornelia was close to tears. She started to wring her hands.

Pietje moved over and leaned into his parents. He looked up at his father. "But we have your accordion, Pappa! And we got the radio on the wagon!"

"Where is it all?" Henk asked quietly.

"It's all stored in the back. Except for your accordion," Cornelia whispered.

"Where's the accordion, then?"

Pietje smiled and pointed at his *Opa*.

Henk looked over at his father. "You have my accordion, Pap?"

His father nodded. "It's on the living room mantle, son."

Suddenly, the Queen, having finished her speech, was replaced by an announcer.

"You are listening to Radio Orange
on the European Service broadcast
with the BBC in London—"

Henk smiled. He turned to look at Pietje again. Pietje, too, had grown taller. He glanced over at Beppie. A few weeks. How could so much change in a few short weeks? The world. His children. No home.

CORRIE AND THE ROSE ACCORDION

"Pietje," Henk said, "get the accordion. We should make our own music," he announced as he took off his coat. "Let's forget about this hell for a little while."

Chapter 7
September 1940

Little Corrie jumped back in surprise as the tower of painted wooden blocks she was building toppled with a loud clatter down onto the old wooden desk. Sadly, she looked over at another tower a little boy had constructed across the room, and she wondered if his wooden blocks were better than hers. Corrie was humiliated. She sat back and angrily swung her legs back and forth under her wooden chair. Looking around, her eyes fell on students' etchings in the wooden surface next to her. She leaned forward, patted her big pink ribbon to ensure it was still there, then picked up her thick pencil amongst the fallen blocks. With zest and her tongue sticking out, she traced the deep etchings in the wood as she once did the tea caddy.

"Children, I have a new word for you. Remember what yesterday's new word was? Anyone?"

Corrie looked up at the nun at the front of the class. She sat back and looked around for another classmate to volunteer.

"Mine?" asked the little boy with the perfect tower.

The nun nodded. "Precisely. And what does it mean?"

"A small bomb under the ground to blow your legs off."

Some children laughed and giggled.

The nun's lips made an 'O,' and she shook her head. "Correct. But children, that isn't funny. I know it sounds funny. But it's a very grave thing."

Corrie looked around at the other students. Some squirmed in their seats, embarrassed. She then studied the smart little boy's face wondering why everything came more easily to him. She forgot the word already. But she remembered it took your legs off. She would never forget the awful image of her without legs.

"Correct. Well done, Emile. Yes, they are small bombs the Germans put under the surface of the earth in places where they do not want anyone to go. They have big signs telling everyone to stay away. But that is a problem when you are young and can't read. So, the word for today is—" The nun turned to the large old blackboard and took a thick piece of chalk from the ledge. She scratched at the black surface. Everyone leaned toward the front of the room. Corrie's forehead creased as she tried to distinguish the separate letters.

"Anyone know what this word is?"

No one offered.

This word says '*prikkeldraad.*' Barbed wire." The nun proceeded to draw a circular tube out of rounded lines. Then she added quick little taps on the lines she drew. She stepped back and pointed at the drawing with the chalk.

Little Corrie recognized it. The coiled mesh that started showing up everywhere they went.

"Whenever you see this *prikkledraad*, you stay away. It could hurt you very much. And even if you somehow climb over it, there is a good chance the *moffen* will shoot you."

Corrie gasped. As did some other children.

Suddenly, a familiar wail cut through the air, obliterating any other sound. As if by magic, they could suddenly hear incoming planes. Their droning props and engines almost blocked out the wail of the siren. Corrie's heart jumped into her throat as she pushed her chair back and ran over to stand in the line that dutifully formed at the door. A small, low rumble shook the ground beneath them.

Corrie started to cry, which encouraged another little girl to cry.

"Now, now. Everything will be fine. Just follow me. Everyone hold hands." The nun took the hand of the first child in line.

Corrie, still hiccupping in grief and fear, turned and took the little boy's hand behind her while the little girl in front of her grabbed hers. Her grip was tight, and though it didn't really hurt, she still cried as if in pain. "Ow!"

"Everyone, stay calm and follow me. We'll be safe in the basement." The nun slowly led them down the busy hall. Other older students left classrooms, and all migrated in the same general direction. The halls echoed with cries and excited chatter, and the constant encouragement and soothing voices by the many teachers who led them down, down, and down into a specially-dug bomb shelter in the basement. After they were all huddled into the large accommodating hole, the sirens sounded very far away. Not as threatening. But the reverberations in the walls and ground continued. A door slammed. Corrie looked up at two light bulbs hanging from the cement ceiling. They swung and created moving shadows that did not do anything to comfort Corrie.

"Now, everyone!" One of the nuns moved into the center of the crowd. "Let's sing, shall we? *Vader Jacob*!" She took out a tuning pitch and blew in it. She hummed. It was hard for them to hear clearly, but the children tried to hum the right note.

Suddenly, the light bulbs in the shelter flickered. Dust sifted through tiny cracks above their heads as the walls and ground rocked once more.

No one felt like singing. Even the nun.

September had been a terrible and terrifying month. Corrie had been going to bed dressed because every night, it seemed, the British bombed, trying to get at the German installations in their city. Corrie understood that the Germans were like harmful germs in their country and that their friend, England, was trying to find and kill them. Make Holland better. But she was shocked when she realized they killed innocent children like her, too. She couldn't understand why England would do that.

The other day, she had seen that some of the boats which sat in the harbor were bombed by England. The harbor was almost just around the corner across the bridge from her *Opa*'s house. *Opa*'s front windows had shattered during a bombing raid, and they were now covered with wood. Her *Opa* had said not to worry, that he was going to fix them. Everything was going to be okay.

But how could all this scary stuff be okay?

Suddenly she had to go to the washroom. She threw up her hand. One of the nuns came and bent over her.

"Yes?"

"I have to use the outhouse."

"Well, you can't leave now, little one. You will have to wait." The nun had to speak directly into her ear over the noise.

"But, I can't wait."

The nun straightened up and left. Then she came back, meandering through the groups of students, carrying a bucket. Some students watched the nun as she headed for little Corrie.

Corrie was appalled so many understood what Corrie was going to do with that bucket. She violently shook her head.

"Okay, just hold it in until this is over. It won't take very long."

But it did take very long.

Corrie preferred to pee her woolen undies than to use that bucket in front of everyone.

November 1940

"What's this?" asked Cornelia. Henk was getting ready for work and had just handed her a big paper bag. She was ironing the girls' ribbons over the edge of the hot stove when he came into the kitchen. Beppie, little Corrie, and Frans' two little girls, Sientje and Rieky, were waiting for their ribbons before heading off to school. They looked exhausted. Everyone's sleep had been continuously disrupted by bombing raids almost every night. And nearly every night, they spent an inordinate amount of time in shelters.

He eyed a plate of buttered rusks with chocolate sprinkles on the table along with empty bowls covered with the remains of their porridge. Each child had a cup and saucer. They'd had their tea poured, and were reaching for their rusks. Except for little Corrie. She sat playing with one of her dolls and looked miserable. Of all the children, she hated going to school the most, he learned.

Henk sighed and reached for a rusk. He stood as he munched on it, thinking over the last little while. They'd been sharing his father's home for six months now, and winter was setting in with its freezing rain and grey days. It was getting crowded in the house, and though he loved being with his father and other siblings, he craved privacy.

He absently watched Cornelia place the broad, flattened ribbons on the table and took the bag he'd given her. She looked inside and pulled out folded material. She looked at it in wonder. "What?"

"I know they've rationed material now. I figured you can make dresses with this or shirts. Or slippers. I forgot to give it to you last night." Henk finished the dry biscuit and, still chewing, reached for his shaving brush from the sink. He soaked it, took his jar of shaving powder, and swished the brush around and around. He lathered the shaving cream on one cheek and took a step toward a tiny mirror to the side of the sink, continuing to lather the other cheek and his neck. He watched his wife in the reflection of the mirror. She studied the material.

"But this is the material used for mattresses. It's on our stuffed mattresses."

"I know." He picked up his razor and started shaving, making a funny face as he did so.

He heard little Corrie laugh. He hadn't realized she was watching what he was doing. He stuck his tongue out at her in the mirror. She stuck out hers. He continued to shave, and everyone could hear a grating sound as the blade traveled over his chin.

"Sounds like it's dull," muttered Cornelia.

Henk looked at the razor briefly before continuing with careful strokes on his cheek, then down to his neck. "It'll do for today." He didn't want to take the time to sharpen the blade. Always being precise and proud of how he looked, he had become somewhat lazy since coming to his father's home. No one said anything for a few moments. The only sounds were the razer scraping, the sizzling of the kettle of hot water on the stove, and little Corrie's humming as she played with her doll. He took a small towel off the side rack, wet it with hot water from the kettle, then wiped off the residual shaving cream.

Heavy footsteps approached the kitchen from the dining room that had been converted to a sleeping area for Henk and his family. Henk turned to see his brother-in-law Frans enter, fully dressed, with starched collar and cuffs, though still unshaven. Frans curiously eyed the material on the table as he passed. Henk stepped aside to let Frans look at his unshaven face in the mirror.

"Henk. Isn't that stealing? What if you lose this job?"

Henk rinsed the towel with cold water, then wet it again with the hot from the kettle. He handed it to Frans, who took it and put it over his face. Frans sighed.

"Things are getting desperate. Cornelia said yesterday the girls need more clothes. Beppie is starting to wear Cornelia's old clothes, but they're too big, and she takes them in. But even then, she looks ridiculous in mature women's clothing."

Frans turned to look at Beppie, who, in turn, looked down at herself. She pushed her chair back and walked over to the back door to get her coat.

"Your ribbon," reminded Cornelia.

Beppie dropped her arms. "A ribbon? With this old lady's dress?"

Henk looked at his eight-year-old. "Do what your mother says, Beppie. She's doing her best."

"Well, I hate it. The kids pick on me at school."

"Soon, no one will, Beppie. We are all in the same boat!"

"Not everyone," she argued as she shook out her tattered gloves from her coat pockets.

"You see what I mean?" Henk looked pointedly at Frans. "And little Corrie simply has nothing to grow into." He rubbed his face and neck with another dry towel off the rack. "Ah, that feels better," he muttered.

"*Ja*, doesn't it? It always feels good to shave," added Frans, distractedly.

Henk turned to see Cornelia cross her arms and continue to stare at the material. She shook her head and covered her face.

Henk stepped to the table and picked up the material. "What do you think, girls? Would you want to have a new play dress made out of this?" He smiled.

All three nodded. Henk saw Beppie stand at the door, sulking. Then he unfolded the material and tapped his wife on the shoulder. "*Kijk.*"

Cornelia dropped her hand and looked down. She watched him hold it up to his chest and pretend it was a dress. The girls giggled. He saw that Beppie did as well.

Cornelia fingered a long streak of blue in the material. "It's faulty?"

Frans stepped closer and looked.

"We couldn't use this for the mattresses. I didn't steal this. I asked the foreman if you could have it to sew dresses with."

Cornelia nodded. She reached out and hugged her husband and then let him go to wipe away a tear. "I'll share it with Antonia for Rieky and Sientje."

"Okay." Henk turned and looked thoughtfully out the back kitchen window. Then he stepped toward the kitchen door beside the sink that led to the cramped back porch where they kept Poekie now that it was getting too cold and wet outside. He opened the kitchen door, then the next door leading to the outside staircase.

"Go on, Poekie," he whispered to the dog. He watched Poekie hurry down the steep staircase to do his morning ablutions. Henk wondered how his dog didn't end up tumbling down those stairs headfirst, as he watched the comical sight of Poekie's black and brown bulbous behind sway from side to side with each step.

Henk raised his face to inhale the fresh November air laced with a hint of ocean, stale beer, and rain-drenched horse manure. A chorus of birds sang and twittered among the tall trees and bushes despite the misty rain. In the distance, horses, carriages, the odd locomotive, barges, a foghorn, and bicycle bells played a symphony of rich sounds. Even the swish of the canal waters sang as a barge puttered by.

A Phoney War. That's what they called it. Germany took over, made some changes and then suddenly, nothing. That only lasted about a month. For a little while, the only things that changed in the days following that five-day war culminating in Rotterdam's destruction were that the Queen and government left, Churchill took over for Chamberlain, and England and the other Allies had officially declared war on Germany. A curfew of 8:00 pm was set under threat of death by Seyss-Inquart, and rations limited the use of electricity, oil, charcoal, gas—and most recently—meat.

A couple of weeks before, the tides turned. The Phoney War was suddenly over, and the German strongholds scattered through the city was continuously targeted by the British RAF. Quite often, the bombs missed their marks and innocent people lost their homes or, ultimately, their lives. Planes were shot down, barges were sunk, harbors were strafed, people were mangled. Collateral damage.

There were rumors that people living in other parts of The Netherlands were looted by the Nazis; their copper, brass, and other metals for the good of Nazi Germany. And he heard that Jewish councilmen were banned. Rumor also had it that Jewish professors were forbidden to teach.

As Henk stood deep in thought, Pietje suddenly came bounding into the kitchen. Pietje pushed past his mother, and grabbed a buttered rusk off the plate.

As he ran past his mother, back to the front of the house, Henk called after him. "Pietje! Say good morning, excuse me, and thank you!"

After a moment, Pietje slunk back into the doorway. "Good morning Pappa and Mama. *Oom* Frans. *Meisjes*. Excuse me, Mama. And thank you, Mama."

"Where are your books?"

"I didn't have any homework last night." He took a quick bite out of the rusk, dropping crumbs and chocolate sprinkles onto the floor.

Cornelia looked down at the crumbs. Then she looked up at Henk, fearful he would lose his patience with Pietje again. She turned and picked up the ribbons she had flattened and chose one. She motioned to Beppie at the door to come over. Beppie frowned and sighed but stepped over to let her mother tie the ribbon in her hair.

Henk saw Beppie look over at Pietje and stick her tongue out. Pietje did the same. Henk looked at his son with disappointment. "I heard from your school. You're not focusing on your lessons, and you're acting like a clown during class. You keep this up, and they'll put you a year back again."

Pietje took another bite out of the rusk. His eyes darted to the old clock over the stove. "I'm not the only one, Pappa. It's hard when you have to run to the shelter all the time. I don't know why we bother going to school."

Little Corrie looked up suddenly. "*Ja*. Why do we bother?"

Henk tried to hide a smile. "Regardless. We can only keep moving forward. This war might end next year, and then what happens after you've let your studies lapse? You end up paying for it. The war is not an excuse, Pietje. Besides, where are you going so early in the morning, anyway? It's not even 7:30. Have you brushed your teeth?"

"We're playing soccer out on the field for half an hour."

"In this rain?"

Pietje nodded.

"Did you brush your teeth?"

Pietje nodded again.

"Who is organizing the match? The school?"

Pietje shook his head. "No, but the other guys are playing."

Cornelia frowned. "The Boy Scouts?"

"The Scouts have been banned," offered Frans at the sink.

"Yes, I thought I heard that somewhere," added Cornelia, looking at Frans.

Henk shook his head. "No, Pietje. Hitler Youth, probably."

Pietje shrugged his shoulders. "I just want to play soccer. I don't care with who."

Cornelia reached out to her son. "No, not with the Hitler Youth."

Henk waved at him, "Play today, but find out if it's the NSB or Hitler Youth. If it is, then no more soccer after today."

Pietje again said, "Okay."

"Teeth?" asked Cornelia.

Pietje turned to her and bared his teeth even though he hadn't finished chewing.

Disgustedly, she waved him on.

Pietje looked at his father.

He also waved at him to go.

Pietje turned and disappeared, but not before he grabbed a second rusk off the plate.

Henk looked out the back window again at the dark grey sky. He could hear props in the distance. A Messerschmitt. A loner. He is watching probably. No siren.

Cornelia moved and stood in the doorway where Pietje had stood. "I think we should have rabbits, Henk."

Henk turned to look at her. The heavy bombing over the last few weeks had drained her, he noticed.

Frans chuckled. Henk looked at him quizzically, then at Cornelia.

"Uh uh, no pets," he said, shaking his head. "They cost too much, and the children eventually don't take care of them. You have fleas and other problems with Pap and the family. And rabbits? Are you crazy? They multiply so fast before you know it, you have—" He stopped, and his look turned into a blank stare. His high cheekbones flushed crimson.

Cornelia crossed her arms over her work shift and leaned against the door-jam again, waiting for the penny to drop.

He nodded. "*Ja*, okay. We should have rabbits." He hung the towel back up. "And then we'll have rabbit pie, roast rabbit…" He smiled.

"Rabbit stew, stuffed rabbit, rabbit croquettes…" added Frans, smiling. He had shaved half his face.

"You can make things out of rabbits," Henk said as he unrolled a sleeve.

"Yes, I can make warm muffs for the girls this winter, fur slippers for everyone, fur hats, fur mitts, I can make good presents for *Sinterklaas*. And Pietje will have something to occupy himself with. He can be in charge of the rabbits. He needs a major distraction."

"Well," he said, rolling down the other sleeve. "I guess I'm going to make a rabbit cage." He quickly buttoned up his starched cuffs and opened a drawer. He took out an old hammer. "I'll scrounge up some wood at work today."

"And while you're at it, why don't you make a nice pigeon pen for the window," said Frans, wiping bits of shaving cream from his shaved face.

Henk's eyes shone at his brother-in-law. "Well, aren't you a smart one."

Something odd happened just then. No one knew what it was at first, but then it dawned on both men: The birds stopped chirping, and a car back-fired. For a moment, it was as if the whole world stopped making noise. Then suddenly, the sirens went off.

"The birds always seem to sense a siren coming. Have you noticed that?" asked Frans.

"Goddamit, not again!" swore Henk, not answering Frans' question.

Everyone got up to go out the back door. Henk's family used the pub's coal and beer cellar as a bomb shelter.

"I'll get Pappa and Antonia," yelled Cornelia as she headed out of the kitchen to look for her father-in-law and sister-in-law.

Suddenly, feet stomped up the back stairs, and Pietje burst in, eyes wide.

"How'd you get to the back so fast—" Henk yelled.

Pietje held up a couple of sheets of paper. "We have orders to move," he yelled back.

Henk looked at Cornelia who had just returned. His sister, Antonia, stood behind her. Then he looked past them at their sleeping quarters in the dining room. He slapped Frans' shoulder. "Well, Frans, it was a pleasure. Now we can get out of Pap's hair and make more room for you guys."

"*Oom* Frans and *Tante* Antonia are moving too," cried Pietje.

Little Rieky and Sientje cheered from the table.

"Here!" He thrust one of the papers to his *Oom* Frans. Frans adjusted his glasses and read the form while the sirens wailed.

"It's from the *Regeeringsgebouw*. We have to immediately report to them and pick up keys for our new homes." Then he read the other letter meant for Henk. "Well, I guess we're not quite neighbors. We're moving about eight blocks apart, I see."

"Henk, we must go!" Cornelia led Antonia and the children past Henk. The roar of heavy artillery boomed through the walls of the house from a nearby anti-aircraft gun. Henk motioned to the girls. "Get your coats and hats on. We're going to the cellar. Now!"

Little Corrie grabbed her father around the thighs, crying. Henk quickly caressed the top of his daughter's head. "Don't worry. Go with Pietje!"

All the women ran out with Pietje. Henk listened to them stomping down the back stairs. Frans looked back at him, waiting. Suddenly, his father showed up in the doorway.

"Let's go!" yelled Henk. He got his father's coat and helped him down the stairs. Poekie, waiting in the back courtyard, joined them rushing into the coal room.

Once everyone squeezed in and crouched under the massive beams of the pub, Henk pulled Beppie and little Corrie close to him. He looked over at his wife. The stress had found a crack, he saw. Cornelia sat on a large burlap bag of potatoes with her head on her knees, sobbing.

Henk breathed hard as he slowly reached out to Frans. With shaking hands, he took the papers Frans still gripped in his hand. He peered at them in the gloom. "Well, Frans. I think we can take the time this morning to see where the Nazis have found it in their hearts to place us!"

Frans didn't answer. Instead, he motioned with his head to Cornelia crying and his own wife, Antonia, crying beside him.

Henk looked at Cornelia's bowed head and shaking shoulders. "We drink, they cry. It's probably better to cry," he yelled.

Suddenly, the sounds of heavy artillery stopped. After a moment of quiet, the siren wailed steadily, meaning all was clear.

"Well, the coast is clear, everyone!" Henk stood up into a half-crouch and perused the cellar. He looked back at Frans and nodded for them to go.

"Can I come, too, Pappa?" asked Beppie, hopefully.

"Where?"

"You're going to the new house?"

Henk looked down at her and the other children. "No, you best go to school. You'll see where we'll live soon enough."

"Oh, I hope I have my own bedroom this time!" cried Beppie softly, wiping her tears with hands covered in coal dust.

"No, I need my own room, too. You're still small!" yelled Pietje.

"You can sleep in the new rabbit cage."

Henk, surprised, looked over at Cornelia. She was wiping her wet cheeks with coal dust-covered hands. She smiled.

Henk grinned at her. "That's funny," he said.

Frans chuckled as he turned and made his way out of the cellar door into the light rain. "Well, still alive and well!"

Henk turned to follow but first looked back once more in time to see Cornelia reach out to tousle one of the girls' hair. While still perched on the burlap bag, she took a corner of her work shift and spit into it. Then she rubbed Beppie's face with it, partially taking away the coal dust.

He took a deep breath. Every day seemed like diving into the deep end of a dry pool. He ran a dirty finger under his blackened-starched collar and went back upstairs to get his cap.

Chapter 8
November 1940

Frans' old car chugged and shuddered along *Hofweg*. Frans stopped abruptly when the Traffic Officer at the intersection swiveled his tall sign to read, "Stop." The Officer blew his shrill whistle, held up his white-gloved hand, then motioned for other traffic to move forward.

"Kind of silly driving the car. We could've walked in almost the same amount of time," Henk said as he watched the many bicycles, Wehrmacht Jeeps, and the odd civilian car pass by.

"*Ja,* but I knew it was going to rain again," reasoned Frans with an impish smile.

"Wimp," teased Henk.

They watched as their milkman went by on his delivery bike, looking forlorn. A miserable-looking baker cycled by, towing a small wagon of bread covered with a heavy canvas tarp.

"Everyone looks so sad," Henk muttered. He brooded over the rising price of bread. There were now strict rations on natural gas and electricity, severely limiting everyone-including the merchants. He looked over at a corner and saw barbwire surrounding a building. A German soldier stood on guard overlooking the intersection.

"Must be some secret stuff," mumbled Frans.

Henk nodded, continuing to look around. "People seem a little shabbier, too."

"Like us," said Frans, smiling.

Henk leaned back into the horse-hair-stuffed seat and opened his window. He lit a cigarette, a Lucky Seven, and threw the match out into the street. Though everything went on somehow, under the new leadership of Seyss-Inquart, many things didn't look nor feel right. Horse manure didn't get swept up as quickly. Dust from heavy equipment, continual bombing, and marching of soldiers clung to shop windows and homes. Armed soldiers generally stood at all major intersections. Newly-built bomb shelter entrances spiked the surfaces of open areas with gaping mouths leading into dark depths. Their signs said, "*Openbare Schuilplaats. Alleen voor publiek op straat.*" 'Public Shelter. Only for the public on the street.'

What honestly frustrated Henk was that newspapers were highly-censored. Germany was always the victor. Ever the grand Father country. Most sad of all, stories of Jewish places of business forced to shut down. Signs reading, *Joden niet gewenst* were almost everywhere he looked.

"I wonder if there are new restrictions about parking at the *Binnenhof?*" muttered Frans.

Henk flicked the ash from his cigarette. "Probably giving right of way to the *moffen.*"

The traffic cop whistled shrilly, cutting through their ambling thoughts, and held up his white glove to passing traffic. Satisfied, he swiveled his sign to "Go" and motioned to Frans to continue on through the intersection.

Frans put the car in gear and slowly crossed the intersection. He stuck his left arm out straight to signal a turn. They turned toward the *Regeeringsgebouwen.* Army jeeps lined the front of the barb-wired entrance. Enormous piles of sandbags were laid against the sides. Frans slowed down. He pulled to a curb. "I'll park here. I doubt they'll let us into the courtyard."

They got out of the car, adjusted their caps and ties, and marched through the archway of the government buildings. As they mounted the stairs, Henk couldn't help but notice that some of his fellow Dutchmen were in friendly conversation with some of the *moffen*. He disgustedly watched one give a Heil Hitler salute before walking away.

They entered the main square. Huge swastika banners hung from the grand upper windows. Henk watched as an officer, glistening in polished leather and brass, suavely floated down the elegant stone steps at the far end. Over to the side, he saw SS Storm Troopers standing in line along the length of the courtyard. The sight of them put a shiver up his spine.

"They're a different animal," muttered Henk, as he flicked the cigarette away. It suddenly tasted bad in his mouth.

They passed a sizeable sign on one of the columns. Henk walked closer to read, *"All Jews must receive their Identification Papers! All Jewish businesses must Register!"* Henk didn't say a word, but he felt both anger and grief. His face hardened, as he continued on. The two of them finally entered through the doors into the grand entranceway.

An NSB Government Official stopped Frans and Henk.

"Your Identification Papers!"

Henk looked with disdain at the Dutchman extending his hand.

"I don't have them yet," muttered Henk. Frans searched his own pockets.

"Sorry, forgot."

An altercation behind them caught Henk's attention, and he swiveled around to see a soldier dragging a man by the neck of his shirt. The man protested loudly.

"But I've worked here for fifteen years!" he cried. "I'm a civil servant! I have five children to feed!"

People around him stopped, looked, and then nervously moved on.

Henk watched as the soldier let him drop. He saw another soldier join the first and he kicked the man in the side.

"As of today, all Jewish civil servants and professors are fired from the *regeering*!" he yelled to everyone within listening distance. Then he turned to the man on the ground. "Your children are of no concern to anyone, Jew."

Henk couldn't take it. He went to help, but Frans quickly grabbed his sleeve. As they stood wondering what to do, they watched a man in spectacles wearing a grey suit limp into the grand hall, to the side of them. There was something very grand and very familiar about him, but Henk couldn't place him. The man waved the two soldiers over to speak to him. They hurried to him and saluted. In hushed tones, he appeared to admonish them. He motioned to everyone around the hall while he spoke, and then to the man who was struggling to get up off the ground. The two soldiers looked back at the man, saluted once more, and hurried back to the man. They lifted the man by his arms and dragged him through the grand doorway. At the top of the stairs, they threw him down.

The man with a limp and spectacles nodded, straightened out his suit jacket, and disappeared again into the adjoining hallway.

"*Godverdomme!*" Henk muttered to Frans. "That was *Six and a Quarter*."

Frans turned to him, frowning. "Who?"

At the Reserves, we called him *Six and a Quarter*, because of his name and limp."

Frans still looked confused.

"Seyss-Inquehart, *Ses en een kwart*," said Henk.

As Frans blinked at him, Henk ran over and down the grand stone steps to the gentleman. The man hadn't been able to get up and was still struggling, shaking like a young willow tree. He was emotionally overwhelmed, crying softly. Henk bent down and helped him up. He brushed his coat down for him and then stepped to the side and bent over to pick up the man's glasses. He noticed one of the lenses was shattered.

The man nodded silently, as his shaking hand took the glasses. He was not able to put them on, so Henk took them and carefully placed them on the man's nose. The shattered lens was a shocking image, especially when a trickle of blood snaked down the side of the man's nose. Henk immediately took out his handkerchief and dabbed at the blood. He held it out for the man to keep.

The man bowed his head, gratefully took the handkerchief, and slowly turned to painfully descend the grand stone stairs.

Henk watched the stunned man stumble away. Suddenly, the man turned and raised his hand at him before continuing on. "*For the Grace of God*," thought Henk. He nodded and waved him on. He felt his own body shaking, his legs trembling. He secretly felt relieved he wasn't a Jew.

"Henk!"

Henk looked back at Frans. He nodded and slowly walked back up the stairs.

"You would do well to mind your own business. That man was just a filthy Jew," said the official, waiting beside Frans.

Henk's body shook with each heavy heartbeat. "Man, let us go through," he almost spit. "We were summoned to come and pick up keys."

"The law states that everyone over the age of 15 must carry their government-issued Identification Papers. Are *you* Jews?"

"Ach! No, we are not Jews," yelled Henk, staring the Dutchman down. "Look, here are the papers." Henk took out his Notice.

The official took it and looked at it coldly. "Spinozastraat," he said disdainfully. He gave it back, looked at Frans' Notice, as well, which Frans held practically under the official's nose. "Van Ostadestraat." He sniffed and finally waved them through.

"Next time, there will be grave consequences if you are caught without your Identification Papers. I would suggest you get them processed today. And make sure your wives and older children do the same."

"Hey, who was that German man with the glasses who talked to the soldiers?" Henk knew very well, but he needed to hear the man say it.

"That, *meneeer*, is the *Reichskommissar* of the occupied Netherlands, Arthur Seyss-Inquart."

"'Zes en een kwart,' you mean," sneered Henk.

The man ignored Henk, sniffed, and turned away from them. He approached more people entering the grand hall.

Frans and Henk looked at each other wordlessly. They proceeded, following signs. Their footsteps echoed along the marble hallway.

"These *NSB* people are working with the devil, Frans. That traitor. They're making it too easy for the *moffen*. Who does he think he is, lording over us like that? What's the difference between a Dutchman working for the Nazis and the Nazis themselves? Nothing!" Henk was furious.

"There are ears, Henk," Frans was careful to whisper, looking around them as they walked.

They passed people waiting in lines, it seemed, at every department door. Many looked unkempt, and others bore signs of wounds and scratches.

"Refugees from Rotterdam, I think," whispered Frans.

"No, they've long ago settled somewhere. These are our own people because of these senseless bombings." Henk shook his head. "It's getting pretty dangerous, Frans." He looked down at his work boots as he continued down the hallway.

"I've never in my life seen people oppressing another person so cruelly. Not even bullies in grade school," whispered Frans. "And that guy pushing us around. It's these damn NSB Black Shirts. They're brown-nosers. They were the guys who roughed us up on *Prins* Bernhard's birthday. Remember?"

Henk grimly thought back on that day in June. It was a fabulous opportunity for a non-violent gesture of resistance. Hundreds of *Haagenaars* hung Dutch, and Orange flags out their windows to commemorate the birthday of the Queen's husband. Though outlawed, people still insisted on putting flowers at the *Willem de Zwijger Statue* at the *Noordeinde Palace*. Mostly *Prins* Bernhard's favorite flower-the carnation. It wasn't long before the *NSB* Black Shirts—their own countrymen—came and cruelly roughed-up many of the people, who remained stubbornly united as a group. Finally, German planes had to dive at them from above, forcing everyone to leave.

Henk wanted to resist them every which way, just to frustrate the hell out of them. Especially after witnessing such ugliness against a fellow human being. Danger lurked not only from planes with no faces, bombs with no particular name, but now also by the boots of officers.

"Despicable," muttered Henk. He felt intense remorse and terrible pain in his heart, but at the same time, he knew he was one of the lucky ones. There were so many others who had far more reasons to feel miserable than him.

"What are you doing?" yelled Frans.

They had just returned from picking up keys to their new homes and Henk's identification papers when they looked up to see a German soldier standing by Frans' car. The soldier held out his gloved hand when he saw them approaching. The car was packed with heavy-looking wooden boxes. The back boot sat open, and two more boxes of thrown-together wooden slats poked past the lid.

"Keys," demanded the soldier.

Henk pushed Frans back protectively. He motioned to the car. "This is my brother-in-law's car. You must be mistaken."

"All articles that are useful for the Wehrmacht will be confiscated. We are confiscating this vehicle for the good of Germany. Your keys." The soldier stood stubbornly, his rounded helmet snugly clasped on top of his head. He put a hand on his holster.

Henk looked back at Frans and saw his face drop.

"But we need it to move our things. We just picked up the keys to where we're assigned to live. You took our homes. We can move to our assigned homes immediately." Frans pushed his glasses up his nose and blinked nervously.

Henk saw that Frans was sweating profusely. He, himself, was feeling hot under his starched collar.

"We need this car," Frans bleated.

The soldier motioned with his outstretched hand. "Identification papers."

Henk held out his new identification papers for the soldier to check over. The soldier glanced at them and handed them back. He reached toward Frans.

"I left them at home," Frans said, miserably.

"You must always—"

"We know. He just has to get used to carrying them," Henk interrupted him. He looked down at the car. "What if we make your delivery for you, and we promise to bring the car back after we are finished moving. That is if you still need it after that." Henk hopefully read the soldier for a positive expression.

"I will demand one more time. Your key." The soldier unsnapped his holster.

Henk and Frans helplessly looked at the holster.

The soldier suddenly looked up above their heads and roughly called out. He motioned to someone behind them. "*Commandant!*"

Henk and Frans turned around to see a lieutenant, slowly make his way down the stairs toward them. He tapped a truncheon against the broader portion of his uniform pants as he took his time taking one step at a time. Light glistened off the highly-polished boots.

"You have a problem, sergeant?" he said, as he joined them.

Henk heard Frans moan and turned to see him bow his head. He slowly turned to the soldier and surrendered the car keys. Then silently, Frans turned back, shrugged, and slowly took a few steps away from them before he looked back at Henk.

Henk gave the soldier, and then the lieutenant, a dirty look before following Frans. He dug into his pocket to see what change he had. They would have to take the *tram* back. More than that, after work, they would have to tell the children they were going to be put to work. He and Frans needed many hands to move if they were to do it on foot and by bicycle.

Frans dug his hands in his pockets, as well, and stared at the ground as they walked away from the soldiers and headed to the *tram* stop. "If only I didn't insist on using the car when we could've walked. I'd still have the car." He shook his head.

Henk patted him on his shoulders. "That's okay, Frans. Eventually, they would've taken that flea trap away. anyway."

An 8:00 p.m. curfew was put into effect almost immediately after the Wehrmacht defeated The Netherlands. Henk looked at his watch and figured how late they could leave from work. He'll have to remind Cornelia to have supper ready early so they could have everything moved by curfew.

Earlier, while Frans checked his new abode on Van Ostadestraat, Henk checked his at an alley situated at the bottom of Spinozastraat.

Henk was shocked at the disrepair. It was one of many squalid little homes built to house impoverished little old men and women. They were tiny single dwellings with a single bedstead built into the wall in the main living area. The kitchen was nothing more than a corner. A few objects were left behind, he saw. As if the former occupant had been torn away in the middle of the night. There were humble little cups and saucers, some chipped. Books, and a Bible. The bed in the wall had a straw-filled mattress covered in a sad-looking woolen blanket. It looked like a haven for bedbugs. There was also one little petroleum-fed single-burner for cooking that was left in the kitchen corner. The woodstove was tiny but would do. And the attic—well, the attic was cramped and low-ceilinged. Here and there, Henk could see that the roof needed repair. Debris from bombing raids had fallen on the roof, and rain liberally dripped through the batten-board ceiling. An old mattress lay on the floor and looked like it had been soaked numbers of times by the elements, its fibers almost destroyed by weather and mold. Henk's nose wrinkled.

Henk left for work straight from Spinozastraat, and met Frans along the way. Henk was strategizing as to what he was going to say to Cornelia later.

"It's just a shit hole in an alley, Frans," Henk said, frowning. "Cornelia's going to be so upset."

Frans looked at his brother–in-law. "I'm afraid the same will apply to your sister, Henk. But I think ours is a little larger, I don't know why. I'm sorry."

"Well, it is what it is," Henk offered.

They hurried along the road in silence. Henk looked over at his brother-in-law. He looked devastated and knew it was because of losing the car to the *moffen*.

"Frans, they did you a favor. With severe rationing of gasoline, unless you have a horse to pull the car as a carriage, it was eventually going to become a useless weight around your neck, anyway."

"Perhaps you're right, Henk." Frans sighed. "But losing the car along with news of these hovels assigned to us? In one day? Antonia's not going to like any of this."

Henk put a hand on his brother-in-law's back as they walked. He frowned, watching the pavement pass underfoot. "It is what it is," he repeated. "Ours is a tiny home, but we will have our privacy. We can't go on living like this at Pap's house, however hospitable he is to us all."

"Right," Frans choked. "Kings of our own little castles again. Well, at least they're for very little rent and the *Regeering* takes care of the maintenance."

Henk laughed. "Now, that's the biggest pile of horse shit I've heard to date!"

"Does it have indoor plumbing?" Cornelia asked, hopefully.

Henk stopped and held his fork halfway to his plate. He had to think for a moment and realized he couldn't remember sinks. Henk did, however, recall an outhouse within the house itself. He stuck his fork in the small piece of *worst* allotted him and chewed heartily. "Well, I don't know about the kitchen, Cornelia. But the outhouse is in the house itself."

"What? No flushing toilet?" She looked aghast.

"No, a pit and a hole in a piece of wood." Henk kept chewing. He was in a hurry.

"I'm not going to sit on a hole over a pit," announced Beppie.

Little Corrie pitched in. "I'm not either! I might fall in!"

Cornelia covered her face and moaned.

Henk looked around the little table at his children. They were too easy a mark for jesting and couldn't help but smile. "The last tenants left their chamber pot for the upstairs," he added, joking. He turned to Beppie for effect.

Beppie's face dropped, and she crinkled her nose. "Nope. Never," she said.

Cornelia dropped her hands. "Well, it is what it is."

He laughed. "That's exactly what I said to Frans!"

Cornelia fiddled with the front of her apron as she stood, thinking. "I'll start packing what little we have," she said sadly. "*Kinderen*, after you finish, you will help me clean up and gather our things together."

Henk got up and gave her a kiss on the cheek. "I'm off to work for an hour or so to make up for this morning. I will be back before 7:00."

Cornelia silently nodded.

Their new place was only about eight blocks away, but the rain, black-out, and early dark hours made it dangerous. Even if it was still before the 8:00 curfew.

Though drenched, Henk didn't mind having to tow the wagon back and forth with the bike. For the second-to-last trip, Henk and Pietje loaded the large radio into the small cart. When, finally, everything of importance and size had been moved, Henk took Pietje along into the pub downstairs to grab a very quick little *biertje* before heading back upstairs.

"Are you sure everything's in this basket?" Henk asked Cornelia. He looked around the swept dining room. It felt good to release the room back to his father. His father didn't want them to go, but understood it was best. Henk had given his father a massive hug and promised to come for supper every Sunday like before the war.

"I'll see you Sunday. We'll try and find some liverwurst!" He grinned at his dad.

"Just bring yourselves. Good luck." *De Heer Gelauf* blinked and shook his son's hand. "If you should need anything, let me know."

"Thanks, Pap. We'll be fine."

Cornelia and the girls put on their coats and hats, and joined Henk and Pietje down the dark back stairs into the rainy night.

Cornelia opened a large black umbrella over her two daughters. Pietje clambered onto the back of his father's bike. They both wore oiled ponchos, with Henk's poncho covering the basket in front of him.

"Okay, we'll see you at the house! Be careful when you cross the roads!" Henk yelled as he pushed on ahead with Pietje. "Poekie, come!"

Henk waved at Cornelia and the girls, before he and Pietje continued into the dark rain with an excited Poekie racing after them.

Little Corrie waved and watched Poekie's wet, sleek back racing after her father and brother. *So much going on,* she thought. It was such an adventure. Staying at her *Opa*'s house was a lot of fun, spending time with her cousins and playing Hide and Seek all the time. There were so many different corners, and pieces of furniture to hide in and behind. And she was so happy her cousins were going to live not far from them. She clung to her mother's hand as they marched in the rain, all watching the bike and dog disappear around the corner.

She could feel her mother's grip tighten over her hand. "Beppie, take your sister's hand, too."

"Do I have to?" whined Beppie.

Little Corrie offered her other hand to her sister, who begrudgingly took it. As quickly as they could, they raced over the wet pavement stones to the corner and continued to the next street. Suddenly, she heard a car's wheels squeal, and a horn honk long and hard. She heard bicycle bells chiming. They moved on, and as they turned another corner, she saw people with their bikes standing in the middle of the road looking down at something.

Little Corrie's ears perked up. She caught the nuance of a noise that appeared familiar and yet it wasn't. When they moved a little closer, her mother stopped her and Beppie.

"Wait here, *meisjes*," she said as she handed the umbrella to Beppie.

As little Corrie stood obediently waiting beside Beppie, she watched her mother stop at the edge of the crowd. A truck suddenly pulled up in the rain, its headlight shining on the group.

Then little Corrie understood what she was hearing. Over the noise of the rain drumming on their umbrella, she could hear her father. The crowd opened for her mother. As Cornelia walked through, Corrie could see past her and saw her father kneeling on the wet cobblestones clinging to Poekie.

"What happened!" Little Corrie could hear her mother's call. She and Beppie scurried over the wet cobblestones to be closer.

"*Moffen*. They came 'round the bed in an old black car and ran right over it. It's a black dog on a black night. *Mevrouw*, so I could see how it happened, poor dog. But the *moffen* drive like they own the road. They knew what they did, and they didn't even stop. They didn't care. I'm sure it was the SS."

Little Corrie looked at the woman who spoke to her mother. A stranger. Strange neighborhood.

The woman straightened her bike and shook the rain off her rubber rain kerchief. "It's almost 8:00, *mevrouw*. Best, you get home with your girls." She put her leg over the bike's middle bar and set a sure foot on the peddle. She pointed to Poekie and her father with a chin. "Do you know that man and dog?"

Her mother nodded. "That's my husband and our dog."

The woman's hand suddenly went to her chest, over the wet rubber coat. "*Ach, mijn medeleven mevrouw*. I'm so sorry, *mevrouw*. Condolences. Such sad days and times." She kindly patted her mother's arm. "You hold fast." She pushed at the pedals with a grunt and rode off across the road. Corrie watched her disappear into the dark.

Little Corrie moved towards her father, but her mother stopped her. "Stay under the umbrella, Corrie."

"But Pappa—."

"I know. Pappa is upset. Beppie, you go with Corrie to the corner. I'll be right back."

Corrie and Beppie walked further, off the road, and turned to wait obediently at the next corner. Corrie watched, heartbroken, as her mother scurried back to the thinning crowd.

Suddenly, there was a deep rumble in the ground and air. Sirens went off, calling everyone to shelters. The noise was deafening, even in the rain.

Corrie let go of Beppie and ran to her father. As she looked at the shadows of man and dog on the wet cobblestone, headlights came around the bend with the roar of a different kind of engine.

"*Achtung*!"

Corrie looked up wide-eyed at the bright headlights. The few cyclists that were left scurried off. The sirens continued to wail relentlessly.

Corrie, heart-pounding, saw through the rain a tall, black figure in a long leather coat step out of the back of the car. She read the authority the German carried in his gait as he swiftly walked toward them and the body of their dead dog. Corrie looked down at Poekie, now drenched in light. She gasped at the sight of one of Poekie's eyes hanging out of its socket in the glare. Poekie's teeth were bared. It was a horrific sight. She felt a wail about to burst from her throat but swallowed it.

"You have a bombing raid and curfew," he yelled over the sirens. "I suggest you all take the children and go home." Above them, searchlights cut through the rain against the low-lying clouds. Distant guns fired. Corrie, still crying, looked up and saw planes exposed briefly by the strong pillars of light. One tiny plane burst into flame and exploded. It took a long time for the rumble of the explosion to reach them.

The German also watched the action in the skies above them. "Eindhoven," he announced loudly, calmly. "Nothing to worry about here. *Geh Raus*." He looked at his watch and held it up in the light from the car behind him. He wiped the rain off the face of his watch. He dropped his hand. "Four minutes. *Geh raus*! NOW."

Little Corrie looked down at her father. His face was wet from the rain and tears, his eyes swollen and bloodshot. He looked up at the German officer. "I have to take—"

"*Bring den Hund schnell von der Straße!*" The German motioned to his driver, who got out and ran over.

The driver grabbed Poekie by the hind legs and threw him over to the side, onto the sidewalk out of the way. Then he quickly followed the German officer back to the car. They got in and immediately sped past Corrie and the others, and disappeared into the darkness.

The rumble of the distant fighting continued all around them. Flashes of silent explosions were the only light to see by. Slowly, the sound of the explosions echoed off the low-lying clouds. The rain stopped. But the sirens kept wailing.

"Mama," Corrie tugged at her mother's coat. Her mother didn't notice and focused on helping her father up. As gunfire rattled in the distance, her father finally struggled to his feet. Pietje grabbed his father's hand while Corrie and the rest doubled-back to their grandfather's house.

Corrie began to cry. Beppie, as well. Corrie felt overwhelmed with grief and fear. The world was suddenly a crueler version of the one she once knew.

A short time later, as they huddled together reunited with her *Opa* on top of the filthy, black coal in the cellar, she shivered with cold and shock. She realized it was the first time she had ever seen her father cry. And she couldn't get rid of the image of Poekie and his eyeball hanging out of his head.

It was the first time she saw death's ugly face.

Little did she know, it would be far from the last.

Chapter 9
June 1941

Corrie hummed to herself as she played with her mother's black leather purse. She loved how the clasp magically clicked shut and open with her fingers pushing or pulling at the steel mechanism on top. There was something mysterious about women's purses. Absolutely all women had one. She knew they had coin purses in them, too. Perhaps lipstick. A comb. But she had seen other strange things going in and out of her mother's bag, as well. So, she just had to see what was within the beguiling depths.

She put her hand in and rummaged. She pulled out a lace handkerchief. The one her mother spat into to wash Corrie's face. She gently put it to the side of the stone stoop she sat on. The stoop was cold to the touch, but the air was pleasant, and more comfortable than the stifling heat in the little hovel they now called home.

Her mother was cooking the wash over the stove, and hanging the clothes on hemp ropes in the tiny back courtyard where they kept the rabbits. She knew her mother would be busy for a while.

"You stole Mama's purse."

Little Corrie looked behind her to see her sister, Beppie, standing in the doorway.

"No, I didn't. I'm just looking."

Beppie closed the heavy wooden door and sat beside her. She leaned into the purse to see what was inside.

Corrie pushed her away. "Don't. I got it first."

Beppie pushed in return. They were just about to get into their usual bickering when Corrie's attention was caught by a strange little girl and boy turning onto their lane off Spinozastraat. They were both carrying a large, heavy, steaming bucket between them.

Beppie stopped pushing and looked as well.

The little girl motioned the boy to lower the bucket in tandem with her. Water splashed over the sides, spilling onto the dirty cobblestones. The girl stepped toward the sisters as her brother shyly stayed in place. He looked at Corrie and Beppie. Then he looked down at the cobblestones.

"*Dag*," said the girl. "I'm Rebecca. What's your name?"

Little Corrie fidgeted before answering. "Corrie." She looked at the girl's beautiful leather shoes with what looked like new laces, then she looked down at her own torn hand-me-down shoes. Her father had created space for her growing feet by cutting open the toes to expose the dark blue wool of her socks. She noticed a hole was forming on her right foot and bent down to bunch up the yarn, hiding the gap. She looked up to see Rebecca eyeing Beppie. She turned to Beppie beside her, who was frowning at the newcomer. "She's my sister, Beppie."

Rebecca turned toward the entrance to their lane and pointed at the little boy. "That's my brother, Saul." She waved at her brother to come forward.

A door opened at the little hovel across the lane. A woman with black hair, slim, wearing a maroon dress, stood holding a baby in her arms. She looked at the children. "Rebecca, Saul. Come in. I need that water." The woman disappeared into the house, but left the battered door open.

Corrie couldn't remember when or how these neighbors ended up on her lane. She couldn't recollect anyone new moving into the lane, though she guessed it must have happened during school.

"When did you move here?" asked Corrie, handing her mother's purse to Beppie as she stood up. She walked with Rebecca to Saul and put her hand on the bucket handle. She tested the weight of it. "My mama heats the water with the stove," said Corrie.

She figured Rebecca's family had more money than they had if they could afford to get hot water from the baker around the corner.

"Diapers," Rebecca simply said.

"We're having a baby," offered Corrie. "Mama said I wouldn't be the baby anymore. Can I see your baby? They come through your belly button."

"My mother ate the baby, and then it came back out," Rebecca said. She turned and, with an exaggerated grunt, got a hold of the pail. Saul did the same. The two of them carried the bucket to their front door, water splashing liberally over their shoes. Rebecca turned and smiled at Corrie before she and her brother disappeared through the door.

Corrie scrambled past Beppie on the stoop, into the main room. She looked behind the small armchair before running to her mother in the kitchen corner. Corrie searched the floor, then ran to the bedstead in the wall and pulled aside the curtains to look inside. Finally, she found the doll she had left there earlier that morning. Her doll hadn't liked being up in the attic anymore and insisted on sleeping in the bedstead with Corrie's parents.

"You come with me," Corrie said as she held it up straight. She looked into its face and studied it as a mother would a little child. It was the English doll with the long lavender Victorian dress. It had a dirty face. She scrambled away from the bedstead and took it to the armchair. With the doll still in her grasp, she spat into a corner of her woolen skirt and wiped the dirty face. "There, that's better. We're going *op bezoek*."

Corrie got out of the chair, and over to where her mother stood, back to stirring the wash in the big pot. Her mother's belly had grown. She noticed her mother resting her left hand on the bump as she stared down into the boiling wash. She looked drawn. Her hair hung over her eyes. Corrie was going to hug her around the middle, but it had gotten so big.

Her mother became distraught when she found out that milk and potatoes were rationed the day before. Corrie heard her cry a lot. Just two more items on the list of things that the *Regeering* put on ration. It seemed these days, Corrie was always hungry. Even her doll had complained about it just the other day.

Corrie looked past the doll to the corner where the radio once stood. Her father sold it when they discovered a new baby was on the way. He bought a bag of flour off the black market because her mother had become weak and sickly. Her father reasoned they could always go to his father's house to listen to the radio. It was no real sacrifice because they were only allowed to listen to heavily censored German broadcasting. And when they tried to get Radio Orange on the BBC, there was always loud static placed there by the *moffen* to make it impossible to listen to the news.

She turned and walked back to the open front door, stepped past Beppie, and stopped to carefully fold up the long lace train of the doll's dress. She swung the doll under her arm as she walked over to Rebecca's house. At the stoop, she took the doll's hand and pretended it knocked at the door. Then she banged it with the side of her fist.

The door opened. Rebecca looked at the doll wordlessly, then disappeared into the house. In a moment, she was out with her own doll. Corrie saw it was a beautiful blonde-haired doll with longer lashes than Corrie's. Corrie's eyes widened, and she smiled.

Rebecca plopped down on the cold stoop, and Corrie joined her.

Corrie and her dolls had found their soul mates.

Henk had gone to the harbor to see if his brother-in-law had some herring for them. Not long after moving to Spinozastraat, both Frans and he had lost their jobs at the mattress factory. The Germans replaced them with young, bedraggled Polish prisoners, at no cost, and the factory now made upholstered seat cushions for German army vehicles.

Henk was stunned when he heard rumors that Polish prisoners were shipped in to take over their paying jobs. Who were these prisoners? Were they criminals? Some of them appeared to be quite gentlemanly. Hungry and tired. Wearier than he. He shivered at the thought of their miserable lives.

Seagulls screeched and swooped down over his head, distracting his thoughts. He took in the North Sea air as he made his way past bundles of stinking nets and barrels. The smell of fish offal permeated every article on the old weathered docks. The pungent aroma assaulted his nostrils. The ocean air was tinged with the smell of rotting fish.

He stopped and readjusted his cap to keep the sun out of his eyes as he looked around the few fishing boats that were tied to the wharf. Most of the ships and barges had been confiscated by the Germans, though Seyss-Inquart, the *Riechskommissar*, allowed a few boats to be used by the Dutch. Most of the catch was sold at the harbor. Very little made it to the market. Lately, Henk brought home more and more mussels and clams, as they were far cheaper. Frans, now working as a fisherman, was able to help out with the odd herring. Henk miserably wondered how long that would last.

Suddenly, he heard a familiar whistle and looked around.

Frans was at a long, old, wooden table covered in fish scales. It stood next to a pile of netting and cork floats. Henk saw the flash of a knife arcing through the air. Frans looked up from where he was gutting fish and smiled. Frans had lost a tooth the month before, so strangely, he looked a little more relaxed. He was proud these days of the deafening whistle the gap made.

Henk strolled to the pile of fish nets and stepped down onto the wharf where Frans was toiling away. Henk watched Frans deftly cut out the intestines of a massive herring and flip the contents into the oil-slicked waters. Seagulls fought over the entrails, splashing the oily rainbow surface with their wings and taking off with bits of intestine in their beaks.

Over the cacophony of gulls, a low rumble rolled over them from the sky. Both men shielded their eyes as they looked over the choppy North Sea.

Three large British bombers hung in the bright blue sky. They slowly headed North along the coast. Frans and Henk heard nearby German coastal guns firing from new bunkers along the dunes. The bombers were just out of German range.

"The poor suckers up north. They're always bombing the hell out of Ijmuiden, and, where?" asked Henk.

"Den Helder. The German navy."

They heard low rumbles from further north.

"Well, we have our share here," said Henk grimly. He took out a checkered handkerchief and wiped his nose. "Damn, this summer cold." He folded it up before stuffing it back into his pocket. Though the weather had warmed up, he and Frans still wore frayed shirts, ties, and stained collars. Henk plucked at the woolen vest Cornelia had just made for him. She found a sweater she liked at the *markt* and unraveled it, knitting vests for him and Pietje out of the reclaimed wool.

Frans took some gutted herring, threw a bit of seawater over them from a wooden pail, and handed them to Henk.

Henk, looking around first, took out his handkerchief again, and wrapped the fish. "Did you get that saw from Pap's?" asked Henk, moving closer so as not to be overheard. There were ears everywhere.

Frans pushed up his greasy-looking glasses and nodded. "I've already done mine. I'll come over later with it and help put a hatch into your floor before we listen to the broadcast tonight." Frans looked around and stiffened.

Henk turned to see a group of armed German soldiers sauntering past. They were laughing, joking, trailing cigarette smoke.

He watched Frans wave at one of them, who returned the greeting.

"Doesn't hurt to seem friendly," Frans muttered.

"Keep your enemies close, right?" Henk nodded in their direction then turned away. His mind was still on the hiding spot they were creating. "It's not as if we have a lot to hide, but what we have, we don't want to lose to the *moffen*. Cornelia has a gold necklace and earrings. We have that brass water jug that someone gave us for a wedding gift."

"Well, it's the principle of the thing. The *moffen* are taking everything. Our food, our supplies. What? Now they want all our metals, gold, brass? I'd like to see them try."

"It's just a matter of time, Frans."

"Well, I'm not going out of my way to make it easy for them. I've hidden everything I could under that floor. You should, too. As if our few belongings will make such a big difference to the glorious *Wehrmacht* War Machine!"

"What'ya find under the floorboards? Stone?"

"No, nothing but sand."

"Much room?"

Frans shrugged. "About thirty *centimeters* or so. Enough room for small things. And a bunch of sand fleas."

Henk nodded, then pointed over to the few fishing vessels tied to the inner harbor walls. "No room for another fisherman yet?"

Frans looked over at some of the men in their bulky woolen sailing sweaters and Portuguese caps. One was coiling wet rope. Another was sitting on the cabin of one of the boats, smoking a pipe. The man with the pipe looked over at Henk and waved before turning away, leisurely sucking at the smoking tobacco. That man had kindly registered with the authorities that Henk was a member of his fishing crew, saving him from being allocated to work for the Germans. But he couldn't afford to actually pay Henk to work, though he allowed Henk a couple of herring once a day. Henk was extremely grateful for the risks this man took on his behalf.

All unemployed Dutchmen were required to sign up for compulsory labor for the Wehrmacht. This gesture of the man helped buy Henk time to find a job that actually paid.

Frans shook his head and peered over the sparkling waters of the harbor. "Henk, if the *moffen* take one more boat away, there won't be room for a whole crew. I wouldn't hold your breath." Frans frowned deeply. He suddenly jumped and faced Henk. "Oh, forgot to tell you. They took Herman early this morning."

Henk felt a shiver up his spine. This was too close to home; a brother-in-law was taken. He quickly thought of how terrible that was for his sister, Willie. "Oh, God. That's terrible. What is she going to do with the flower shop? Run it herself? I should help her!"

"The shop is now closed."

"What do you mean?"

"The *moffen* are using the shop as a supply depot."

Henk looked down at his feet. He noticed fish scales on the leather. "Oh, Lord." He looked up at Frans and then back at the German soldiers. "Even though he tried so hard to make friends with the *moffen*? That didn't work very long, did it?"

Herman, their brother-in-law, had become friendly with the young German soldiers who came in to buy flowers for their newly-found Dutch girlfriends and favorite whores. But business was otherwise bad, and he had to finally close shop. There was a downside to this tactic of being friendly with the enemy: They knew practically everything about you.

Frans looked at him, squinting. He lowered his voice. "Willie said as soon as he put up a notice on the door that the shop was closed for business, the *moffen* were at their house taking him away at gunpoint."

"Where'd they take him?"

Frans shrugged. "Willie doesn't know. She's hoping they'll let him write once he gets to where he's going. Some work camp in Belgium, probably."

Henk thought of how long he'd been without work. Months now. "At least they're not quite organized here." He thought of the baby coming. How was he going to feed another mouth in the middle of a war? "I'm so relieved I'm safe for the time being." He looked over at the captain with the pipe. The man was now on the wharf, checking the side of the boat. Henk whistled at him.

The man straightened up and looked over at him.

"*Bedankt*," he called out, holding up the fish.

The man nodded, smiled, and waved.

Henk turned to Frans. "Well, see you later, around six."

Frans took a deep breath of the pungent air. His raw red, scale-covered hands deftly threw another herring onto the wet wooden surface of the table. He pressed the flashing, flopping body down with his left hand as he cut off its head and sliced the soft white belly in two swift moves. He looked up and squinted through his greasy glasses and nodded. "*Ja*, I'll see you. *De mazl.*"

Henk walked into their lane and looked at a man sitting with a little carving knife on a stool near his house. The man bent over a small piece of wood while a young boy stood by watching closely. There were shavings on the cobblestones around their feet. The man's shirt sleeves were rolled up high into the upper arms exposing firm, hairy forearms. He looked up, smiled, and then quickly cleared shavings off his lap. He handed the knife and wood to his son. Henk couldn't help but overhear their conversation.

"Here, Saul, you give that a try. Slow, steady, but precise sideway slices. Remember to cut away from yourself."

Saul nodded at his father before peering at the knife. He kept his hands on the piece of wood and carefully balanced the little knife in his hands before sitting on the stool his father vacated.

"Henk, I have good news for you." Dovid Aaronson grinned at Henk as he walked closer. He looked down at the rolled fish in Henk's hands. "You've been to see Frans."

"Yes, our daily fish," Henk said, smiling back. "What's the good news?"

"Well, I told my boss how beautifully you built that rabbit cage of yours, and you had done a very nice job on the leaks in our roof and your own. You know how to use a hammer. My boss managed to get that contract mending rooftops in Wassenaar where some of the higher-ranking German officers live. A lot of shrapnel's done damage after that bombing raid back in July. He needs more help so I told him you were available."

Henk stepped back. He blinked. "*Ja*, well, thank you very much." He lowered his handkerchief roll of herring to the dusty, dirty cobblestones and grabbed Dovid's hand. He pumped it happily, grinning.

Dovid grinned back and slapped Henk on the shoulder. "See, did I not tell you all would work out?"

"Yes, you did!" Henk nodded, grinning. "You're far more positive than I am, Dovid. I tip my hat to you." Henk wondered how the man could be so happy. In February, Nazis arrested over 400 Jews in Amsterdam for absolutely no reason. This happened right after all Jews were to hand in their weapons. Everyone was so upset at the Nazis for singling out their Jewish friends and neighbors, that tens of thousands of people went on strike. The strike spread across the center of Holland, including the tram and train operators in The Hague. The whole shocking business made him that much more aware of the 'Jewishness' of his friends and neighbors. He never forgot how that gentleman was treated by the Nazis back at the *Regeering,* the day Frans lost his car. The Nazis' strange obsession with the Jewish portion of their population became more frighteningly apparent each day.

"Please. Let's celebrate. Come inside; I'll tell you all about the job. And we'll have some beer!"

Henk bent over and picked up the bundle of herring and smiled. "I'll come right over. I'll just give this to Cornelia and tell her the good news."

He was relieved to be coming home with something positive to offer, for once. He took a deep breath and sighed with satisfaction as he stepped into the dark little house. He looked over to where Pietje and Beppie were arguing over something, and didn't even bother to address it as he usually would. He walked right past them, placed the bundle of fish onto the kitchen table, and went out back where Cornelia was hanging wash. Henk stepped up and hugged her from behind. As he did, Henk saw little Corrie to the side, crouching beside the rabbit cage and holding a baby rabbit in her arms. He smiled and closed his eyes, letting the sun soothe and warm his tired face. Suddenly, Henk felt a slight stir under his arms.

New life. "Ah!"

Life kept moving forward regardless of what people did to each other. So, with a smile and love for the tiny being inside of Cornelia, he decided to think more positively.

He stepped back and walked through the house again. He knew why Dovid suggested to come in for a beer instead of the usual offer of going to the pub. He didn't let on that it was because Jews were no longer allowed in public eating houses, cafes, and pubs. And yet, Dovid extended the invitation with no hint of anger. No sign of resentment. Not even that he was aware of it.

Perhaps, he will try to be as gracious as Dovid and find the good in everything.

Little Corrie sat on the floor along with Beppie and Pietje as they watched their *Oom* Frans sawing into their floor. Every once in a while, he wiped away the spreading sawdust. Corrie looked over at her father, who crouched nearby with a large burlap bag at his knees.

"There, finished. Now we just need to create support around the hole and finish what will be the hatch cover," Frans explained. He stood up, bent over, and wiped sawdust and shavings off his worn corduroy pants.

Her mother went to the corner and took out an old straw broom. She wordlessly handed it to Frans. He took the broom and swept everything into a pile.

Little Corrie leaned forward to look through the hole, curious as to what she would find. She was too far away and couldn't see enough, so on her hands and knees she crawled closer. She poked her face through the hole and looked around. It smelled musty and she could smell the outhouse. Sand. Like on the beach in *Scheveningen*. But there wasn't much room. She was surprised as to how close the ground was to the floor.

"Watch out little Corrie, I have to get through," her father said.

While her *Oom* Frans worked on sanding down the edges of the hole in the floor, her father put down the burlap bag, accidentally exposing a shotgun.

"Wow, I didn't know we had a gun!" Pietje cried suddenly. "Can I see it!"

"*Godverdomme*, Pietje! Keep your mouth shut! There are ears all around!"

Pietje withered under his father's angry gaze.

"Pietje, that's okay. We all need to get used to having to be careful of what we say," Frans said softly to his nephew. He turned to his brother-in-law. "Henk, there's no one around. He made a mistake."

Corrie looked at her mother, who suddenly turned and went into the small water closet. Little Corrie knew her mother had been quite ill, and she'd been spending much time throwing up in the hole in the wood. It was that, or she lay down more and more in the bedstead in the wall.

"Whose gun is that?" asked Frans.

"It belongs to Dovid across the way." Henk rewrapped the shotgun with the burlap covering and carefully lowered one end of it at an angle to lay it on the sand below.

"*Ja*, I heard that Jews were not allowed to own any weapons. You know if you get caught with this, you're in big shit?" Frans stopped sanding and waited for little Corrie's father to reply.

"We're in big shit one way or another." Henk turned to Pietje and snapped his fingers. He pointed to a small box he had fashioned to hold some of their brass, copper and other metal objects they didn't want the Germans to take.

Pietje gently pushed the box toward his father, who then carefully lowered it through and shoved it to the side in the sand. He leaned back on his haunches and looked through the hole.

"There." He looked at the children, and seemed to be thinking.

Corrie watched him, wide-eyed. She sensed the danger in what her father was doing.

Their father pointed at them. "Do not tell a soul what we are doing here. Understand?"

"It's a secret!" little Corrie announced.

Her father placed a finger on his lips.

"It's a secret," little Corrie whispered.

Her father nodded. "Precisely."

"But secrets are bad, too, sometimes, Pappa. Right?"

Her father shook his head. "Not this one, *schatje*. Not this one. You mustn't tell a soul."

Secrets weren't good, little Corrie thought. She learned that in school. But her Pappa was teaching her otherwise. She decided to listen to her father, instead.

"You would save the whole family by not telling anyone." Henk looked at her steadily until she nodded. Then he looked at Beppie and Pietje, who also nodded.

Frans took a few pieces of batten and fashioned a frame around the opening in the floor. The space below was so shallow there was hardly any room to swing the hammer. At the same time, her father measured some more batten for the bottom of the new hatch cover.

Her mother returned from the back and walked over to the bedstead. She sat on the edge and slowly lay down on her side, clutching her bulging midriff.

Henk noticed, and looked at his wristwatch. "What shall we have for supper, Cornelia?"

Her mother didn't answer.

Her father turned to Corrie and said, "*Schatje*, you ask Mama what to do for supper. Can you do that? Can you make supper and let your mother rest?"

Little Corrie, stunned, looked over to her slightly older sister, Beppie.

As if reading her mind, her father pointed at Beppie. "I have other things Beppie can do to help, but you can follow your mother's directions when it comes to cooking. Okay?"

Little Corrie, now all of six years old, was a bit frightened at the prospect of using that small petroleum burner. "I need help with the burner."

"That's okay. I'm sure you'll get the hang of it. I'll show you later. You go and ask your Mama what she would like you to do. It's 5:30 now," he said, looking again at his watch. "If you work quickly, we could go back to *Opa's* and listen to some music on the radio before curfew."

Corrie stood over the burner, listening to the hiss it made as it heated the pot she had on to boil. Her mother had instructed her to peel five potatoes, clean some of the carrots, and chop them along with onions. A dash of salt in her palm. It started to smell very nice. Her mother had instructed her to test the potatoes with the end of a fork. She did, and burned her hand on the steam, but didn't want to complain. She was proud to be cooking for the family. Wait till she told Rebecca.

After supper, Henk took her, Pietje, and Beppie to his father's house. A little later, they sat around the large dining room table with tea and cookies. A few of her aunts were there with their families, too. Her *Tante* Willie was there, sometimes crying and wringing her hands, while the others tried to comfort her. She'd been drinking *jenever*, and quite teary.

Listening to Verdi on the radio calmed her down. When the chorus cut in, everyone intertwined their arms and swayed to the music. Listening to music on the censored broadcast was still better than having no music at all. They all closed their eyes and sang along, already knowing the words very well. It was a quiet, slow waltz mellowing everyone's heart. Corrie saw her aunts crying with *Tante* Willie. Corrie thought, what sad times these are, but she knew the music soothed their souls. Was it wrong to enjoy some of the things the enemy allowed?

She saw her father choke up. He continued to sway with everyone as he looked over at her, Beppie and Pietje.

Suddenly, Pietje stood up and pretended to be an opera singer. He swung his arms around and made faces, making the young ones howl. Corrie laughed too, but intuitively knew he was disturbing the older relatives who were sad and deep in thought. She looked at her father to check his reaction. A little while ago, he had been excellent. Nothing seemed to bother him. But that only lasted a few days, and he became easily upset again. Especially by Pietje.

Her *Opa* watched too. "A little light fun is probably what the children need," he said to her father.

Everyone nodded, and no one said a thing when Pietje continued to make fun of the music.

After all, even Corrie understood that none of them had asked for any of this. Especially the children.

Chapter 10
September 1941

Little Rebecca gently patted Corrie's back with the flat of her palm. She was trying to comfort her. They stood in the gloom of the cloakroom at the end of their classroom. This was where students hung their coats, took off their dirty shoes or boots, and where they left their lunches during the day.

Even though Corrie's shoes had the toes cut off, fixed with cumbersome thick layers of used rubber as new soles, someone had stolen them.

"What's going on in here?" asked their teacher, surprised to see them.

They both looked up at the tall man. Little Corrie wiped her eyes. "I have no shoes." She cried as if her heart had broken. She felt her teacher's hand on her shoulder.

"Corrie, are you sure they're not here? Shall I help you look again?" He looked around the cloakroom.

"They're for sure not here," offered Rebecca. "And I know who took them!"

Little Corrie also knew. It was the new boy in their class who was barefoot. Some of the boys bullied him and made fun of the fact he had no shoes to wear. Not even *klompen*.

"Well, you have nice thick socks, at least, and they will protect your feet. Still better than going barefoot, right?" He turned and looked down at Rebecca. "Rebecca, you live on the same street.

Could you please walk Corrie home? Perhaps her parents could find her another pair."

Corrie cried anew. What pair? How? There were no other shoes for her to inherit. New shoes were out of the question. Oh, the shame. She wailed.

Rebecca took Corrie's hand. They were both seven now, and little Corrie had a new baby sister at home, which really upset her life. She cried over losing her shoes. But she also cried because she was no longer the baby of the family. All the attention went to the baby, who never stopped crying. Worse than that, she now always cooked while her mother took care of the baby. She hated that baby with all her heart.

Rebecca led her out of the cloakroom, and out of the school. Corrie padded quietly beside Rebecca for a little while without taking her eyes off the pavement. Corrie didn't want to step onto glass, nails, garbage, dog poo, horse manure. She was suddenly so aware of the dangers of walking outside in socks without the protection of shoes.

Dust clouds swirled around them as large green, army trucks trundled past. Only once did little Corrie look up to see soldiers with their guns standing up in one of the vehicles, swaying and bouncing along with the truck.

The soldiers and workers had been busy. They built large and long cement walls to keep enemy tanks out in case they came in from the sea. Now it was a very long walk to get to school and back, and most of it was along the canal where bombs had fallen and destroyed barges. She heard there were smaller boats inside one of the big barges and heard her father tell *Oom* Frans that these little boats were for the *moffen* to use once they landed in England. She guessed someone in England found out and sent over bombs.

Corrie's mind drifted to England. Her mother had once shown her clouds far away along the horizon when they were on the pier in *Scheveningen*. She told her England wasn't very far away by boat, and especially not by plane. She finally understood to where the Queen ran away. It wasn't that far, at all.

She looked at Rebecca, at the yellow star pinned to her sweater. She wished she had one. She loved brooches and craved beautiful things, but no one let her have one. "We should go to the beach. I can show you where England is. That's where the bombs come from," she said, keeping up to Rebecca.

"Pappa said we can't go on the beach anymore," Rebecca said.

"Why," asked Corrie.

"Because we are Jews."

"Because you wear that pretty broach?"

"Yes," answered Rebecca, also looking out for Corrie's feet.

"Then you can take it off before we go there."

"I have to wear it."

Corrie gingerly stepped around a puddle. "Why?"

Rebecca shrugged. "I think because I am Jewish."

"What is Jewish?" asked Corrie, looking at Rebecca closely.

"Because we believe in God," Rebecca said.

"But we believe in God, too."

Rebecca looked at Corrie and shrugged. "Maybe because I have black hair?"

"But Mama has black hair, too."

"I don't know. It's too much for me to think about," Rebecca said, sighing dramatically as only a child could.

They finally reached the end of their lane on Spinozastraat. From where they were, they could already hear Corrie's baby sister crying. Rebecca dutifully led Corrie to her front door. She knocked on the door. Corrie went to turn the knob, but Rebecca pushed her hand away. She again knocked at the door. They waited, listened to a baby wail until Corrie's mother opened it, rocking the crying baby. She looked down at them surprised. She looked at the doorknob.

"Was the door locked?"

"No, *Mevrouw* Gelauf, the *Meester* said I was to help Corrie come home. I am delivering her to you," she said proudly.

"Hello, what happened here?" Corrie's mother looked at her dirty socks.

Little Corrie wailed with fresh tears. "Someone stole my shoes."

Her mother waved them inside and closed the door behind them. Corrie immediately went to the armchair, sat on it, and studied the bottom of her socks. She pulled them off by the toes and threw them on the floor, disgusted.

"Where did they go? Who stole them?"

"Someone new in our school. The boy was barefoot." Rebecca stood politely by the door.

"Bare feet?" Cornelia shifted the crying baby to her other arm and shook her anew. She shrugged. "We'll see what we can do."

Rebecca turned to go.

"You want to play with our dolls?" asked little Corrie, hopefully, flushed from crying. She got off the chair and padded to the corner behind her chair. She lifted her favorite Victorian doll and turned to walk barefoot to Rebecca.

"Corrie, no," said her mother. "I need your help. You can play with your dolls another time, maybe."

Corrie looked over at her mother and baby sister. She glared at the baby.

"But you can stay, Rebecca, if you want to keep Corrie company."

Rebecca shook her head while eyeing the baby. "I have to go home."

Corrie saw her mother eyeing Rebecca's yellow star.

"Mama, Rebecca got a new brooch. I want one."

Her mother shook her head. "Corrie, that's not a brooch. Rebecca, I'm sorry to say, it's supposed to be sewn on."

Rebecca looked steadily at Corrie's mother. "I know," she said softly.

"Why, Mama? It's a brooch."

"No, it's not a brooch. Rebecca is Jewish. Only Jews wear the Star of David."

Star of David? Who is David? "Can I have a Star of David?" she asked meekly.

Little Corrie's mother sighed and looked around. "We have some carrots left, Corrie. I'll give you money so that you can run to the vegetable merchant and buy some green beans. Also, ask if they have any old vegetables they're throwing away. See if they'll give you any for the rabbits.

"But, I have no shoes!" shouted Corrie.

Her mother looked down at her own feet. She stepped out of her shoes. "Here, wear mine. We'll ask Pappa if he could find you some *klompen* at the *markt* tomorrow on his break."

"Can Rebecca come with me?" asked Corrie.

Her mother eyed Rebecca's Star of David. She was sad, Corrie could tell. But it could be because the baby was always fussing and crying. No one slept a wink at night. Her mother nodded.

"If her mother allows her."

Corrie quickly went to the dish that had a few coins in it and grabbed a net bag. She put on her mother's shoes, but they fell off as she walked.

"Wait, Corrie." Her mother went to the armchair and bent over to pick up a newspaper on the floor. She handed it to Rebecca. "Here, Rebecca, you tear up some paper and crunch it up into the toes of the shoes. That will keep them from falling off. And thank you." Corrie's mother smiled at Rebecca.

Corrie stood, humiliated, and sad, as Rebecca did as her mother instructed. She allowed Rebecca to lift her foot and take each shoe to squish paper into the toes. Finally, she gently put them back on her feet. It occurred to Corrie then that Rebecca was a perfect friend. There was something powerful and beautiful about Rebecca.

Finished, Rebecca stood up. "Let's see if Mama will let me come with you." Corrie followed her out. Another adventure, at least. She looked down at the coins in her hand. She had no idea if what she had would buy a lot. But she trusted the grocer would know.

She was grateful when the door closed on the baby's cries. She watched the shoes as she shuffled across the cobblestones to Rebecca's house. They were still quite loose. She stopped to adjust one of them. As they stepped up to Rebecca's door, it swung open, and Rebecca's mother stood holding her toddler. Corrie saw that she also wore the Star of David brooch.

"What happened?" Rebecca's mother looked down at Corrie's feet and the over-large shoes.

"Someone stole Corrie's shoes at school. She has to wear her Mama's shoes. Can I go with Corrie to buy green beans at the grocer's?"

Rebecca's mother put down the toddler, who was half-naked and wore only a diaper and rubber pants. She went further into the main room, and the two little girls followed her in.

The toddler stood wavering on his feet as he sucked on his fingers. He looked at Corrie and pointed at something in the sky. Corrie looked out the door. The toddler laughed, showing two front teeth.

Rebecca also laughed and bent over to hug her tiny brother. Then, with a grunt, she lifted the toddler, who was half her size. Rebecca smiled as she bounced her little brother in her arms. Corrie couldn't understand why Rebecca liked her little brother so much. Maybe because he didn't cry day and night like her baby sister, Henny, did.

Rebecca's mother came back, holding a pair of girl's shoes. "Try these on, Corrie. They are Rebecca's old shoes and don't quite fit her. See if they fit you."

Corrie's mouth dropped open. She was saved from humiliation! She eyed them as if they were the most expensive pair of shoes in the world. She allowed Rebecca's mother to lift each foot, place the shoe on, and tie up the laces. They indeed fit.

Rebecca put her foot next to Corrie's to show the comparison.

"No *klompen* for you!" announced Rebecca.

Corrie smiled for the first time since discovering her shoes were missing. She hugged Rebecca's mother and turned toward the door, clutching at the coins and net bag in one hand and her mother's shoes in the other.

"You come straight home. And if you hear sirens, you go to the bomb shelter right away. You hear?"

"*Ja*, Mama," said Rebecca.

Corrie took Rebecca's hand as she opened the door and skipped down the stoop. Together, they kept skipping over the cobblestones to her house where she placed her mothers' shoes on the stoop. Then they skipped to the end of their lane, then turned right to go over the canal bridge to the grocer.

"Over my dead body. It's slave labor!" Henk was furious. "What do they think we are, morons? That we should report to them and say, yes, take me away from my family. I would love to be your slave?"

"They say men between the ages of 18 and 40. If they do take you, I will be here to care for your family," said *de Heer* Gelauf.

"How can you, when the family is so large! That means all the men in our family except for the wives and kids! You can't take care of everyone!"

"Then, do your best not to be taken."

Henk sat back in his seat at the dining room table. All men were required to report for work wherever the Reich wanted to place them. No pay. They were taken away in droves. "How can this be possible? It's morally despicable."

"Then we won't report like Pap says, Henk. What are they going to do, come and shoot us because we refuse to go?"

Henk snorted at his brother-in-law, Frans. "I wouldn't put it past them!"

Frans sighed as he sat back, as well. He fingered the blue willow teacup in front of him. "We could always hide or be somewhere else." He shrugged.

Henk fumed. "Like where?"

Frans shrugged again. "When we know they're coming, we hide under the floor. How about that?"

"Listen, *jongens*, it could be worse. I'd rather you have this problem than the ones our Jewish friends are having," offered *de Heer*.

Henk looked at his father. He thought of Dovid and his family. Such gentle people.

"And you noticed, they didn't say Jews were to report for slave labor like the other men. What did you think? That they were getting the royal treatment? Be happy you're not Jewish." The older man took a sip from his cold tea. No milk or sugar these days. Soon there will be no tea, Henk thought.

"No. That's something else that bothers me. Why treat people like animals just because they are Jewish and then turn around and say, hey, we care for you. You're special. We set up a whole new promised land in Poland just for you. You believe that crap?"

"Many do," offered his father. "Perhaps it is true. Even though they treat Jews like animals, maybe they just don't want them mingling in with the proud Aryans."

"Pap, Poland is part of Germany now. Why would they send people from one place in their domain to another place in their domain? It doesn't make sense." He shook his head. He thought of how a German soldier threatened Dovid at work because his Star of David was pinned and not sewn on to his clothes. Henk slapped the table. "Right, I need a *borreltje*. I need a distraction. Let's play some darts," he said, as he turned to Frans. "Shall we?"

"It will do you good, Henk. A *borreltje* wouldn't hurt," said his father.

"You coming?" asked Henk of his father.

His father, a little slimmer these days, shook his head. He'd gotten greyer, Henk noticed. Paler. He suddenly realized that, of course, his father fretted about the welfare of his large ever-growing family. How much more could his father bear? Fifteen kids, in-laws, grandchildren. Henk realized he didn't have it so bad. Especially now with the new job. And he doesn't get roughed up because of wearing a Star of David incorrectly.

He pushed back his heavy chair, and Frans followed him out through the kitchen.

"Where'd all the little old ladies go to?" someone asked down along the sticky bar.

Henk's ears perked up. He was quietly enjoying his *borreltje* with Frans after a game of darts. They were in deep thought.

"What little old ladies?" asked another.

Henk didn't recognize the two gentlemen. Frans and Henk had been going to a pub between Spinozastraat and Van Ostadestraat and hadn't been to their father's haunt for a while.

"You know, the ones on Spinozastraat. They disappeared. To where? The *moffen* moved families in after they took their homes away. It's like the Great Charlemagne's Move all over again." The gentlemen laughed.

There was a pause. Henk didn't want to look over as yet. He wanted to make sure there weren't any Nazi informers listening. He turned quietly and leaned back into the counter and looked around.

There were a few men here and there. Two were playing darts over by the far wall. No German soldiers. Only one man alone at a little table. He might be an NSB man; he might not. Either way, it would be better if these two men kept their voices down. He turned back to face the bar again and locked eyes with their father's friend, Bert the bar owner.

Bert motioned slightly to the men over at the side. He looked down and continued wiping his counter with a wet rag.

Henk moved closer to the men. "It may pay to keep your voices down. You never know who is listening."

The man with his back facing Henk turned around. He wore a cap similar to his and held a cigarette. He looked over at an ashtray, tapped the cigarette, and stepped back so Henk could see the other gentleman.

"Why, what's it to the *moffen*?" asked the first man. "It's not a big secret."

Henk leaned into the bar and spoke in their direction. "I also want to know where they went. What do you think happened?" Henk looked around one more time. "You see, I live there now. And I wondered the same thing about the little old man or woman who lived there before us. I mean, where would they be now? It troubles me very much."

The other man leaned in toward Henk, past his friend. He also wore a cap, a black one, and his hands indicated he probably worked with coal. "I bet you they killed those poor little old people."

Henk leaned further into their space. He felt Frans shuffling closer behind him. "Why do you think that?" Henk asked quietly.

"Goddam, would I know, except that maybe they were in the way. They're not of any importance to the *moffen*. Maybe they wanted their gold teeth?" The man shrugged and tapped his cigarette against the ashtray.

Henk watched the man play with the ash in the ashtray. Everyone was quiet for a moment longer.

Henk's heart was skipping beats. "They wouldn't do that, truly?" he whispered, frowning.

The man motioned with his hand. "Oh no? Where did they go then?" He leaned in closer. "Hitler got rid of anyone who didn't measure up to the super standards the Germans all of a sudden have." The man counted on his fingers. "In Poland, you know what he did? First, he got rid of the mentally handicapped. Then he got rid of the very crippled. Then he collected all the homosexual men and took them away." The man wiped his brow with the back of his cigarette hand. "Take them away to where, right? He killed them."

Henk stepped back and took a deep breath. He felt sick to his stomach. What was this nightmare unfolding around them?

"That's enough of that!" announced Bert. "Henk, play some accordion for us. We need something to lift our spirits!"

The two men stood back. One dragged on his cigarette; the other took out a handkerchief and blew his nose. Before putting his coal-stained handkerchief back, from underneath his black eyebrows he eyed Henk.

Henk stepped back. He nodded. "*Ja*, okay. Where's the accordion?"

Bert bent down and brought out an old accordion. "It's not as nice as yours, Henk, but you can still bring the magic out of these keys, I'm sure."

The man with the cigarette raised his hand. "Good, some music. Some nice Dutch accordion music. What is your name, by the way?" he asked.

"Henk Gelauf, and this is my brother-in-law, Frans Riep."

"Gelauf. Your one of Piet's sons?" he asked, pointing to the ceiling.

"Yes," smiled Henk. He took the hand that was offered and shook it before slipping on the straps of the accordion. Henk ran his fingers over the keys to limber up. It was a little stiffer than his, but he could still get something out of it.

Frans stood up and pulled his stool over for his brother-in-law to perch on.

Henk leaned against the stool and started playing the "Too Fat" polka. Light, fun, and funny.

The few men in the pub came to life, singing along, swaying to the happy tune. People from outside poked their heads in or pressed faces against the grimy window. Some sauntered in to join the fun.

As Henk played, he saw an SS pass by the window. The man walked back and peered in through the door. Henk's heart dropped but kept playing as the German walked through the door and looked around.

The German turned, stepped through the door and back out into the street. Henk saw him craning his neck to look in the distance. The soldier made a motion with his hand summoning someone to the door. He smiled, then nodded, then walked back in. As Henk played, the men tried to ignore the soldier. Frans started clapping, and everyone clapped along, as did the soldier.

Suddenly, a second soldier, heftier than the first, walked in and made his way to his comrade. They relaxed, leaned against the wall and clapped along. They laughed and sang, but in German, to the tune, they knew so well.

"From the front, I can see that back
You're too fat for me,
You're too fat for me,

You're too fat for me,
And I don't want you,
I don't like you,
'Cause you're too fat for me.
You're too fat.
Far too fat,
Far too fat for me! Hey!"

The first German hurried over and slapped Henk on the shoulder. "That was very, very good. You are good! It's so nice to hear music from home." His accent was heavy, but his Dutch was good.

Henk nodded, smiled, didn't know what to say.

The soldier turned to Bert and yelled, "A drink for this man!" He waved his comrade over. "Look at this accordion. My father used to play the accordion."

Bert put a *borreltje* on the bar and pointed at the soldier. He nodded and grinned. "I'm not supposed to, but this is a special occasion. Fritz, have a drink with me?"

The other soldier, Fritz, walked over. "*Ja*, okay."

The first turned to Bert and put up three fingers.

Bert poured two more *borreltjes*.

The first held up his drink as the other gave Henk his and kept one himself. "*Prost!*"

"*Prost*," said Henk.

All three tossed their drinks back in one gulp.

Henk shivered with the lovely searing heat that went down his throat. Then he put his glass down and looked around nervously.

The first soldier pointed at the accordion. "Is this your accordion?"

Henk shook his head.

Bert spoke up. "No, it belongs to the pub. You should see Henk's accordion, however. A beautiful bright red accordion, so polished you could check your teeth in it. And the inside has a pattern of roses."

Henk looked at Bert, askance.

The first soldier fingered the accordion. "That is a very special accordion. I know. My father once had one with a pattern in its baffles. They create a beautiful effect when you play them." The soldier sobered up and looked more intently at Henk. "You live around here?"

Henk looked around the room before answering. "No."

"Where do you live?"

"Just across the bridge on the other side of the canal."

The soldier straightened up. "Where on the other side of the canal. I wouldn't mind seeing your accordion sometime."

Henk caught his breath. He coughed. "Spinozastraat."

Both German's turned to look at Frans.

Frans swallowed. "Van Ostadestraat."

Both Germans repeated after him. "Van Ostadestraat."

Frans nodded. "*Ja*."

"Do you have your identification papers with you?" asked one of the soldiers, holding out his gloved hand.

"Wait," said Bert. He held up his arm and motioned to the rest of the men. "This is a place where we can all relax. Perhaps you can ask for identification papers on the street, but here... Please, have another drink on the house on me. And if you have girlfriends, come when you have some leisure time. I guarantee you I can make you feel quite happy and make a nice little date for you. You can impress the lucky girls."

Fritz stepped forward and put a gloved hand on his comrade's shoulder. "Sounds good, old man. We will be back."

The first soldier stepped back, looked around, and then nodded at Bert. He pointed a gloved finger at him. "We will take you up on your promise."

"Please do," said Bert, grinning like a Cheshire cat. "Come anytime." He smiled and nodded, but Henk could see sweat breaking out on his forehead.

The soldier pointed at Henk, "One day, friend, I would like to see your accordion." He held up a finger. "Spinozastraat!" He turned to his companion. "Let's go, Fritz!"

All watched as the soldiers left the pub. Their departure suddenly lightened the heavy feeling in the air.

Henk turned to face the bar. "I have to go," he whispered to Frans.

Frans frowned. "Where are you going so fast?"

"I'm going home to hide my accordion under the floor."

Chapter 11
September 1942

"Someone knifed a soldier in the back last night!" Pietje, tall, thin, and pale, ran breathlessly into the house.

Henk put down his heavily-censored newspaper. "Someone in the underground killed him, no doubt."

"He's still lying there, on the street corner!" Pietje nodded, turned and left as quickly as he came.

Henk put his paper down. "Pietje! Stop!" He got up and quickly left the house. As he ran out of the lane onto Spinozastraat, he looked back and noticed little Corrie following close behind him. He stopped and pointed back down the alley.

Corrie stopped and looked at him. She had grown a few more inches, but only in height and not weight. Her long blonde braids were unruly, and her clothes were nothing but rags. Ever since they stopped attending church, they worried less about clothing. They were just happy to have things to wear.

Henk had stopped praying and hoping for the best. It was his decision not to go to church any more, even though Cornelia wanted to keep going. He just plain stopped and gave up. If God was there, why didn't he do something to stop this nightmare? Henk found it easier to accept the nightmare; the bomb raids; the sirens. It took less energy to be miserable.

He sternly looked at Corrie one more time before pointing up the lane once again.

Wordlessly, she lowered her head and turned back for home. He stood and watched her disappear through the door before turning and resuming his chase. He felt helpless, he couldn't play the role of a protective father anymore. Too many dangerous and awful things happening at once these days. His hands were tied in so many ways. And Pietje simply didn't stop getting into trouble. Usually nothing serious, but extremely aggravating. Henk couldn't be everywhere all at one time. He had to get Pietje before he got into trouble with the *moffen*. Where there was death through violence, there was always more to come. And in spite of reviewing the reasons why he didn't go to church or why he no longer relied on God, he quickly said a prayer to Him to keep Pietje safe until he caught up to him. Lately, the *moffen* had started shooting people at random in retaliation to acts of resistance, and he didn't want Pietje to be in the wrong place at the wrong time.

Little Corrie sat on Rebecca's stoop. They were comparing the dresses they had made out of bits and pieces of cloth left over from a dress Rebecca's mother found at the flea market. She cut it up and sewed a whole dress for her daughter and herself, and gave the girls the remnants to play with.

"Look, she looks just like me!" Rebecca said proudly. She held up her doll showing off the little cobbled-together dress that matched her own.

Corrie looked up and smiled. She liked the dress and the idea that she matched her doll.

"Corrie!"

Little Corrie stirred. It was her mother again. She knew she needed to care for her little sister, Hennie. She'd begun to walk and was being a pest these days. She hated her. So, she ignored her mother's call.

Rebecca pretended not to notice. She was brushing her doll's beautiful, yellow hair, though the hair had gotten matted beyond repair in spots. It was still a beautiful head of hair for a toy.

"Corrie!"

Corrie squirmed. Then she dropped her hands and let the doll rest on her lap. "I have to go."

Rebecca silently let her friend leave.

Corrie turned and gave her doll to Rebecca. "Will you babysit my doll while I babysit my stupid sister?"

Rebecca smiled at the doll and carefully collected the long, frayed lavender lace dress into her arms.

"She says thank you," said Corrie. She looked down at Rebecca for a second before moving on.

Rebecca held up Corrie's doll and waved the arm at Corrie. "*Dag*, mama!" said the doll through Rebecca.

Corrie grinned. She raised her hand and waved. "*Dag*, baby." She turned and skipped to her front door, opened it and closed it behind her.

It was getting cold and wet again, so they kept their door shut to keep the cold out and keep what heat they had in the house. It was harder to find anything to burn in the stove these days and the house sometimes just wasn't getting warm. The coal that the German's allowed the Dutch to burn in their stoves did not burn very well. So, it was harder to clean the wash. Stained diapers and clothes hung from one wall to another. It was dank, smelly, and everything hung in the way when you tried to do something in the house.

Corrie went over to little Hennie, pushing aside the odd garment hanging off the washing lines. Hennie sat in a wooden playpen their father had fashioned together, and played with a wooden figure his father had carved.

"I have to stand in line for soup. You take care of Hennie." Corrie's mother put on a coat from one of the few hooks at the door. She bent down and picked up a banged-up pail. "You make sure Hennie has her bottle of sugar water while I'm gone. I don't know how long this will take. If your father comes home before I do, tell him I'm in line at the soup kitchen. There's some old bread in the cupboard, but he may want to wait. He can soak it in the soup. Other than that, make sure Hennie doesn't hurt herself. And change her diaper if she needs it."

Corrie miserably looked at her little sister. She had a snotty nose, big eyes and massive blonde curls. She was teething and dribbling spit.

Hennie looked back at her, mouth open. She was a thin child.

"Where's Beppie," asked Corrie.

"She's with Pietje. They're standing in line for more coal. They might take a while, too."

With that, her mother left her alone with Hennie.

Corrie sat helplessly watching little Hennie play. Suddenly, little Hennie made strange faces as she did pushing motions with her torso.

Corrie sat up and slapped at the playpen. "Don't you dare shit your pants!" She smelled the pungent smell of a filled diaper and pinched her nose. "Eeeeeew!"

Henk walked from work, Dovid by his side. They crossed the street to avoid another store with glass windows shattered. Henk tried not to see the ugly graffiti denigrating Jews. Another Jewish establishment destroyed. He looked over at Dovid and the Star of David sewn on his chest. He looked away, adjusted his cap, and took out a cigarette. He didn't offer it to Dovid. Dovid didn't smoke.

Lately, Cornelia sent the children out to find cigarette butts. She ripped the butts open for the remaining tobacco and then rolled cigarettes when she had enough to fill the papers. He looked down at the roughly-rolled cigarette and thought of strangers' shoes pressing down on butts in the street. Of lips and teeth that clenched them. People's breath all over them. But it was war and times were hard. It was better than having nothing at all to smoke. He pulled out a match and lit up while cupping his hands. He flicked the match into a puddle. It had rained earlier, and everything was wet and cold.

He was thinking of the latest news Dovid shared with him; that Jews weren't allowed to go on the beach anymore. But more importantly, the possibility he would soon lose his job because he was a Jew.

Henk asked Dovid why he and his family didn't just leave and go to another country. But Nazi Germany controlled all of Europe and Dovid told him that the United States wasn't accepting any Jewish refugees. He spoke of a ship full of Jewish refugees which was turned away from every port it tried to enter, the rest of Europe, the United States of America, and South America. They had nowhere to go. So, the ship came back to home port.

And Poland? Ugly rumors were sifting back, that it wasn't the Promised Land, after all. That those who were taken there, were never heard from again.

What the hell did that mean?

They slowed down and waited for a troop of stiff SS to goose-step past them. They were evidently on their way to the *Regeeringsgebouw*, where they did their training. To Henk's eye, the soldiers seemed to be getting younger.

"Jew!" One of the soldiers spit in their direction.

Henk and Dovid jumped back and looked at the gob at their feet. Henk was about to run after the soldier, but Dovid held him back.

"It's not worth getting killed over this," he whispered into his ear.

Henk looked at the marching soldiers' backs. He thought about the day when Pietje had alerted everyone a soldier had been knifed in the back and was left on the street. In retaliation for the death of that one soldier, they did precisely what Henk was afraid of. They went door to door and randomly pulled out 25 men. There didn't seem to be any organized thought behind it. They just wanted 25 warm male bodies. They lined them up in the street for everyone to see and shot them all. Dead and left to lie, as a clear message to everyone else. He was so relieved to have run after Pietje and dragged him home before that happened. They might easily have become two of the random twenty-five.

It was becoming a bloody Hell.

Bombing had also stepped up again. Japan had bombed Pearl Harbor and single-handedly brought the Americans into the war arena against Germany and Japan. Since then, the Americans attacked the Germans during the day, filling the skies over The Netherlands with a blanket of darkness. They dropped bombs on military outposts and suspected ammunition depots all over the country. Amsterdam and the northern coastline seemed the get the worst of the action but The Hague received its share.

At night, the Brits flew over The Hague, sometimes bombing the same suspected German installations. Other times, they crossed overhead on their way to attack Germany. The Dutch rarely had any peace at all. It was starting to show on everybody's nerves.

Henk sucked on his cigarette, coughed, and removed some loose tobacco from his lips. Again, he found himself relying on the old habit of prayer.

A *Kadish*, as Dovid would say.

So, he prayed a *Kadish* to God that there be an end to the nightmare before long.

He didn't know how much longer they could hold on without losing their minds.

"Corrie, I want you to take Hennie in the baby carriage and stand in line for bread. Here are the ration cards," Cornelia announced.

"Can Rebecca come?" Corrie hated being alone with Hennie. Corrie was still, after all, only eight years old, and Hennie, though underweight for her age, was still a bit heavy to lift and carry. But the baby carriage would make it easier, and she could put the bread in with Hennie. Also, it would be a lot less of a chore if Rebecca kept her company.

"If her mother allows her to come along. It's not safe out there. When they see those yellow stars…" Her mother stopped short of saying why.

Corrie noticed that no one wanted to talk about Rebecca and her family having to wear that Star of David anymore. And she couldn't understand why having a Star of David was so dangerous.

Corrie went out in the tiny courtyard and pulled the baby carriage out from under an overhang next to the rabbit cage. She shook out the little blanket that was in it, slapped the small flat pillow against her skirt to get the dust out, then pushed the hood all the way back. Corrie maneuvered the baby carriage to the back door and struggled getting it through. Once inside, she bent over the playpen and motioned to Hennie that she wanted to pick her up. Hennie, now learning how to walk, pulled herself up by holding on to the rungs, her skinny little legs shaking under the weight. With a grunt, Corrie pulled her out and got her head first into the baby carriage. Hennie didn't cry. She just squirmed around until she was safely on her back. But she did whimper when she couldn't get a grasp on anything to help her sit straight.

Corrie reached in and helped her into a sitting position.

Her mother came over with the ration books. "Here, Corrie. Let's hope the line-up is not too long."

Corrie put the ration books into the corner of the carriage and rolled the baby carriage closer to the door. Her mother opened it and helped her jostle the carriage over the threshold, down the stoop and into the lane. Corrie pushed the carriage, almost as high as her chin, to Rebecca's front door. She knocked only once before the door swung open. Rebecca stood expectantly.

"Wanna come? I have to go and stand in line for bread. We can take turns pushing the carriage."

Rebecca leaned over to look at Hennie bouncing in the baby carriage.

Hennie grinned back at her, slobbering.

Rebecca disappeared into the house and came back, putting on a large, heavy sweater. Corrie noticed that there was a Star of David sewn both on the sweater and her blouse underneath.

Together they pushed the carriage to the entrance of the lane, and stopped to tuck Hennie in a little better against a cold breeze from the canal. Corrie, very carefully, raised the dirty hood to block out as much wind as possible.

"I still remember sitting in this baby carriage. I was the baby once."

"Everybody was a baby once," replied Rebecca, her nose getting red from the cold dampness.

Corrie looked at Rebecca as she huffed and puffed. The notion that everyone was a baby once never occurred to her. She thought she was the only one who was ever special.

They pushed the carriage to the bridge and over the canal, straining as they went up the incline of the bridge, then had to hold it back when it wanted to roll down the other side. There weren't as many bicycles on the road now, as the Germans had taken many of them away. And bicycle parts and tires weren't readily available anymore, keeping others off the road.

They hurried into town toward the harbor and passed one of the German anti-aircraft batteries set up throughout The Hague. A young girl in brown hair with a woolen vest over a red dress, stood smoking a cigarette with a soldier beside a massive gun. She was giggling at him while he played with her hair. She wore red lipstick.

Corrie and Rebecca stopped to stare, astounded.

The girl looked over at Corrie and Rebecca. "What are you looking at?"

Corrie looked over at Rebecca. She held out a hand to keep the carriage from shaking under Hennie, who was bouncing up and down.

"Cat got your tongue?" The girl took a drag from the cigarette, flicked the ash, and then crossed her arms, smiling.

"You shouldn't talk to *moffen*," offered Corrie.

"I'm sorry? What did you say?" The girl walked toward them, cupping a hand to her ear.

"I said, you shouldn't talk to *moffen*," Corrie repeated, looking over at the German soldier.

The girl looked her over, from the top of her head to the top of her feet. She took another drag from her cigarette, then flicked it onto the road. "Is that so? Who do you think has food to eat and cigarettes to smoke, huh? You should learn more about what you have between your legs. You'll go farther in this rat's nest. That is, once you grow up, *kind*."

Corrie looked from her to the cigarette she'd thrown on the ground. It lay in between cobblestones, still smoldering. She stepped over, picked it up and pinched the burning edge. She put it into the corner of the carriage.

"It's like that, is it? Here." The girl took out a very fancy cigarette case and held it up for them to see. "A gift to me from you know who," she smiled, motioning to the soldier behind her. She opened up the cigarette case and offered it to Corrie and Rebecca. Rebecca went to get one but the girl suddenly took it away. "Not you, you filthy Jew. Blondie here."

Corrie gasped and looked at Rebecca, wide-eyed. Then she turned back to the girl and reached out. She took two cigarettes but the girl snatched one back.

"I don't want you giving this one a cigarette." The girl sniffed at them before swaggering back across the road to the German soldier. The girl leaned back against the mound of sandbags placed in front of the large gun and crossed her arms, giving the soldier a bright smile.

Corrie looked around and saw people looking at the girl in disgust. Curious, she thought. Life seemed unfair. You do good; you have nothing. You cheat, you survive a little better.

Rebecca pulled at Corrie's jacket. "Let's go before they run out of bread."

Corrie turned, put the cigarette into the corner of the carriage along with the cigarette butt.

They made it to the baker's, but there was a long line as usual. They obediently maneuvered the carriage into line and waited. Others around them played with Hennie and then turned away to wait.

And wait, they did. When they were only a few spots away from the door, the baker announced they had run out of bread for the day and to come back the next day. People complained and moaned; they were not happy.

Corrie's stomach growled. She quickly undid the belt around her middle and tightened it by one notch.

"What are you doing?" asked Rebecca.

"Mama said that when I'm hungry, I have to tighten it. It helps take the hungry feeling away. I don't feel the pain so much."

Just then, they heard a heavy drone mounting in strength. Corrie and Rebecca stepped away from the storefront and looked up over the rooftops toward the North Sea. They could see American bombers, in haphazard formation, almost overherad.

"They're going to Germany," offered Rebecca. Then they saw the bomb bays open and bombs fell. The sirens wailed just as the ground shook under an explosion somewhere.

They looked around, aghast. "Where's the bomb shelter!?" Corrie cried to someone rushing by.

"Follow me!" yelled the woman.

Rebecca and Corrie ran like the dickens, pushing the bouncing carriage as fast as they could. Little Hennie was thrown around and bounced from her back to her behind, and almost on her head. She started to wail along with the sirens. They made it to the entrance of a bomb shelter, and were just about to push the carriage down the stairs when someone took the carriage away from them.

"No carriages, we need room for the people. Here, let me help." It was an older man, eager to help. He lifted Hennie out of the carriage just as another explosion shook the earth around them. Shrapnel came from somewhere, and dust, smoke, and grime quickly overtook the street. The kind man led Corrie and Rebecca through the smoke and dust, and down the dank steps into a large bunker. Light bulbs hung from the severely-cracked ceiling, though it took a while for their eyes to adjust.

Hennie started to cry. The man shook her gently, but soon it was so noisy, no one could hear her cry anymore. They quickly grabbed a spot on a bench and sat down. Corrie took Hennie from the gentleman and put her on her lap. She could feel that Hennie needed changing. She looked underneath quickly and saw a very wet spot on her woolen skirt. It was hard doing the wash these wet days. Corrie hoped to rinse it right away when she got home but Henny might have to walk around half naked if the other diapers aren't dry by the time they got home.

That is, if they didn't get killed and managed to get home.

Soon, the rumbles became fewer and farther apart. They heard rumblings in the distance in between the staccato noise coming from the anti-aircraft guns from above them on the street. Slowly, even that settled down, and Corrie heard Rebecca breathing heavily next to her. By now, Hennie had calmed down as well. She was sucking her thumb.

When the girls finally made it back to the street, Corrie saw that the baby carriage was missing. She looked around desperately. She handed Hennie over to Rebecca, who almost fell back under the weight. "The baby carriage. Where's the baby carriage!?"

She ran into the middle of the street and looked up and down. She started to cry.

Rebecca caught up to her, looking around.

"Someone took the baby carriage," she cried. Looking around feeling entirely helpless, she didn't know what was worse, losing her baby carriage or having someone stealing their ration books.

"What happened?"

Corrie turned to see Pietje standing next to them.

Corrie cried. "Someone stole the baby carriage."

"Those assholes!" yelled Pietje. Now twelve years old, he considered himself an expert on assholes. "Wait till I find them. Where'd they go?!"

"We don't know," Rebecca said.

Pietje looked up and down the street. "Well, you can't hide a carriage like that. One day we'll see it, and I'll give them a fist in the face, I will!"

"But that's not all you lost," offered Rebecca.

Pietje looked at Corrie. "What else did you lose?"

Corrie raised her arms in despair. "Everything! The baby blankets, the baby pillow, a cigarette butt, a good cigarette, and our ration books!"

"What!?" Pietje stood staring at her in disbelief. "Corrie—"

"I know!" She was beside herself in anguish. How will they survive without their ration books? It was the middle of the month!

Pietje bent over her. "Corrie, you and Rebecca go over there and sit down with Hennie. I'll be right back."

Corrie looked over to where Pietje was pointing. A pile of sandbags towered at the end of the street. Corrie and Rebecca took Hennie to the bags and settled down on top of the first row. Corrie took the distraught child onto her lap. Hennie tried to reach for Corrie's hair, but Corrie impatiently pushed the little hand away.

Rebecca patted Corrie on the back. "We'll share our food with you, Corrie."

"I'm so in trouble," cried Corrie. "Mama will be so upset."

They waited and watched as people moved back and forth in their various chores and journeys. Soon, Pietje came running up to them, out of breath. He flicked a blonde lock of hair out of his eyes.

"Close your eyes."

"Why?"

"Both of you. Just close your eyes."

Both Corrie and Rebecca closed their eyes. Corrie tried to see through a squint.

"Ah, ah. Close your eyes!"

Corrie dutifully closed her eyes.

"Hold out your hands."

They held out their hands.

Corrie felt something odd placed into her hand. She squeezed it. A ball? She held it to her nose. It was one of the most beautiful things she had smelled in a long, long time.

"Open them."

Corrie opened her eyes. "An orange!"

Pietje grinned and flicked the blonde tendrils out of his eyes once again. "Go ahead. Peel it. But eat it before you get home."

Corrie didn't want to know why she shouldn't take it home. She didn't need any more encouragement. Rebecca and Corrie dug their nails into the tough peel. With dirty fingernails and their teeth, they were eventually able to peel the oranges and tear apart the succulent pieces. She bit one in half and put the other half into Hennie's mouth, who spit it out with a frown.

They laughed.

"Eat it, Hennie. It's good for you."

Hennie picked the piece up again and tried unsuccessfully to find her mouth with the soggy orange piece.

Pietje stood by, took the odd piece, and carefully collected the peels. They smelled so beautiful. "You can dry these and put them in your underwear drawer. Keeps the undies smelling fresh."

"If we had an underwear drawer," laughed Rebecca.

Suddenly a large truck full of men standing in the back rumbled past. The men all looked miserable. Some had their hands covering their faces. Others smoked cigarettes while they clung to bundles of clothing.

Corrie watched the truck turn onto the bridge, then left onto Van Der Duynstraat.

"Wait here. I'll go see what that's all about." Pietje ran after the truck.

Corrie ate the last piece of orange and brushed debris off her lap. Between Hennie peeing on her and the orange spray, her skirt had quite a day. She would have to hand wash it before she went to bed. But at least the orange took away some of the pungent aroma.

She stood up, lifted Hennie as far as she could, and walked toward the bridge.

"Wait," cried Rebecca. She caught up and together they took turns carrying Hennie. At one point, Corrie tried to persuade Hennie to walk on her own, but she only sat down on the ground and cried.

"She's so overdue for a diaper," fretted Corrie.

Hennie started to wail even louder, pulling at her rubber pants.

"You better take it off. I think the wet diaper is burning Hennie's skin."

Corrie looked at Rebecca and then looked around. She placed Hennie back on her feet and proceeded to take off the heavy, urine-soaked diaper. First, the stinking rubber panties, then off with the diaper pins. The diaper was so bulky with urine it dripped onto the sidewalk.

"Ew," said Corrie, disgusted. Corrie held the sodden diaper to the side as she stared at a thick red crusty rash all over Hennie's behind. "That's not good."

Rebecca looked close at Hennie's skin. "Diaper rash. But bad." She straightened up. "Here, give it to me," said Rebecca.

Corrie was only too happy to hand over the despicable thing. She wiped her hands on her poor skirt and didn't notice until the last moment what Rebecca was doing with the diaper. She looked just in time to see her swing the dense mass into the canal.

Corrie gasped. Then she laughed as she looked down at Hennie, half-naked. She already seemed to be much more comfortable. Corrie bent down, hefted her up, and tried to wrap as much of her skirt around Hennie's feverish bottom as possible. Not for the last time, did she wish she had no baby sister. It was nothing but trouble. She couldn't wait to get home.

As they passed the bottom of Van der Duynstraat, she saw Pietje standing at the truck, talking to the men. It had parked in front of a house from which a German soldier was pulling along another man. A woman ran after them crying, pushing a bundle of clothing against the soldiers back. She was pleading.

As they stood and watched, Pietje suddenly took off away from the truck and ran like the dickens toward Corrie and Rebecca. As he caught up to them, he was out of breath, and looked upset.

"They're dragging men out of the houses—anyone between 18 and 40. We have to warn Pappa. Rebecca, we have to tell your father. I'll run ahead."

"No, wait! We can't carry Hennie anymore. I need help!"

Pietje ran back, grabbed Hennie, held her up, and noticed there was no diaper, but didn't say a thing. He ran off with her bouncing in his arms. "Come, quick!"

Corrie and Rebecca ran as fast as they could. When they got to their lane off Spinozastraat, Rebecca went straight to her house to see if her father was home. Pietje had already disappeared into their house.

By the time Corrie ran into the main room, Pietje was excitedly talking to their father and mother.

"I'm telling you, Pappa, you have to hide under the floor!"

"Where is Hennie's diaper?" asked Cornelia when she saw the half-naked child. Then she reached out to touch the sensitive skin. "Oh dear. Here, give her to me." She took Hennie from Pietje.

Henk held up a hand against the commotion. He had been reading the paper and still clutched it in his right hand. "Slow down, Pietje. Tell me again what they said."

"The *moffen* have to fill a quota of men today for working somewhere in the work camps, factories, no one knows. So, they're going to houses where they know the men are between the ages of 18 and 40."

"We heard of this before. It was voluntary," added Henk.

"Not anymore, it isn't. If the *moffen* find you, you go by gunpoint. You have no choice!"

Corrie panicked. If they took their father, and they had no food stamps for the rest of the month, she was sure they would die.

"Pappa, please hide!"

Henk looked at his daughter. He frowned, turned back to the chair he was sitting at, and slapped the paper onto the seat cushion.

"Henk," Cornelia said softly, cradling Hennie.

Without another word, Pietje pulled the kitchen table away and dragged the rug from the hatch. He quickly opened it and stuck his head down the hole. He suddenly looked up. "Come on, Pappa, there's room. You just have to lie there."

"Henk," Cornelia said again, not as softly.

The rumble and sound of a truck reached their ears. Corrie squealed.

"Henk!" Cornelia cried. "Get down there, please!"

Henk, without another word, got on his stomach and squeezed into the hole. He could just make it through. He squirmed further forward so that his legs finally followed him underneath the floorboards. Quickly, Pietje put in the hatch cover. Corrie helped him put the rug back over the hole while their mother returned the table.

Pietje ran over to the shelf in the kitchen corner and grabbed a school book. He grabbed a chair and sat down at the table. He looked over at Corrie and hissed. "Play with Hennie. Put her in the playpen and play with her! Mama, pretend you are cooking or something!"

Boots marched down their laneway. They heard knocking on a door across the way. Then they heard a bang on their door.

Corrie, her heart pounding in her chest, looked over at her mother and Pietje. Pietje saw her face.

"Stop it, stop. Act normal. Don't look so frightened. Sing a song!"

As their mother walked to answer the door, Corrie summoned up her courage and sang loudly to little Hennie.

Hennie watched her closely but suddenly jumped when there was a sudden booming voice at the door.

"*Mevrouw*, is your husband home? We are looking for Hendricus Gelauf."

Corrie momentarily stopped singing, but after looking at the soldier briefly, she turned back to Hennie and continued to sing a little louder. In the background, she could hear her mother.

"My husband is not home from work as yet."

"When will he be back?" The German soldier was mean and rude. He peered around the sad little house with disdain. Then his sharp eyes fell on Pietje, and he motioned to him.

"Is this your son, *mevrouw*?"

"Yes, but he is only twelve."

"He is big for his age."

"Yes, despite not having enough to eat," her mother said angrily.

The German looked around one more time. "We will be back," he said before he disappeared back into the lane.

Henk lay in the damp sand. He felt a bug crawl up his leg and wanted so much to swipe at it but didn't dare move. Henk heard every word spoken. He could also hear the soldier's boots stomping around the lane. He heard the truck start and someone giving the order to move on.

He lay there, his heart pounding. Too close. His family needed him. How dare they take away the bread winner? How could women and children possibly survive this Hell on their own?

Henk waited to make sure the truck was far away before he finally leaned sideways to find whatever bug was crawling up his pant leg. Above him, he heard the table and rug scrape away and the hatch lid lifted. He squirmed through the sand, finally able to stick his head up through the hole.

"Well," Henk said. He was speechless. He looked over at little Corrie who had climbed into the playpen with Hennie. They both looked at him through the rails of the pen.

He saw Pietje looking down at him, pale and shaking. His wife, Cornelia, looked drained. Grey in the face. Skinny. He frowned. The scare frightened him into being on high alert. Suddenly he saw everything in a new light. Colors were brighter. Noises more distinct and clear. The smallness of the house hit him as if looking at it for the first time. The smell of the indoor outhouse was overwhelming. How did he not get bothered about it before? The mold-smelling wash hanging from the lines across the room and above his face looked sad and stained. The bedstead in the wall looked dark. The grimy walls were ugly! The change was overwhelming. He climbed out and moved to the armchair. He felt for it like an old man and slowly lowered himself into its soft cushion seat. He frowned and focused his eyes on a small bright orange item on the rolled-up carpet. He stood up and walked to it. He bent over and picked it up.

"Orange peel," he muttered. He looked up and saw Pietje look away, move back to the table where his school work lay and pretend to study.

Henk looked at Corrie. Wide-eyed, she looked back at him. She shrugged and shook her head.

"Where'd this come from?" He turned and held it up for Cornelia to see. She reached out and took it. She closed her eyes and smelled it. "Hmmm. Orange." She looked at the peel. "I don't know where it came from."

Henk looked at Corrie again. He motioned to her. "Corrie, out. You're far too big to be in there." He watched Corrie climb out of the playpen. He held up the peel. "Where did this come from?"

Corrie looked down. "I don't know," she said feebly.

He exploded. "Who stole this? Because we certainly do not have the money to buy this. So, it had to have been stolen. Who stole this?"

It was either Corrie, Beppie or Pietje. More than likely, Pietje. He lunged forward and grabbed Pietje by the scruff of his neck. "Where did you steal this from?"

"Stop, Henk, stop!" screamed Cornelia.

Everyone looked at her.

She scurried over to Pietje and put a protective hand on her son. "Pietje just saved your life," she whispered tearfully.

"I will have no stealing in this family!" Henk yelled, pointing to the floor. "No one in this family steals!"

Corrie began to cry. Then Hennie, still half-naked, also cried.

Henk unbuckled his belt, looking intently at Pietje.

Pietje gulped as he watched what his father was doing.

Cornelia stepped in front of Pietje.

"Move, woman!"

Cornelia's face hardened. "Our son is starving. He is growing into a young man, and more than any of us, he needs food. He needs nourishment. So what if he steals an orange?" Her voice became shrill. She motioned to the house and to the two children in front of her and started to cry. "What did they steal from us, huh?" She pounded her thin chest. "Look at what they've done to us. So what if he stole an orange? He's probably stealing from an NSBer, a Nazi sympathizer! Well, I have no sympathy for them! So, you leave my son alone! He just saved your life!"

At that moment, Beppie crashed through the door. She looked at her father and ran up to him. "I saw them taking men away!

I thought you'd gone! I thought they'd taken you away, too!" cried Beppie.

Henk looked down at Beppie's blonde hair and put his hand on her shoulder. He patted her and briefly covered his moistening eyes before looking around the room in a hot daze. "Not to worry," he croaked. "Your brother saved the day."

Chapter 12
March 1943

"What was that?"

Henk looked over at Pietje, who was looking through a tattered magazine depicting the many planes that were up in the air. He had gotten into the habit of identifying every German and Allied aircraft flying overhead.

At first, Henk thought Pietje had heard a plane and was trying to identify it.

He listened, as did Beppie, Corrie, and Cornelia.

Cornelia was spreading alum over a stretched rabbit hide while Corrie looked on. Beppie sat brooding.

There was no plane droning overhead, but Henk did hear a dog bark. Somewhere a truck sounded as if it was moving away from them. He didn't remember hearing it arrive. It was already past curfew, so there was very little going on in the streets—just German patrols.

Then Henk heard it. A wail. A female wail, broken-hearted, frightened.

The hair on the back of his neck rose. He hurled out of the chair and raced to the door. Carefully, he opened the door a tiny crack and peeked out. The lane was clear. Then he heard clearly that the wail came from Dovid's house.

He closed the door and reached for his worn jacket and cap.

"Stay here, it's Dovid's wife, I think. I'll see if there's something wrong with Dovid. I'll be right back." He motioned for

Pietje to turn the light off before he opened the door. Suddenly, the room was dark, and he disappeared before anyone could say another thing.

He quickly crossed the small lane. There was just enough moonlight to see where he was going as no light escaped through the black-out curtains in the little homes. He peered at brilliant stars above him. The war had brought darkness, and with darkness came nights of magnificent star-filled skies.

His ears perked up. He could barely hear it, but it was Dovid's gentle voice. He arrived at their door and very softly knocked. He waited as he looked at the outline of their *mezuzah* nailed to the doorframe.

He could sense them dousing their lights, there was a movement in the curtain at the window. Enough starlight to see it flutter. Then the door was unlatched and opened.

Henk stepped through the door into the darkness.

"My friend, you shouldn't be out," said Dovid somewhere in the shadows of the house.

Light filled the room and he saw a distraught *Mevrouw* Aaronson at the table. She sat with her hand over her face, wild wet eyes staring over her fingers. She shakily held a piece of paper.

"Do you need any help?" asked Henk, frowning.

Dovid, his eyes soft and dewy, gravely shrugged. He stepped over to his wife and took the paper gently from between her trembling fingers. He wordlessly handed it to Henk.

The first thing Henk saw was the official stamp of the German Reich. That familiar stylized eagle. It sent a cold shiver up his spine. Then he read the contents. He put it down before he even finished it. His heart beat faster as his mind raced.

"It sounds so matter of fact, doesn't it?" asked Dovid softly. He gently took the paper back. "Please arrange for your gas and electricity to be turned off by this date. Ensure that you have only one suitcase for each member of the family. Be ready by the appointed time on Monday, March 15th, at 13:00 hours," he read. Dovid lowered the paper and stared at the wall.

Henk felt dumbfounded. "They don't tell you where you're going at all?"

"No."

Mevrouw Aaronson looked up. "I know where we're going. We're going to our deaths." She slammed the table top. "I've heard the rumors."

Dovid put his hands up toward his wife. "*Ja*, but *schatje*, these are just rumors. Perhaps the story of Poland being our Promised Land is true. Shouldn't we see the positive side of things?" Dovid moved closer and sat down to face his wife. "*Schatje*, please. The children are listening."

Henk looked over at the crib, where the Aaronson's three-year-old slept. He was sleeping there now, innocent, cherubic, and undisturbed by their commotion. He looked over at their bedstead and saw Saul's drawn face poking out, watching intently. So quiet and always watching. How old was he now? Seven? There was movement behind the boy. Slowly Rebecca peeked out sadly from behind her little brother. Henk looked away and around the familiar setting. He looked at the brass menorah on a side shelf. They had managed to save it despite German soldiers constantly looting everything. Next to it stood their wedding picture in a wooden frame. He looked at a portrait on the wall, which he knew was a painting of *Mevrouw* Aaronson's father, a rabbi. He looked back at the letter in Dovid's hand. It was precise. *Be ready*.

"They don't give us much notice wherever they are sending us—less than a week. I was wondering if you wouldn't mind watching over our things until we send for them. They seem to imply that everything we own will follow at a later date."

Henk looked at Dovid askance. Dovid truly believed what he was saying, even while he was wearing the sign of death—the large yellow Star of David with the letter 'J.' Henk nodded. "Yes, of course. Just give me the key when you leave, and Cornelia and I will take good care of your things."

Dovid stood and put a stable hand on Henk's shoulder. "Thank you, my friend." He turned to his wife and motioned to Henk. "See, *schatje*? We have good friends and neighbors who will watch over our things." He turned to Henk again. "I could always write to you where we are going. We could make arrangements then." He smiled broadly. "And who knows? You could even come and visit us once the war is over, *ja*?" He turned to his wife. "*Ja, schatje?*"

Mevrouw Aaronson fidgeted with a handkerchief she had hidden in her lap. She looked up, her face wet with tears. She wiped her nose with the handkerchief and nodded. "*Ja*. And *bedankt*, Henk."

"*Heel graag gedaan*," he said quietly. He blinked.

"And we should have a gathering before we go." Dovid motioned to his wife. "We can have my wife's amazing chicken soup if your brother, Frans, wouldn't mind sacrificing a chicken for the celebration? Of course they would be invited."

"All of them?" asked Henk, as he looked around the little house.

"Yes! The more the merrier. Rebecca and Saul love to play with their children. We can offer some Manischewitz wine, maybe even manage to make Chala bread?" He looked questioningly at his wife.

Mevrouw Aaronson shrugged and waved her hand.

Dovid shrugged, "Maybe."

"We'll slaughter a rabbit for dinner," offered Henk. "Cornelia can make that stew you like so much, though I'm not sure of what potatoes and vegetables we'll be able to scrounge on such short notice. But it's a good idea. What day and time shall we gather together?"

"How about Sunday afternoon at 4? If your brother wouldn't mind bringing over the chicken for my wife to pluck and cook first thing in the morning, then we should be ready."

"Sounds good. I'll go tell Cornelia." Henk reached out to take *Mevrouw* Aaronson's trembling hand. He patted it lightly.

"These rumors we hear, they are very, very terrible. I cannot, in my heart, believe that humankind would be so cruel to itself. It's been bad, I know. Sometimes truly bad. I'm not making excuses for the *moffen*. War is war. But these rumors…" He frowned and shook his head. "Then this truly must be Hell on earth. But somehow, I can't believe that humankind has come to that form of ugliness and cruelty. I hope this helps."

Mevrouw Aaronson, her big black eyes looking at Henk so hopefully, nodded and smiled. "Of course. You're right."

Henk let her hand go, saluted to Dovid, and waited for them to douse their light before opening the door to return home. As the door closed gently behind him, Henk reached up, kissed his fingers and shakily touched the *mezuzelah* as he had seen Dovid do. With burning eyes staring at it in the darkness, he prayed briefly that the Angel of Death chose not to come to this home of kindness and gentleness. And that, indeed, rumors were after all only rumors.

Saturday afternoon, after the morning's half day's work, Henk found himself holding a hefty ax behind Frans' little home on Van Ostadestraat. He bounced the ax slightly in his right hand. He checked its edge with his left.

"I like to let them roam around freely every-once-in-a-while but only while I'm with them. Too many people stealing too many things these days," muttered Frans. He stood by holding a fluffy white chicken, its comb and wattle bright red. Its head jerked this way and that, eyes focused on Henk, then the chickens down on the ground, then at Frans' face. Around Frans' feet were about five more chickens picking at the ground. Off to the side was their little cage with their nests. "Is that sharp enough?" he asked.

"*Ja*, it's sharp enough," said Henk.

"Now, *nee*, I don't think so, Henk."

Henk frowned and studied the blade's edge. He shrugged and grunted. "*Ja*, I think it is."

Frans motioned to Henk to move to the chopping block.

Henk looked over at all the children standing around them. Frans' two girls and little boy, his two girls, and Pietje. They all insisted on watching as if they hadn't seen the beheading of a chicken before. Truthfully, it had been a while as Frans didn't usually slaughter his chickens. He kept them as egg-layers. He was able to get relatively good returns on selling his eggs on the

Black Market, so he was genuinely sacrificing something out of the goodness of his heart on behalf of Dovid and his family.

Henk again tested the weight of the ax and flicked his thumb on the edge. He nodded and stepped to the chopping block.

Frans walked over and carefully lay the chicken down, all the while soothing it with caresses and little cooing sounds. "It's okay, *schatje*." He nodded as he kept two hands on her, stretching her neck. The chicken clucked softly.

Henk held up the ax over his head and then lowered it to center it over the chicken's neck. Than he lifted it again and, with a grunt, let it drop down onto the chopping block. Henk screwed his eyes shut against the blood splatter.

"Ew!" squealed Corrie from the side.

Henk looked down, and to his horror, he saw he had only sliced half-way through the chicken's neck. He watched as Frans let go of the chicken to take out a handkerchief to wipe blood away from his eyes, but when he let go of the chicken, it flapped its wings and flew off the chopping block, scaring the hell out of everyone. The men both looked on as the bird mutely and frantically fluttered all around the little back yard with its head hanging down its neck.

The girls screamed as it came close to them. They pushed each other out of the way. Pietje screamed and pushed the others out of the way, tripping over Saul. Henk screamed and fell back, tripping over Saul.

"What?" Frans yelled, wiping his eyes before peering around. He suddenly spied the chicken with its head flopping around its neck, and he fainted.

"That poor chicken!" Everybody laughed, including little Corrie. She had just finished explaining what had happened to the chicken as she saw it, after everyone else had a go at it. Her rendition was just as gruesome as everyone else's. Everyone rolled with gut-wrenching, pant-peeing wholesome laughter.

She looked over at Rebecca, laughing, who had also been laughing at her version of the story. They hugged each other and covered their mouths as they continued to giggle.

They all huddled around the Aaronson's table after they finished a lovely and generous supper. Quite a change from the standard fare, but two animals had sacrificed their lives for their feast, which meant those poor animals no longer provided eggs or little bunnies for their bellies. But Corrie, as everyone else, thought they were worth the sacrifice.

"How does it feel?" asked Corrie, looking down at the rabbit muff her mother had made as a parting gift for Rebecca. Rebecca had one hand dug into the luxurious fur even though it was stifling hot in the little house.

"I love it," she said as she turned to Cornelia, sitting beside *Mevrouw* Aaronson. She smiled at her. "Thank you so very much, *Mevrouw* Gelauf."

"Nice and warm, isn't it?" Cornelia smiled at Rebecca and winked at Corrie.

Corrie grinned and was very happy for Rebecca, though she knew she was losing her good friend. As she looked at her sister, Beppie, it occurred to her that Rebecca was actually more of a sister than Beppie was, certainly. Suddenly she felt quite sad. Beppie was no fun to be around. Who would she hang around with after the Aaronsons left? Cousins Sientje and Rieky were just a tad too far away to see anytime she wanted.

"Well, a toast, my dear, dear friends," announced Dovid. He pushed back the wooden box he was sitting on and raised his arm.

Everyone else stood up from whatever they managed to find to sit on. Frans and Antonia had taken two small chairs along from their home, as had Henk from across the lane. Chairs and boxes scraped as everyone got into position. They waited, smiling at Dovid.

"To our dear, dear friends and all their lovely children. We do not know what we would've done without you. Honestly. You all have been very good to us." He motioned to Frans. "Frans, thank you and your wife for sacrificing such a giant chicken. The poor tortured thing!"

Everyone laughed.

"To Cornelia for that lovely rabbit stew. And to my dear friend Henk, you are a good brother to me."

Corrie watched her father look down at the table. She thought he was going to cry. His bottom chin quivered for a split second before he looked up again with sparkling eyes.

"No, Dovid. It is you who did so much for us. I wouldn't be working at a job, keeping the wolves at bay. We can still buy the odd thing because of you."

"Hear, hear," said Cornelia, as she raised her glass even higher.

"Time for some music, Pappa," announced Corrie as she looked hopefully at her father.

Henk turned on his seat and looked back at the door where the accordion case sat.

Corrie pushed back her chair and hurried to the door. "I'll get it!" She picked the case up and lugged it with a grunt back to the table. She stood by watching as her father placed the case onto the wood floor and unlatched the locks. Out came the beautiful polished rose accordion.

"Ah, it's so beautiful," said *Mevrouw* Aaronson.

"Wait till you see when he pulls it apart!" Corrie said excitedly.

Everyone watched as Henk slowly pulled the two sides apart with a long hiss to expose the rose pattern in the bellows.

"I've never seen such a beautiful accordion," announced Dovid.

Corrie watched as Henk looked down at the scratch and nick at the top under his chin. She watched as he looked over at Pietje, who in turn, looked away.

"Yes, it's beautiful. So, what should I play?" Henk ran his fingers over the keys.

"You're Too Fat for Me!" yelled Corrie.

"Well, I know for sure I won't offend anyone by playing that as we're all on a perpetual diet!" He smiled as everyone else laughed.

"That's for sure!" agreed Dovid. "We need to eat more. Please! And drink up!"

Henk started playing the happy polka as everyone slurped at the sweet thick liquid in their glasses and cups, swaying contentedly to the music. Then he stopped and looked around.

"What's the matter, Henk?" asked Dovid.

"Is it too loud? I don't want to bring attention to us."

Corrie watched Dovid's face as he frowned and thought about it.

Pietje stood up. "I'll take a peek on the street."

"Be careful, Pietje," said their mother.

Pietje nodded. He went to the door and paused. Dovid stood up and turned off the one bulb over the table. They heard Pietje open and close the door. Corrie had a brief look at the dark cobblestones out the door before it shut.

Corrie listened to the breathing around her. Then she giggled as Rebecca leaned in and quietly said, "Boo." Frans' two girls, Sientje and Rieky on the other side of the table also giggled. They waited patiently, listening for noise outside the house. Then they heard Pietje's footsteps running through the alley on the cobblestones.

The door opened, and Pietje's dark figure stepped in. The door closed. "No one up or down the street. I even ran to the bridge and couldn't see any patrol anywhere."

There was a big sigh around the table. A scrape of the box signaled Dovid getting up again to turn on the light. Suddenly, the room was bathed in light.

"No one will bother us. I really don't think we're too loud," Dovid added, smiling.

Everyone relaxed as Henk continued to play the happy tune. Corrie proceeded to drink more of the sweet liquid, and it felt good going down her throat. She was nine years old now, an old soul. It felt good to have a nice glass of something that made her feel so cozy inside. She felt her cheeks flush. She put an arm around Rebecca, who grinned back at her. They touched their glasses together one more time, as adults did, and they downed the liquid as they swayed and bounced to the beat of the polka. Suddenly, she inhaled, ready to sing along with the chorus, but she hadn't swallowed the liquid completely and she went into a coughing spree. That made Rebecca giggle while she hadn't entirely consumed the Manischewitz wine herself, and it went up her nose and sprayed out.

That made them both laugh even harder. Even Rebecca's little brother, Saul, laughed out loud.

"Rebecca," scolded *Mevrouw* Aaronson. But she smiled.

Corrie's father looked over, as well, as he played. Though he tried to sound strict, he was smiling. "Okay, girls. That's enough drunken rivalry! Dovid, no more for these maidens!"

Monday arrived. Corrie got up extra early to get the porridge ready on the one burner for the family. Then she put out the bowls and spoons. What little bit of milk they had, she put in a small glass jug. Their ration of milk for the week. But this was a special day. Somehow, she wanted the extravagance of the night before to continue as part of the festive feelings, reflecting their hope and best wishes for the Aaronsons and their exciting trip.

Hennie stirred where she had been sleeping in the playpen. Corrie craved some quiet time alone to do things she wanted to do. It figures her little sister would know precisely when she was about to do something she liked. If only Hennie would sleep until after her mother woke up. She wouldn't have to be responsible for changing diapers all the time.

Corrie looked over to see little Hennie turning, and pulling herself up by the frame of the playpen. She watched her gnaw at the wood. Hennie made noises, trying to get Corrie to come over and get her.

Corrie turned her back on Hennie. "I don't see you," she whispered to no one in particular. She picked up the comb that was lying on the wooden trim along the wall. She positioned the tiny, spotted mirror so that she could see herself combing her hair. She wanted to do her braids in such a way that they could loop back and form two circles. She needed uninterrupted time to do it correctly.

Hennie started crying.

Corrie ignored it.

Hennie's cries increased in volume.

"Corrie, please help your little sister," her mother mumbled from the bedstead in the wall.

Corrie was upset. She walked to the bottom of the tiny rickety stairs that led to the attic. Beppie never helped, and there she was, snoring under the covers upstairs.

Hennie cried even more.

"Corrie, take care of your sister," demanded her father, from somewhere in the bowels of the bedstead.

"I'm doing it!" Corrie retorted.

"Watch your tone, Corrie!"

She dropped her hands from the stair rail and walked, defeated, to the playpen. She bent over, and with a loud huff, as a good martyr should do, she lifted Hennie who was now a year and a half old. She couldn't quite get her over the railing and accidentally let her slip back into the pen onto her behind. Hennie cried anew, this time she was swiping at her right ear. Corrie took no notice of it.

She tried again, and this time got her clear over the railing.

She carried Hennie to a blanket in the corner of the room next to the coal stove and started to take the soiled diaper off. As she focused on her work, she could hear someone getting out of bed upstairs. Steps pounded down the old stairway, and Pietje appeared at the bottom, yawning. He had slept in his clothes the night before. Partly because he was afraid of an air raid, but mostly because he was tipsy.

Corrie held out the drenched and full diaper to Pietje. "Shake this out into the toilet."

Without a word, Pietje took the diaper carefully between two fingers as he pinched his nostrils tightly with his other hand.

CORRIE AND THE ROSE ACCORDION

Beppie came running down, headed straight to the water closet. Pietje was bent over the hole, trying to shake the contents of the diaper into the darkness below.

"Get out of my way," demanded Beppie. "I have to go."

"I'm not finished," retorted Pietje. "You'll have to hold it in or go outside."

"I can't wait!" she yelled.

"Okay, already." yelled their father from the bowels of the bedstead. "Cornelia, please move. I'd like to get out."

Corrie looked over to see her mother's body squirm out of the way for her father to climb out of the bedstead. He looked at Beppie and Pietje. He pointed at Beppie to move over and sit on a kitchen chair. "Pietje, do it quickly. Or do it outside. Let Beppie use the toilet."

Beppie stuck her tongue out at Pietje.

"Pap, Beppie stuck her tongue out at me!" Pietje yelled from the bowels of the water closet.

Henk raised his voice. "How many times do I have to tell you, Pietje, you are the oldest. Act like it for a change!"

"Henk," Cornelia said softly from the bedstead.

Henk took a deep breath. "Today is a special day. Our friends are leaving for the Promised Land. Let's make it a nice departure for them, okay?"

"Are you going to work at all," asked Cornelia, climbing out of the wall while straightening her old, worn nightgown.

"Just for the morning. I'll be back before the Aaronsons go. Say, who made the porridge already?"

"I did!" offered Corrie.

"Is it ready to eat?"

She nodded happily. Pleasing her father pleased her. She turned back to little Hennie and carefully dabbed at the diaper rash with a wet cloth before putting baking powder all over Hennie's behind. "And you, Hennie. Do me a favor," she whispered. "Don't pee or poo today!"

Corrie and Rebecca sat on Rebecca's stone stoop at their front door, playing with their dolls. "Goodbye," Corrie said, as she held her toy up to Rebecca's. She positioned the arms to reach out, and they put the dolls together as if they were hugging goodbye.

Mevrouw Aaronson opened the door and held out her purse and a small net bag full of onions. "Rebecca, take these and put them on a dry spot on the cobblestones. Or on the window sill. Wherever they'll keep from falling over."

"*Ja*, Mama." Rebecca twisted around and took the two items.

"Can I hold your mother's purse?" asked Corrie. She had always admired that beautiful purse. There was a purplish sheen to the black leather, and the gold clasp was especially fancy, with its filigree pattern.

Rebecca handed the purse to Corrie. Little Corrie stood up, put it on her arm, and pretended to be a mature woman walking around.

Rebecca laughed because if anything, Corrie looked more like a country girl in her fur-lined *klompen*.

"Corrie, could you please give this to your mother?" *Mevrouw* Aaronson asked as she held up the almost empty bottle of Manischewitz. Corrie took it and looked at it. She was tempted just to open and drink it all up.

"This stuff is delicious. I fell asleep right away," offered Corrie.

"Yes, we had a good time last night, didn't we?" agreed *Mevrouw* Aaronson.

But *Mevrouw* Aaronson's face showed a sleepless night. She looked drawn and had dark circles under her eyes. Corrie could tell she was worried. Very, very worried.

Mevrouw Aaronson looked at her elegant thin wristwatch. "They will be here soon. Corrie, did your father come home yet? We don't want to go without saying a good farewell."

"Not yet, *Mevrouw* Aaronson," offered Corrie. She looked over at her friend. "I'll be right back, Rebecca." She raced off to her own house with the bottle, all the while still holding the purse over her arm.

She scrambled through their door. "Mama here's the rest of the wine from *Mevrouw* Aaronson."

Cornelia turned from the stove. She had been boiling the leftover chicken bones that had already made soup at the Aaronsons'. Corrie knew her mother wanted to suck every bit of goodness out of those bones a second time. She watched her mother wipe her hands on her work shift and take the bottle. Her mother unscrewed the top and smelled the pleasant aroma. She smiled. "That's nice."

She put down the bottle, untied her work shift, and went outside with Corrie.

"Almost time," she said, as she walked forward to hug *Mevrouw* Aaronson.

Dovid poked his head out the door and stepped out with a hammer in his hand. "Good afternoon, *Mevrouw* Gelauf. And how are you today, on this glorious day?" He turned to the *mezuza* and deftly loosened it off the door frame.

"Very well, thank you." She looked up at the sky. A beautiful pure blue peeked shyly through the grey March clouds. "Nice day for you to be traveling. No rain, I don't think."

Dovid looked up at the sky and nodded. "Beautiful." He disappeared into the house and reappeared with three suitcases. He placed them by the onions.

Corrie realized she still had the purse over her arm, and dutifully put it down on top of one of the suitcases. She reached back to make sure her braids were still looped and satisfied they were. She wanted to look nice for the Aaronsons.

Dovid came out with two more suitcases while holding their toddler in his arms. Their other young son, Saul, shyly followed in his wake. Dovid put the last bag down and lifted his little son's arm and waved it at them. "Bye, *Tante* Cornelia. Bye, Corrie."

Corrie smiled and waved back at the toddler. She looked around and saw that Beppie and Pietje weren't there. She ran to their doorway. "Pietje, Beppie! It's almost time!"

Suddenly, they could hear the motor of a heavy truck come down Spinozastraat from the direction of the canal.

She yelled up the stairs. "They're going! Come!"

"*Ja!*" yelled Beppie. Pietje came rushing down, his shoelaces untied. He flicked blonde hair from over his eyes and excitedly passed Corrie into the lane.

Corrie looked around. No Pappa. She looked over at the entrance of the alley and saw a big, dark green truck come to a stop at the opposite curb. The truck's doors opened, and two soldiers jumped out with their rifles. They ran into their lane and stopped amid a cacophony and clatter of sounds. They peered angrily at everyone.

Corrie blinked. Rifles. Surely, they didn't need guns to pick up families heading for the Promised Land. Protectively, she moved closer to Rebecca. Rebecca reach out to Corrie and held her arm.

"Who is *Meneer* and *Mevrouw* Aaronson?" The soldier's voice echoed in the small alleyway.

Both Rebecca's parents, looking confused, slowly raised their hands. Dovid smiled slightly, curious, looking at the rifle. "We are they. Lovely day, yes?"

"And which are your three children?" the soldier demanded, ignoring the greeting.

Dovid turned and pointed at Rebecca, his son, and toddler.

"Leave your suitcases here; we will come back for them later."

"May I ask, sir, how much later? I have clean diapers in one of them, and I will need to change my son's diaper." *Mevrouw* Aaronson said shyly, clutching with fear at the neck of her coat.

"You will not need to worry about that."

Mevrouw Aaronson's face fell. In shock and confusion, her dark eyes darted around the alley and settled on Corrie's mother, who looked back at her, confused.

The second German waved them toward the truck. "Sir, follow me." He stepped forward and grabbed Dovid by the collar. Dovid's face dropped. He hurriedly put down their toddler, who had started to cry out of fright.

Rebecca ran and swept her little brother into her arms and scurried back to Corrie. Corrie reached over and held Rebecca close to her. She put her other hand on the toddler.

Mevrouw Aaronson grabbed Saul and clung to him like a wild animal as she watched the soldiers drag her husband out of the alley to the truck. He strained to look back, his eyes locking onto his wife briefly. A third soldier appeared at the gate suddenly from the back of the truck. He stomped into the lane, and grabbed Saul from *Mevrouw* Aaronson, who began to claw at the soldier's arm. Saul screamed and also feebly clawed at the soldier's gloved hands as he called for his mother. But he was helpless against the soldier towering over him.

Corrie stood, stunned. Strangely, the world slowed down. Her breathing slowed to a crawl. Words, screams, cries were strangely convoluted sounds. She saw *Mevrouw* Aaronson slowly reaching up into the air, willing for her son to fly back to her arms.

Corrie slowly looked terrified over at Rebecca, who clutched at her, still hugging their toddler. Corrie searched Rebecca's face and saw the look of horror that contorted her beautiful face. *Rebecca, let us fly straight up out of this alley and go to the beach. Where the sun shines, and we can create sandcastles. Watch the surf, see the water sparkling on the North Sea where we can skip along the boardwalk and sing our favorite songs.*

In slow motion, Corrie saw Rebecca disappear as if a monstrous slow tornado pulled her and the toddler away from her and out of her line of vision.

Corrie blindly looked on at nothing. Suddenly, her body gasped and turned in time for her to see a soldier cart Rebecca and the toddler to the truck. Rebecca was leaning back into the soldier's grasp, her shoes scraping the cobblestones as he dragged and pushed her along. Corrie could hear Rebecca yell.

"No! No! No!"

Mevrouw Aaronson raced after them and pulled the toddler out of Rebecca's arms. She turned and raced past the other soldiers, back to their house. She ran in and slammed the door shut behind her, screaming for help.

The soldier marched to the door and kicked it in. Corrie stood by helplessly as she heard the soldier yelling at her in German amidst *Mevrouw* Aaronson's pleas. He reappeared pulling her by the arm, and as they passed, *Mevrouw* Aaronson dropped the toddler.

"Cornelia, take my baby!" she screamed.

Corrie looked over at her mother, who stood with her hands over her mouth in shock.

Pietje jumped forward and grabbed the little one and stepped back to the wall of their house.

Corrie watched. She consoled herself for a moment. Corrie was dreaming. Surely this was a nightmare and she will be waking up soon. But then an alarm went off in the back of her mind and she gulped. Her body convulsed as it suddenly dawned on her that, no, indeed, this was real.

She jumped toward the soldier pulling *Mevrouw* Aaronson. She grabbed at the soldier's back and hung on for dear life. He turned and quickly swiped at her, sending her on to her side on the cobblestones.

Her mother cried and ran to lift Corrie up.

Corrie tearfully pushed her mother away and ran through the gate. She stopped on the sidewalk. Her body shook violently. Her eyes were glued on *Mevrouw* Aaronson. Corrie watched as she squirmed and knocked the soldier's helmet back. Her elbow hit his nose and he cringed. He dropped *Mevrouw* Aaronson suddenly as he grabbed his nose. Corrie saw her eyes almost bug out as she scrambled past her, back into the alley.

The wounded soldier yelled to the other soldier. Corrie twirled around to see the other soldier struggling with Pietje, yanking at the toddler. The soldier stood back, picked up a rifle and was just about to hit Pietje with the butt of it when he realized that his comrade had been hurt. He, instead, grabbed *Mevrouw* Aaronson, and together, the two soldiers bodily picked *Mevrouw* Aaronson up by her arms and legs. Corrie, dumbfounded, watched them lug her to the back of the truck, her fighting like a cat with nails and teeth. Her coat and dress were yanked up in her struggles, and Corrie saw her underwear and torn stockings. *Mevrouw* Aaronson's eyes were popping out of their sockets with fear.

Corrie screamed. "Leave her alone!" She stood, tight and wiry, frightened beyond her wits as she witnessed the soldiers tossing the screaming *Mevrouw* Aaronson into the depths of the truck. The truck shook under the impact. Then they roughly pushed Corrie to the pavement as they hurried back into the alley.

Corrie stood up and helplessly watched as one finally freed the toddler from Pietje. Corrie screamed. "No!" She stood to the side helpless as the one soldier lunged past her and to the back of the truck. Without a moment's hesitation, he physically flung the toddler through the air into the truck. Then the two soldiers yanked up the back ramp and locked it into place while the third climbed back into the driver's seat.

Corrie ran past the two soldiers to the back of the truck to look inside as it pulled away. In the shadows, she saw another soldier sitting guard with his rifle beside *Mevrouw* Aaronson, her wailing face held by Dovid, whose own face was covered in blood. In front of them, she could see Rebecca, looking back at her, frozen in fear.

Corrie started to run after the truck, but it picked up speed and threw up a cloud of dust. Before she lost sight of Rebecca, she lifted her hand. Then, as the truck trundled over the canal, Corrie thought she saw Rebecca wave back. That made her jump and wave frantically, running toward the canal. But the vehicle turned out of sight and disappeared.

She sobbed. Suddenly, someone lifted her into the air.

"Shhh," her father said.

Corrie no longer had breath. She had cried it out and now wailed silent tears of grief. She felt hollow and in suspension, reaching out toward the canal as he carried her back to the alley.

Once through the gate into the alley, her father put Corrie down. She slowly turned to see the two remaining soldiers emptying the contents of the Aaronsons' suitcases onto the cobblestones. She watched, horrified, as they set some things aside and left the rest on the stones while they went in and out of the Aaronson's house. They threw out furniture, pots and pans, bedding. Corrie spied both Rebecca's doll and her own! She'd forgotten she'd left it with Rebecca. Then she saw *Mevrouw* Aaronson's purse. *She didn't even have the time to take her purse! Where would she go without her purse!* Without thinking, she stepped forward to save all three from destruction. As she reached down, her hands were knocked aside by a rifle butt and Pietje pulled her back.

Finally, as they all stood watching in shock, one of the soldiers poured petroleum from the Aaronson's burner over the contents.

Corrie gasped and howled as she watched her doll getting drenched. Her beautiful doll!

Corrie's heart couldn't stand the shock. She trembled and clung to her mother, remembering the two dolls playing together. Then she remembered the lovely chicken soup *Mevrouw* Aaronson made on that burner the soldier dumped on the heap. She recalled how happy they all were for the Aaronson's' good fortune. Just the night before! For the first time in a long time, they all had hope, joy and laughter. They felt so safe and so content as her father played the accordion. It was as if the war hadn't started at all. It all seemed perfect. She yearned for that evening again as she watched the soldier strike a match and toss it onto the pile that represented everything the Aaronsons owned.

With a whoosh, monsters of flames devoured the pile.

In a trance, Corrie watched the two dolls melt in the heat. Their mouths melted into a moan, the eye makeup ran, and the hair burnt to nothing.

She felt her father pull her back and drag her to their front door. She turned, surprised that everyone else was already gone. She took one last horrified look at the flickering flames over her shoulder. They now reached up from between the closely-set homes, into the sky, spewing up a black, sticky plume of smoke. Corrie looked over at the other houses and saw faces at the windows, before letting her father finally pull her into the house. She saw the ugly sight disappear when the door shut.

Stunned, they all quietly huddled in their little house. Corrie watched the flames through the window before her father pulled her to the bedstead in the wall. There, they all climbed in and clung to each other. Though sounds were muffled within the bedstead enclosure, Corrie could still hear the crackle and pop of those flames of destruction and she could smell the smoke wafting into their little house.

The sight of the big, strong, angry soldier flinging the little helpless toddler in an arc like a bag of stinking garbage into a dump truck played over and over in her mind. A child just like little Hennie, her sister. A child helplessly flung through the air, squirming. The image haunted her, burned through her brain.

She looked around in the bedstead and rocked. She suddenly ached to hold and comfort Hennie. How many times had she wished Hennie dead and gone? She frantically looked out at the empty playpen on the floor and over to the kitchen corner as she continued to rock back and forth. She looked beside her in the bedstead again, past Beppie and Pietje and she rocked some more. She rocked as she moaned like an animal in grief, trapped in the bedstead surrounded by her family but not seeing them.

"What are you looking for?" asked her father, his voice cracking.

"Hennie," she cried. "Hennie. Where is Hennie!" She rocked frantically, crying.

Her mother tearfully reached out to her and held her arm. "Corrie. Corrie, stop. Hennie is here." She motioned to Hennie in her arms, sucking nervously at her fingers.

Corrie twisted and looked down. She leaned over and pulled Hennie from her mother. Through tears, she looked into Hennie's dirty face—the little child that was the curse of her existence. The newcomer who took her special status of baby away. The little sister who smelled, and peed, and pooed and did nothing but cause her work—the little sister. Her bothersome little sister. Her little sister who is alive and needed her.

With the image of the toddler in mid-air, she clutched Hennie tightly. She stopped rocking and squeezed her eyes shut as she smelled Hennie's little neck. She kissed her cheek and her little head and then caressed Hennie's beautiful blonde curls. She looked down through the filtered and flickering light of the bedstead and studied Hennie's delicate little fingers. Then she touched her chubby legs and looked at her tiny toes and the tiny toe nails that needed trimming. She couldn't help but squeeze her tightly once again and allow the flood of fear and shock to pour out in heart-rending sobs.

She was never going to allow anything like that to happen to her precious little sister. "I'm sorry," she cried into Hennie's ear. "I'm so sorry I hated you." She sobbed and wiped her eyes.

Hennie reached back with her little arm, grabbed Corrie's braided loop and pulled it loose.

Corrie buried her face into Hennie's neck and stayed in that position until they both fell asleep, surrounded by the rest of the distraught and shocked family, crammed into the bedstead until nightfall.

Chapter 13
April 1943

"They're crazier than I thought if they expect us to report in," announced Henk. He straightened out his back and tried to look calm, but this latest announcement hit a nerve. He vowed never to leave his family, and he never would.

"The *Koningen* announced that we should ignore them anyhow," offered Frans.

They were sitting at the dining room table at his father's house.

Henk looked questioningly at his father. "What do you think the repercussions are if I don't report?"

His father shifted in his armchair at the end of the table. He intertwined his fingers and leaned forward. "I agree. Calling all former soldiers to report shows they're not right in the head. We all know either you will be fighting on behalf of the Germans against the Allies or you're going to a Prisoner of War camp. Either way, I think this is an indication that the records have been destroyed by bombing; otherwise, they'd have everyone's name and at least, former addresses." He shook his head. "Don't do it. Ignore it as the *Koningen* said."

Henk leaned back and tapped an unlit rolled cigarette against his hand. Then he rubbed the back of his neck hard. He winced. A huge boil had been tormenting him for a week or so and he darn well knew it was going to bleed again. He took his hand away and sighed. He knew it was their limited diet and lack of water and soap. "This is getting bad. I keep expecting it to get better, but it's like a nightmare. Watching what happened to Dovid and his family was like watching a scene from Hell." Henk felt a burning sensation behind his eyes. He was close to tears so often these days.

"They've rounded up more Jews in Amsterdam. They're arresting anyone who tries to hide them, too. I heard that those who tried were shot without a trial." Frans was almost whispering. Sitting over a pub frequented by German soldiers was nerve-shattering.

"What else did Bert tell you?" asked Henk. He looked at his father. Bert, the bar owner downstairs, was now the former owner. The *Regeering* took over the pub and allowed Bert to continue working in it while living in his home behind the pub. But he had no control anymore. It was hard, as the locals stayed away, and it seemed that every night, German soldiers took over. Bert couldn't keep up with the demand. The beer barrels arrived, but working alone meant having to do everything by himself. Quite often, he couldn't bleed the pipes, and the beer went skunky. Fortunately, most of the time, the Germans were too drunk to even notice.

But there was a hidden bonus in this odd arrangement—when the soldiers were drunk, they had looser lips. There was one whore who frequented the pub. Her name was Greetje and she lived above the Groeneweg off Spinozastraat. She hung around the soldiers enough that she managed to slip a good deal of new and useful information to the Dutch Resistance. Some of which filtered through Bert to *De Heer* Gelauf upstairs in his flat.

"Talk has it they ship Jews to various camps. Old and young, sick and dying, are immediately killed." *De Heer* Gelauf remained composed as he spoke, though his face hardened. He had gone through the First World War and the Depression, both heavy periods in history. He knew much death and anguish and saw this war as a continuation of misery. But what he heard through the grapevine was more evil and Machiavellian than anything he ever remembered during the First World War. They called that one the Great War. He wondered what they would call this one. He doubted there were enough words in the Dutch language to properly label it for what it was. It was like the gates of Hell had opened.

"What do they do? Take them somewhere and shoot them? Where? Do they keep the children at least?" Henk thought of *Mevrouw* Aaronson. Of their little sons and Rebecca. Then he thought of Corrie. Of all of them, the ordeal with the Aaronsons had a more profound and devastating effect on her. She was quiet, sad, distant, disturbed. And she clung to little Hennie every moment of the day.

"And how is little Corrie doing losing her friend? She didn't say a single word when you were here Sunday. I've never seen her so quiet."

Henk looked up at his father. "What the *moffen* did to the Aaronsons was hellish and she witnessed it all, like the rest of us. It's bound to affect her."

"She's extra sensitive. It concerns me that my grandchildren should know such evil in their lives."

Henk nodded. He had come to tell his father that the *Regeering* had taken away his job, which meant he and Cornelia had to rely on soup kitchens and rations for the children. On the other hand, it also meant he stayed around the house. There was no way he wanted a repeat performance of what he saw the other day. Though the Gelaufs were not Jewish, he felt that with the slew of shootings of innocent people as punishment for everything the Dutch Resistance did, he was worried that his children could be dragged out any time of the day or night to be shot as retribution. Henk took out his handkerchief and wiped his nose; it had begun to run, as if he were on the verge of tears. He pushed his chair back. "*Bedankt voor de koffie*, Pap. I better go back. I need to check the rabbits. Someone stole one the other night and I can't bring them into the house, the cage is too big and they're riddled with fleas. I have to figure out a way to close their cage with a lock of sorts."

Frans got up as well.

Henk looked at his brother-in-law. He had lost his job as a fisherman just the day before. That meant, of course, there was no more free fish for either family. And harvesting mussels was no longer an option as the whole coastline was out of bounds to everyone, not just the Jews. Barbwire and signs indicated mines. No one dared venture to the shore anymore.

"Where are you going now, Frans?" asked Henk.

Frans picked up his cap and adjusted his glasses. "I'm going to check to see if there is any job posting at the *Binnenhof*. You want to come?"

"Going anywhere in this city is a pain with those ugly cement walls. We have to walk so far to find an opening. What used to be across the street now takes twenty minutes to go around. No, thank you just the same." Henk also picked up his cap and threw it on.

"Ah, yes, the great Atlantic Wall. It's a shame they tore all those beautiful old buildings down along the dunes. I'm beginning to think of ourselves as caged rats waiting for the Allies to come and bomb the Hell out of us just to get at the *moffen*." *De Heer* Gelauf was emotionless as he spoke.

A rock, thought Henk. My father is a rock.

Frans pulled at his sleeve. "Come, please, Henk. You may find something on the postings as well. Besides, I'd rather walk with you than walk alone. When they stop me for my ID, I half expect them to say they're arresting everyone with the name beginning with 'F.'"

"Stay strong, boys. This nightmare must soon be over."

"If we should live to see the day," muttered Frans as he left the room.

Henk looked at his father and nodded. They locked eyes and his father nodded back. Henk turned and hurried to catch up to Frans.

Pietje ran breathlessly into the house, startling Corrie. She was down on the floor keeping Hennie occupied while their mother cleaned a slaughtered rabbit.

"Mama! The *moffen* are going from house to house again looking for men! Where's Pappa?"

Cornelia looked up, startled, and wiped her hands as Corrie looked on.

"I don't know. Corrie, where is your Pappa?"

Corrie started to shake and shrugged, her eyes wide. She searched her brain to remember anything her father might have said before he left earlier that day. She remembered seeing *Oom* Frans join him at the end of the alley. "With *Oom* Frans."

Corrie got to her feet. Hennie grabbed her by the legs. Corrie bent down and gently loosened the tiny hands. "Shhh. I'll be right back, Hennie. Here!" Corrie gave Hennie a soft well-gummed sponge ball. Hennie immediately put it in her mouth and chewed on it. Though Hennie was almost two years old, not all her teeth had come in. Her mother said it was because Hennie had never had enough nourishment. Corrie looked out the low little window.

"Corrie, do you know where your Pappa is?" asked her mother.

Corrie thought she had answered. "I saw Pappa with *Oom* Frans."

"They probably went to *Opa*'s or the pub," offered Pietje.

"Not the pub, there's no money," muttered Cornelia.

As they stood, they heard distant screams and guns shooting. *My God, screams again*, thought Corrie. She looked at her mother and brother. "What's happening?" Corrie asked almost inaudibly.

Pietje looked at her. He had grown gaunt, and his stomach was starting to distend. They said it was a sign of hunger, of malnutrition.

"They don't believe it anymore when people say the men aren't home."

They listened to boots marching. Suddenly there was a commotion in the alley. Corrie saw the familiar grey uniforms coming into view. Someone banged on their door.

"Quick, take Hennie," their mother said to Corrie.

Corrie picked up Hennie and ran back to the bedstead. She put Hennie on the bedding and closed the curtains. She turned just in time to see her mother open the door.

Pietje hung back, too. He yanked at his pants, nervously.

The door opened a second before a soldier burst through the doorway. They heard banging on doors further up the alley.

Her mother said something in German to the soldier. She knew it always made the soldier more pleasant, knowing that their mother was German. But for some reason, it didn't work this time. Ignoring her German, he looked around.

"Where is your husband."

"He isn't here."

"Where did he go?"

"I don't know."

The German soldier pushed her aside and went straight to the water closet. He took his pistol out of its holster and shot into the toilet.

The shot was deafening in the little house. Everyone screamed. Corrie shook violently. *Why the toilet?*

The soldier turned and looked at everyone, to read their faces. Another soldier burst in holding his rifle. The first soldier nodded at him. The second one pointed his rifle to the floor and looked up at their mother.

Cornelia stared back and blinked.

Suddenly, both soldiers fired into the floor and the corners, down the middle, under the table. Everyone sprung back. Wood splinters flew everywhere. The kitchen table jumped sideways and a chair was flown to the side.

Corrie gasped and grabbed her ears. She was wild with fear. She had an image of her father hiding under the floor, being riddled by bullets.

Her mother, Cornelia, stood by, shaking. She stared blindly at the soldier.

Hennie wailed from the bedstead. Corrie looked back and saw the curtains move as if Hennie was trying to get out. She ran to the curtains, tossed them back and grabbed Hennie to comfort her. She could've been shot!

She looked back at the soldier, who seemed satisfied that her mother hadn't lied. Then he looked at Pietje.

Their mother put up her hand. "*Nein!*"

The soldier held his hand to Pietje. "Your papers."

"He has no papers. He's still too young," yelled their mother.

"How old are you?" demanded the soldier.

"Thirteen," stammered Pietje.

"You look older than thirteen."

"He's thirteen! Leave him be. I need him. Please. Don't take him away."

Corrie saw the pleading look in her mother's eyes.

He left as quickly as he appeared, leaving the door open for them to hear gunshots and screams at another house.

Corrie lifted Hennie off the bedstead and scrambled to their mother, who stood clinging to Pietje. Corrie looked down at the bullet-riddled floor, then saw a puddle under Pietje. She moved closer to Pietje and burrowed her face into his bony, quivering shoulder.

Henk and Frans stood reading the poster plastered on the cement of the tank barrier they called the Atlantic Wall.

"All radios are to be taken to the *Regeering*," read Frans.

Henk turned to Frans and whispered, "Do you think we should tell Pap to hide his radio? Will they leave an old man alone?"

Frans stepped away and looked down the road at the anti-aircraft gun mounted amidst sandbags. He looked over to the other corner where the Germans had destroyed part of a building to create a better line of sight to the center of the downtown. Between the Atlantic Wall, the sandbags, trimming of buildings and bomb craters, mayhem and destruction ruled. Yet, on the outside, the stoic Dutch did their best to just keep moving. They ignored the guns, and simply walked around craters.

Henk thought of his father's fancy radio as he watched the passersby. Though highly censored, at least the broadcasts the Nazis offered were some sort of distraction and a bit of entertainment. Everyone decided that any fantastic news of German victories was probably bogus, anyhow. They all knew it. So, why now, no radios?

"I'd say don't let him take the chance. Living right over their heads certainly doesn't protect you. All they have to do is run up the stairs drunk and decide to rough up the old man. They may end up throwing him out the window along with the radio."

Henk felt sick to his stomach.

"Pappa! Pappa!"

Henk turned to see Pietje running up to them. He stopped wearing socks long ago and wore an old pair of his father's shoes, too big. Floppy. No laces. He had tied the shoes to his feet with twine.

"What is it, son?"

Pietje stood gasping for air before he could say anything. "Pappa, the *moffen* were at the house looking for you. They went to all the houses looking for men."

"They're taking men away again?" asked Frans, looking pale.

Pietje nodded. "And they shot into the floor. They even shot into the toilet, thinking you might be hiding there."

Henk grabbed Pietje's arm and moved away from the cement wall. "Let's get home," he hissed. They scrambled past the anti-aircraft gun and soldiers. The soldiers looked over at their group and Henk glared back at them. He didn't give a damn if they took notice. What were they going to do? He was no longer going to hide what he felt as their filthy evil came too damn close to his home.

Henk stood looking at the bullet holes. The bullets had gone through the floor, the rug, and into the bottom areas of the walls. Then he looked into the water closet and saw the splatter of sewage on the walls.

He stepped back. "Cornelia, I can't let you go through this anymore." He turned and saw his wife's face turn white. Her eyes bulged.

"What do you mean, Henk?"

"I have to report in."

"No!" cried Corrie. Corrie ran and clung to her father.

Beppie, who had been sitting in the kitchen corner, looked as if she had already given in to shock. Henk saw that Beppie didn't know what he was saying.

"What do you mean, Pappa?" asked Beppie.

He pointed to the floor. "I will not let them come in here and do this again. Next time I might be under that floor." He turned to his wife and spoke with a strained voice. It was a voice of defeat. Of death. Of numbness. Of surrender. "Cornelia, if you can, make me a bundle of something to eat. And put some clothes together for me."

He turned to Pietje. His poor son, who had grown into a tall stick with a distended stomach. A boy about to grow into a man. He will have to develop a little faster. He put his hand on Pietje's bony shoulder. "Pietje, I want you to be the man of this family."

"No!" cried Corrie.

"You take care of your mother and sisters. I know you can do it." He continued, ignoring Corrie. "I know when I come back, your mother and sisters will all be okay. Because of you, Pietje. Because you will know what to do." Henk looked into the eyes that were so similar to his own. It was as if he was looking at his son for the first time in his life. He was suddenly overwhelmed with emotion. He smiled at Pietje. "Okay?"

"Pappa..."

"You'll be fine. Now, do me a favor while your mother gets my things ready."

"Anything, Pappa."

"Please see if my accordion is okay down there and not shot. You take care of it for me. I'll be back to play it again when this Hell is over."

Pietje lowered his head and clung to his father as everyone else looked on in grief.

Chapter 14
July 1943

Henk stood swaying as the train full of pressed Dutchmen pulled out of The Hague station. They had no idea where they were going. While on the platform, in line, he learned which trains transported the Jews. Cattle cars. For people. For women and children, old and lame. Many standing around him had the same stories of Jewish neighbors, friends, their banker, their barber—all taken away in the same hateful manner.

He rubbed his face, tried to rid himself of the vision of Dovid and his family herded into a cattle car. He remembered what he witnessed as he hurried home to say goodbye to his dear friends. He could still hear *Mevrouw* Aaronson's screams. He silently moaned as he took his cap off and covered his face. He had been emotional of late, and he didn't want anyone to see his face collapse in grief. He closed his eyes within the darkness of his cap and willed himself to relax. He smelled the warmth in the wool and a hint of hair cream.

But misery always loves company and he eventually found himself relaxing somewhat with the other men. They were all in the same boat. And their spirits were slightly buoyed by the lovely, colorful and passive resistance the Dutch flaunted as they lined up along the railroad tracks outside and waved at the train along the journey. They cheered at them and waved their orange or red, white and blue flags—even though it was illegal to do so. The people recognized their train for what it was. By the large

Royal Lion proudly displayed along the sides. They knew exactly who were in the train cars being carted away to do the dirty work for Hitler's war.

Though there were Nazi guards on board, and everyone was under watchful eyes, the guards did not react to the display of Dutch pride within or without the cars. And they did nothing to stop them when the men sang popular Dutch patriotic songs.

Henk roused himself. Eventually, he mustered up his Dutch pride, and proudly sang along.

> *Merck toch hoe sterck nu in 'twerck sich al steld,*
> *Die 'allen tijd 'so ons vrijheit heft bestredern!*
> *Notice how strong when the work is required,*
> *The fight for liberty is taken at heart!*

Perhaps they did not understand Dutch well enough, had no inkling of what the lyrics meant. Indeed, one or two of them even smiled and waved a hand to the rhythm of the singing.

Strange times. Even stranger world. Life was so very, very strange.

With every stop along the way, more conscripted men were loaded onto the train. They shared their fears and discovered strength in each other. In spite of Henk's nightmarish concerns for his family and friends, he eventually sensed the excitement of an unknown challenge. Did all these men feel the same? How is it that together they felt so powerful? As if nothing could conquer them. It seemed odd; he had the sensation he was part of a group of boys going to camp. A camp they despised and hated, but all decided to tolerate together.

Apart from the surreal experience of having to use the facilities while being watched by an armed guard, he eventually relaxed and claimed his little turf on one of the seats. He watched windmills, towns, canals, and marshes float elegantly past the windows. He had never traveled this far from home before. He was surprised to discover most of the country was just as ravaged by war as The Hague: bombed craters, coiled barbwire, German soldiers at train stations, and army vehicles and anti-aircraft guns stationed everywhere.

As newcomers crammed into the compartment, Henk welcomed every new face and made a point of getting to know every man around him. Who had children, who weren't married, who was related to whom? After a while, even pleasant conversations carried out in a rocking train took its toll. He found he could not keep his eyes open. He eventually fell asleep to the clicking rhythm of the train and the drone of the conversations around him.

Corrie sat squeezed into the creaking hard, wooden pew between Beppie and Pietje, while little Hennie sat on her lap.

Cornelia, wearing a little black pill hat and a tired-looking drop-waist dress, sat at the very end. She wore mended gloves and rested her hands upon an old Bible. Corrie could sense her mother was deeply focused on the echoing Liturgy of the Eucharist sung by the priest.

The priest's voice sounded calm and reassuring, immensely mysterious in its Latin. Corrie allowed the soothing voice to sink into the core of her grief. She had not had a moment's release from the fear that Rebecca and her family were somehow in trouble. Were the Nazis that bloodthirsty, so monstrous, that they would harm such a nice and innocent girl? A baby? A woman?

She reached up and scratched at the knot tied under her chin. Having left their Sunday hats at their last house in haste, so long ago, Beppie and Corrie wore woolen headscarves to cover their 'shame,' as taught in Catholic School.

They went to church more regularly now, praying for safety, for food, for protection, but mostly for the safety of their father and friends. Rebecca was always uppermost in her thoughts. Where were they now? Were they in a new home? She closed her eyes to the frightening images that haunted her day and night.

At that moment, Hennie decided to bounce, making small gurgling sounds, on Corrie's lap, shaking her out of her deep thoughts. Another baby elsewhere in the congregation bawled and fussed, its cries echoed through the high ceilings and buttresses. Little echoes slashed by people coughing. A single prop plane slowly flew overhead, causing people to whisper and fidget in barely controlled fear. After a few moments, no alarm sounded, so they settled down and listened to the priest once again. The priest did not let it bother him. Nor did the altar boys, so fixated on their duties.

Corrie silently looked from statue to painting to a stained-glass window. The bombing had shattered one of the old windows, and wooden planking replaced the beautiful stained glass. Thin shafts of light filtered through the side edges, casting a sharp edge of light clear across the congregation. It seemed to dance along with brilliant reds, blues and purples of the other stained-glass windows. She watched specks of dust float through the lasers of multicolored light. Dust. Dead skin. Dust.

Apart from that one window, the church was a clean, beautiful, and colorful environment. She looked at the people in the pews in front of her. They wore frayed or stained clothing as she and her family did. She saw one or two people nodding off to sleep. On the other side of the center aisle, two little boys fought, and the mother slapped them both. One cried.

Everyone seemed less dressed, less refined than she remembered before the war. Going to church in *klompen* and bare legs would previously have been frowned upon and ridiculed. Now, people were fortunate to have anything at all on their feet. Children went barefoot on the streets. At least the warmer days bought a bit of time for parents to acquire footwear or anything else essential to their children's survival, by the time the cold months restarted and school began again.

As Corrie watched the proceedings, she noticed that the altar boys looked cleaner, healthier than Pietje even though they were about the same age.

She bent forward to look past Beppie at Pietje, but couldn't. She leaned back instead and looked past Beppie's head at Pietje's ear. He did so much for the family and seemed to know where to scrounge for things they needed. He had taken his role as head of the family, in their father's absence, to heart. But he looked tired. Unkempt.

She leaned the other way to her mother. "Mama," she whispered.

Cornelia, distraught, slowly turned to her and bent down. "Hmm?"

"Why can't Pietje be an altar boy?"

Cornelia slowly straightened up and looked at the altar boys. She then looked past Corrie at Pietje. She bent towards Corrie again.

"That is an excellent idea. We'll ask after mass. It's worth asking."

Corrie felt warm inside. She looked at her mother's wristwatch and saw that it would take at least another half hour before Mass finished, but she couldn't wait to go to the front to accept the Host. Was it sinful to consider the Bread of Life, the Body of Christ, as something to eat? The wafer was an extra little morsel. She even began to think of it like candy—a candy-wafer. A Holy candy-wafer.

Corrie's attention was taken away from heavenly food when Hennie suddenly fidgeted and rubbed her left ear. She was getting a little restless, so Corrie took her tiny hands and played a quiet clapping game, whispering the lyrics into Hennie's little ear.

> *Klap eens in je handjes, blij blij blij,*
> *Op het boze bolleke, allebei,*
> *Handjes in de hoogte, handjes in de zij,*
> *Op het boze bolleke, allebei!*
> *Clap your little hands, joy joy joy,*
> *On the little angry cheeks, all of both,*
> *Little hands way up high, little hand on the side,*
> *On the little angry cheeks, all of both!*

Little Hennie quieted down, clapping on her own.

An older woman with a grey bun turned to look at Corrie and Hennie. At first, Corrie thought she was going to reprimand her for making too much noise, but the lady smiled instead.

"You have a little mother in the making there, *mevrouw*," she whispered to Cornelia.

Cornelia nodded. "For sure." She smiled at Corrie.

It seemed to Corrie, that was the most beautiful thing anyone had ever said about her. She felt quite mature and proud. She wiggled in the pew and sat up much straighter. She felt herself blush, not knowing how to take the compliment. She went from the baby of the family to a blossoming little mother. She guessed it wasn't a bad trade. She flicked both blonde braids over her shoulder. One day, she'll pin them up and see what she looked like as a woman.

Beppie stood behind Corrie and Pietje while their mother held Hennie, standing at the door at the top of the flight of worn stone steps. Birds chirped around them. It was still a very bright and pleasant day. The sun poured down on them as they waited for someone to answer the hefty parsonage door. Cornelia banged the brass knocker for a second time.

Someone scraped something aside and the door slowly opened with a creak to reveal a little wrinkled old nun. She looked with a startled expression at Cornelia, then at the children on the sidewalk behind her. Her watery eyes widened, then squinted.

"*Ja, mevrouw?*"

Cornelia turned to Pietje behind her. "*Ja, Zuster.* I was wondering if the church wouldn't take my son, Pietje, as an altar boy?"

The nun blinked.

Cornelia leaned in, smiling weakly.

The nun blinked again. "I'm sorry, *mevrouw*. What did you say?" She leaned her right ear to Cornelia.

"I am here to ask how my son could apply to be an altar boy."

The nun stepped back and covered her chest with a gnarly little hand. "An altar boy?"

"*Ja,* you do take altar boys?"

The old nun looked stiffly at Cornelia and her tired dress and hat, then looked down at Corrie's *klompen* and bare legs; at Beppie with her frayed coat and unruly hair. Then she peered at Pietje, with his shock of blonde hair over his eyes, his broad bony shoulders, his distended stomach, and knobby knees.

"*Mevrouw*, we do not need another altar boy."

"*Zuster*, please. I need you to take my son as an altar boy. He is growing so quickly and needs more nourishment than I can provide. His father was taken away as forced labor. We are alone. You do compensate altar boys somehow, do you not?"

"Excuse me?"

"The altar boys get paid, do they not?"

"Well, yes, *Mevrouw*, though lately, it's not money we give them. Certainly, we help our boys in other ways. Food, clothing."

"Precisely. Well, then. My son is of perfect age, and we attend this church. We just live around the corner on Spinozastraat."

"Spinozastraat?"

"Yes. Please." They watched as their mother looked down at her worn shoes for a moment. She looked up anew. "May I talk to the priest?"

"The priest is busy, and then he will be resting. He cannot be disturbed." The nun still held that startled look.

Corrie's heart sank. She watched her mother slowly lower Hennie to the top step. Corrie immediately ran up the steps and helped Hennie manage the steps down. At the bottom, she lifted Hennie and turned to watch her mother. Her mother was wringing her hands. Then Corrie, saddened, looked at Pietje and saw the ember of hope fade in his eyes.

"Come on, Mama. The bitch doesn't want him." Beppie loudly announced, turning to leave. She gave the nun a mean look.

"Beppie!" Cornelia shouted.

The nun looked taken aback.

"Stay here! I'm not finished speaking with the…"

Suddenly the door shut with a massive bang followed by a scrape and loud click.

Corrie was astounded. She looked at her mother's back. Then over at Beppie. Beppie stood with her arms crossed, tapping a shoe impatiently.

"Mama," Beppie said softly.

Their mother stood frozen, facing the closed door. Slowly, Cornelia turned on the top step and carefully descended. At the bottom, she turned once more to look at the grand entrance and up at the steeple. Then, tearfully, she looked over at the church. Shock and disbelief etched her face.

"What the...?" Pietje stood with his mouth open.

Cornelia took out her white handkerchief and covered her face. As they stood silently waiting for their mother to overcome shock, they saw her chin quiver. She sobbed for a moment, then she took the handkerchief away from her face. She dabbed the tears in her eyes and blew her nose. They watched as she opened the clasp on her purse and put the handkerchief back in its place. She reached up and took out a hat pin from her pill hat. She took off her hat and looked at it. She brushed it with purpose, looked at it one more time carefully, then tossed it to the side, into a bush. The children watched as it disappeared within its branches.

"Mama, why'd you do that?" asked Corrie.

"I won't need it anymore." Their mother stepped to Beppie and untied her headscarf. Then she removed Corrie's. "We won't need to hide our shame anymore." She stuffed the scarves into her bag.

"Why?" asked Corrie.

"Because we're not going back to that church."

"Never?" asked Beppie.

Cornelia shook her head. "No, not if I can help it."

Corrie looked over at Pietje. He looked down at his own worn shoes. He stuck his hands in the pockets of his corduroy pants with threadbare patches.

"What about *Tante* Dina in Amsterdam?" asked Beppie.

"What of her?" asked Cornelia stiffly.

Beppie shrugged. She was much taller than Corrie now. Corrie had to look up at her. "It's just that, *Tante* Dina is a *Zuster*. Why can't we ask her for help?"

Cornelia looked at her daughter and blinked. She then looked over at Hennie and reached for her. Corrie released Hennie and watched as her mother shifted the child onto her hip.

"Well, I suppose it's a try. I'll write your *Tante* Dina a letter when we get home. But first, Beppie, you come with me. We're going to *Opa's* to pick up a little piece of meat he promised us. I'll take Hennie this time, Corrie. Could you start doing the ironing when you get home?"

"*Ja*, Mama," said Corrie, trying to keep a steady pace in her *klompen* as her mother led them away from the church.

Cornelia led Beppie to the right on their way to the grand Gelauf family house by the canal.

Pietje and Corrie walked in the opposite direction towards Spinozastraat. Pietje was brooding.

"Are you okay?" asked Corrie, almost out of breath keeping up with him.

Pietje flipped the hair out of his face before looking down at her. His eyes were slightly bloodshot. He squinted at her as if deep in thought. "I'm okay." He continued to trudge on.

"No, you're not. I can tell." Corrie frowned, panting.

Pietje kept his hands dug in his pants and swaggered as he walked. "Nope, I'm okay. I'm thinking of a thank you gift for the church." He smiled slyly at her.

Corrie didn't say a word and hooked her arm around his to help her keep up the pace.

He squeezed her arm against himself to give her support, as they finally fell into step together.

"Corrie, where's your pen and ink?"

Corrie looked at Pietje. She stood by the window, looking at the large, black burnt spot on the cobblestones in front of the house. A new family, refugees who lost their home somewhere else, had moved into the Aaronson's house. The concept was hard for her to comprehend.

"Corrie, the ink?"

Corrie turned to her brother, who stood beside the ironing board she had erected a moment before. "Are you going to write a letter to the church now?"

"I might."

"Can you help me write a letter to Pappa after?"

Pietje's jaw was working, Corrie noticed; that usually meant he was upset, though she knew he was trying to hide it. "Sure. But first, I need the ink for something else."

She didn't entirely understand why. She moved away from the window and walked to the ironing board. She took a little stained leather case down off a shelf. She handed it to Pietje.

Pietje opened the case and looked inside. "Thanks."

Corrie picked up the iron that was heating on the stove. She licked her finger and touched its hot surface. It sizzled perfectly. She was about to put the iron to a bed sheet when Pietje turned and rushed to the door. She watched Pietje go out past the front window. *Where was he going with her pen and ink?* "Mama needs it to write Pappa a letter!"

"I'll be right back," he yelled from the alley.

She put the iron back on the stove and hurried out the front door. "Wait, Pietje!" Corrie caught up to him outside their gate. "Where are you going?" she asked.

"You'll see." He looked down at the ground as he raced forward.

Corrie had a hard time keeping up with his long strides. She followed him to the bridge and over the greasy waters of the canal. They clomped past the anti-aircraft gun and sandbags, and up the street to the church.

Corrie looked up at the steeple as they neared the front entrance.

"There's no mass now, Pietje. Why are we here?"

Pietje held finger to his lips. "Shhh. Here, hold this." Pietje took out the little bottle of ink and gave the case back to Corrie. "I'll be right back."

Pietje turned and climbed the steps to the front doors and disappeared inside.

Corrie, heart skipping, ran after him.

In the darkness of the inner hallway, she could make out Pietje unscrewing the cap of the bottle of ink and emptying its contents into the Holy Water font. Corrie's gasp echoed through the vestibule. She watched as Pietje shook the last drop of ink out of the bottle, then turned and bolted, pulling Corrie along with him.

They scrambled down the stairs, but Corrie couldn't run in the *klompen* anymore, so Pietje stooped down and took her *klompen* off. He carried them as he grabbed her hand, and they raced off, not looking back. They ran criss-cross around people and soldiers, through the traffic, bicycles, and the odd wagon. Corrie almost tripped on the cobblestones as her big toe caught on an edge. She could hear the flap-flap of her bare feet hitting the smoothed cobblestones.

"Watch out!" yelled Pietje as he maneuvered her around debris on the road. They avoided horse manure, dog manure, and some glass. She kept her eyes glued to the ground, all the way home.

Breathlessly, they arrived at their gate and ran into the lane, gasping for air.

Corrie grinned at Pietje. Such wonderful courage!

"That serves them right," laughed Pietje.

"But now we don't have any ink to write letters to *Tante* Dina and Pappa," reminded Corrie.

"Oh!" Pietje covered his face in surprise. "I wasn't thinking."

"Oh well, we can always use Beppie's pencils," offered Corrie. "But, Mama will want to know where the ink went."

"Leave it to me. I'll think of something."

He pulled her back into the house. Corrie, laughing, continued with her ironing, while Pietje went out to clean the rabbit cage.

An hour later, their mother returned with little Hennie and Beppie. They came bearing a gift of a ration of beef from their *Opa*.

"Goodness, gracious," said Cornelia as she put her purse and meat package on the table. "It's not Ash Wednesday, is it?"

"No, Mama. Why?"

"We saw people walking around with black dots on their foreheads. They had dots on their shoulders, their chest. Very strange."

Corrie dropped the sheet she was ironing and covered her mouth.

"What's wrong?" asked Cornelia. "Did you hurt yourself?"

Corrie lowered her hands and grinned. "No. But you might want to ask Pietje why people had black dots all over them."

Cornelia stood looking at her blankly. Beppie clapped. She knew.

"Where's Pietje?" asked Beppie.

Corrie pointed to the back. Beppie passed her. "This I gotta hear!" She disappeared out the back of the house. Suddenly they heard Beppie scream and laugh hilariously.

"Oh no," whispered Cornelia. She smiled while covering her face. "I hope no one saw him do it."

"Nope. No one was around. And we ran home as fast as we could."

"Well," Cornelia said, dropping her hand. "Serves them right."

Henk watched as the impeccable German guard stood slapping his baton against his thigh.

"The work week is now a minimum of seventy-two hours, not including the half-hour it takes for you to walk to the factory and a half-hour back. You are still responsible for your chores in the morning and at night. We will punish anyone not properly groomed."

The men grumbled amongst themselves. Cold weather moved in, and they did not have warm clothing. Their living conditions worsened by the day with more forced labor arriving every week. Their facilities were overwhelmed.

They had one razor to share amongst themselves even though they had to report to work looking well-groomed. The food portions, though better than the prisoners' they saw every day in the fields, were still not enough to keep them healthy for 12-hour day shifts six days a week. They were forced to walk in all kinds of weather, be responsible for both their crowded cell and themselves. They only had two working sinks amongst the sixty men to do their wash, with only four holes in the cement floor as washroom facilities. What was worse, everyone had lice, which made their lives almost unbearable. They spent all their spare time looking for and killing lice in their clothing.

Henk scratched at the back of his neck. He watched the guard's monocle twinkle as the man looked around at the silent throng in front of him. Henk thought back at the time he spent at Camp Vught before arriving at this place in Germany while there. It was still in the Netherlands, and he was able to correspond with his wife and children. This camp, however, was only a half-way house where, as labor, they were organized according to where the demand dictated. Though the Germans seemed to treat the Dutch and other 'Aryan' races better than they did the Polish and certainly the Russians, they also ironically received particularily-severe punishments. The Dutch tended to be outspoken and quite often voiced their complaints. Then a few would be thrown into a windowless cell for two weeks as punishment.

Unfortunately, it happened to Henk, though it wasn't directly his fault. It was more by association. He was Dutch. Another Dutchman stirred quite a bit of trouble when the sleeping arrangements were far below par. In response, twenty men were put into these smaller punishment cells where they were only given bread in the morning, and one small bowl of watery cabbage soup in the afternoon. There was no reprieve from the stifling hot cells. They called it the 're-education of the workers.'

Soon after his punishment, they sent Henk to a work camp near Oranienburg, Germany. More onerous work was his fare. Here, Henk met people from other countries; countries he had naively assumed were of lower intelligence or culture. Except for different physical traits and mannerisms, he learned they were basically all like him; honest, hardworking, and watching out for their fellow man. He became excellent friends with many of them. He learned to appreciate the differences.

Whatever the case, they were all in this together.

But damn, he couldn't get used to the fact he was not allowed to write to his family anymore. Somehow the letters from them arrived and were delivered to him once a week, yet there wasn't any accommodation for them to write in return. Not communicating with his family bothered him the most. It was the most unbearable aspect of his new life.

He just prayed that they would trust he was okay.

Chapter 15
September 1943

Henk devoured a letter which he had earlier folded into a tiny square and stuffed into a hidden vest pocket. He reread the message as he sat on the edge of his bunk. He slept on the bottom of a three-tier bed near the end of a long narrow chamber.

"Listen to this," he laughed to his Russian friend, Radoslav. Neither one understood each other entirely in their native tongues, but they both struggled through French. "Pietje put a whole bottle of ink into the holy water at church. Cornelia wanted him to be an altar boy but the nun slammed the door in Mama's face, so that made Pietje so mad. After that, Mama said there were people with black dots on their faces and clothes walking around." He chuckled.

Radoslav looked at Henk quizzically. "*Opyat' taki?*"

"My son, he put ink into holy water at church," he explained in French. Then he made a motion of doing the Holy Cross, making a point of stabbing himself in the forehead, diaphragm, the left shoulder, and then the right shoulder.

Radoslav, short, stocky, and wiry, happily nodded his wrinkled face. He grinned, exposing a gap between his two front teeth.

Henk shook his head in wonder. He continued to read to himself and only then noticed that the letter was written in pencil. He realized that Pietje, of course, used up the entire ink supply they had on hand. He doubted Cornelia had the cash to buy more.

He put Corrie's letter down and unfolded the one from Cornelia.

He frowned as he read the section in which she also wrote of the nun slamming the door in her face. He sensed it hurt her deeply. He was hopeful her letter to his sister-in-law, the nun Dina, would be able to bring about help. He was relieved that his father was able to help with a little meat for his family.

He looked up. He could hear someone crying somewhere in the camp building. A woman? Women bunked elsewhere though some worked in the same building as the men. Indeed, they were virtual prisoners, not just workers hired for no money. They might as well have been prisoners. Though it was hard to believe, they had it far better than those poor souls.

His thoughts turned to the men with whom he bunked. One of the 60-plus men in their chamber was dying. He was taken away the day before for medical help, and they returned him sedated just as the men arrived from their day of toil. He slept for about an hour until woken up for 'supper,' but he refused to eat. He was obviously in pain, and painkillers were wearing out, but there was nothing any of them could do except to take turns comforting him. Henk sat by him earlier as he quietly read his mail. One look at the man told him there wasn't life enough left in him to pull through. He should check on him again, he thought.

Henk got up and stretched, hoping he would never get sick in this godforsaken place. He was worried because every muscle in his body ached. He rubbed the stubble on his shaved head, then scratched under his arm. Damn ugly, despicable lice. He was dying for a proper bath.

He made his way past legs and bodies and arrived at the small cluster of men around their dying member. They moved over to allow Henk to get close enough to see if he'd gotten any better.

"A good dose of *Jenever* would do the trick right now." One of the men said, looking over at him. He was also Dutch. Most of the men there were either Russian, Polish, Belgian, with only a few Dutch.

Henk leaned over and touched the man's forehead; it was hot and moist.

"Pneumonia," suggested one of them.

Late summer rains had started, and they marched without any protection nor means of drying once at the factory. The factory, itself, had sawdust flying through the air continuously, and no one wore a mask.

"You're probably right," Henk agreed.

"We should do something, or he'll die. It's bastardly miserable listening to him suffer like this."

Henk looked up at the guy. Every time they demanded some correction in their treatment from those higher up, whether it was for more food, less heat, more heat, more fresh water—anytime they demanded their rights—someone was thrown into the pit.

The pit was a tiny room with a solid door and one light bulb—just enough room for a plank to unfold from the wall that served as a bed.

But someone had to say something. Henk looked around at the men. A few of them had already suffered that punishment. They always came back weakened, destroyed. He sensed it was time he paid the price. At times, they had experienced little miracles when they found themselves with the right guard in the right mood at the right time. Henk decided to step up to the plate and take his chances.

"Right, then." Henk slowly stood up, listening to his joints crack. He touched the back of his neck where his boil was slowly festering before gently touching his cheek. He had a bad tooth, and there was an isolated feverish spot on his jaw bone. He sighed, walked through the men, and banged at the main door, at which point one or two of them men cheered him on.

Clutching a letter in her dirty hand, Corrie raced as quickly as her *klompen* allowed. She felt her braids bouncing on her back as she scrambled over the bridge, passed the anti-aircraft gun, scurried around a bomb shelter entrance, and breathlessly reached a tall, brightly-painted, red *brievenbus*. She crammed the thick letter through the slot, then bent down to pick up three cigarette butts in the dust and dirt beside it.

"Little poor girl, still picking up someone else's garbage," yelled a woman.

Corrie squinted into the late September sun. She could barely make out the same young woman hanging around the anti-aircraft gun. The young woman smiled at Corrie and held up a burning cigarette. As Corrie watched, the girl flicked the smoking cigarette into the street onto the cobblestones.

"Go get it, little doggie," she said, grinning.

An older woman in an oversized coat near Corrie heard the challenge.

"That slut. Someone should do something about that piece of filth, giving herself to the *moffen* like that. Don't even give that piece of trash the time of day." The woman glared at the girl and then turned to follow the Atlantic Wall down the street.

Corrie breathed heavily. She eyed the smoldering cigarette and resisted scrambling to get it. She sighed and headed back home, but she still had to pass the distasteful young woman.

She quietly kept her eyes on the girl until she passed her, then hurried back toward the bridge. When she thought she was no longer in sight, she quickly studied the sidewalk and searched around for more butts. She spotted a cigar butt! She picked it up and looked at the butts in the palm of her hand. She squeezed them tightly into a ball and put them into a side pocket of her skirt. She slowly made her way home with eyes glued to the street. Her heart jumped when she eyed a coin. With shaking fingers, she picked it up and studied it. It was the new Nazi-inspired zinc quarter. She held it up to her eyes as she continued walking to her gate. She looked around the street one more time before ducking into her alley. Suddenly, she became aware of a baby wailing somewhere. She looked around and saw no one. As she clutched the coin, she hummed to herself the rest of the way.

Eventually, she realized it was Hennie who was wailing, her cries echoing through the alley.

Corrie scrambled straight into the house. There she saw Hennie clutching at her ear while being held by Cornelia. Corrie looked at her mother. She looked terrible.

She suddenly realized her mother was very sick. She looked too weak to be holding Hennie.

Corrie stepped up to her mother, took the wailing Hennie out of her arms. She watched as her mother wordlessly bent over, clutched at her stomach, and stumbled to the bedstead. Slowly, her mother allowed herself to lie down and roll up into a fetal position.

Corrie put Hennie down on the bullet-riddled floor to check where she was scratching. Behind her left ear, there was a boil the size of a pigeon egg. It was as beet red as Hennie's face. She wailed and cried. She was obviously in pain.

She left Hennie and went to her mother.

"Mama?" She stood by obediently, waiting for a reply.

There was none—just a moan.

"Mama, what should I do with Hennie?"

Her mother slowly unfolded herself and looked weakly at her daughter. She pointed at the door. "She needs to go to the hospital."

Corrie looked back at Hennie, who could hardly breathe; she was wailing so much. She tried to crawl to get up but couldn't and dropped down on her behind, crying. She shook her head violently, her blond curls waving in the air.

"There's a little money still in my coin purse," her mother said, feebly. She pointed to her purse on the kitchen chair.

Corrie walked over and opened the clasp of the purse. She searched in the bag and pulled out a coin purse. Then Corrie took the zinc quarter out of her skirt pocket and added it to the coins. She tucked the bag into her pocket and stepped toward Hennie.

"First, let's wipe your nose," Corrie said, her ears ringing with Hennie's cries. Corrie fought to wipe Hennie's nose and cheeks with the hem of her skirt as Hennie wriggled away from her hands. Corrie hiked her up on her hip. In her *klompen*, she left the house lugging a screaming Hennie along the street.

Back to the city center and past the anti-aircraft gun, but this time the sirens suddenly began from a nerve-shattering, ghoulish, low moan to an ear-splitting wail. Distant planes droned in their direction, coming at a fast clip. The staccato burst of the anti-aircraft gun nearby suddenly cut through the air. Corrie saw the bullets shooting up into the sky. A bomb fell somewhere close, and the ground shuddered.

There was a fresh crater along the road beside a house in flames, the fire spewing black smoke. The smoke blinded Corrie. She squinted against the sting, and frantically stumbled to where she knew was the closest bomb shelter. People converged around her with the same intent. They had dust marks on their faces, and their eyes were wiped clear for vision.

Corrie followed the people down the stairs and quickly found a tiny spot somewhere on a coveted bench. The pandemonium outside and in deadened Hennie's cries. But Corrie could hear them as Hennie continued to wail and clutch at her ear.

The bombing appeared to move quickly, and gradually Hennie's cries were what echoed in the shelter. Though it seemed safe to come out, they waited an excessive amount of time before the all-clear signal blasted distantly through the air.

Corrie was afraid that the hospital would close before she could get there. She clung to Hennie and rocked her back and forth, kissing her on her head, her cheek, snuggling her for comfort-both for Hennie and herself. To no avail.

Finally, as the sirens marked all was clear, she exited the bomb shelter with the crowd. She quickly marched toward the hospital. She pushed herself with great physical effort, her klompen marking a hollow drumbeat along the way.

She eventually reached the hospital. She yanked at one of the doors and hurried into the front hallway. The place smelled of ammonia and disinfectant. There were no people waiting in line, and she saw the receptionist window was no longer open. She stepped into the adjoining hallway that led to patients' rooms. She saw a nun in white down the hall.

"*Zuster!*"

Hennie's cries echoed through the hall.

The nun hurried toward them. With her habit spreading out around her in her haste, she had the look of an angry swan. The nun pointed at the door.

"Out! You are disturbing the very sick and wounded." The nun grabbed her by the shoulder and dragged her and Hennie to the front vestibule. She pointed at the sign that said what hours they were open. "Can't you see, you're late. You'll have to come back in the morning."

She continued pushing her out through the front doors and onto the street. "Come back tomorrow."

"*Ja*, but my sister is in pain, *Zuster*!"

"Give her some brandy for now and come back tomorrow!" The nun closed the door. Through the glass, Corrie could see her disappear into the opposite hallway from where they had just come.

With tears in her eyes, she cradled Hennie's head. She knew they didn't have any brandy. Perhaps some of that Manischewitz from the Aaronsons. But she didn't want to take the chance. She instead headed for *Opa*'s house. Surely, he would have brandy, or at least get it from the pub downstairs.

Henk sat miserably on the plank in the dark, hot cell. There was no window save for a slot at the bottom of the door where food was occasionally slipped through. The pail he used needed emptying, and the stench almost made him vomit. He leaned back against the plaster wall, where so many others had scratched graffiti. Pain shot through his jaw and caused his eyes to water. It was getting steadily worse, and he knew he had a rotten tooth. That was all he needed now, another complaint to make to the powers that be. Unfortunately, it was the wrong guard at the wrong time who gleefully found Henk's demands on behalf of his sick companion, an affront on the Great *Fuhrer* himself.

"You are lucky you are not a prisoner—a Jew. You'd be dead now," he announced as he roughly pushed Henk into the cell the week before.

A friendly guard came by a few days later to inform Henk that his sick friend had died. But the guard had more news for Henk. "My friend, I have news," he said, opening the door to the cell. It was the only way of getting fresh air.

Henk inhaled deeply and felt his head clearing.

"You are being transferred. Your carpentry skills are valuable to the Wehrmacht, it seems. Your skills are in high demand these days."

"What do you mean," Henk asked, hoarsely.

"We are taking you to somewhere in Poland. Don't ask me where. I just know. So be prepared."

"Is it because I've been speaking out? Is this another form of punishment?"

The friendly guard shrugged his shoulders and made a face. "Probably, yes. There is too much rebelling going on. The women—" he motioned off to the side and rolled his eyes. "They, too, have many demands, and they were distraught when your friend died. We have our hands full." He wiggled his head. "Besides, a change of scenery would do you good." He leaned in and padded Henk's bony shoulder. "Believe me; I could use a change of scenery, too."

"But I can't," whimpered Corrie. She looked with large eyes at her brother. She was frightened to death of what he proposed.

Pietje looked up at her from where he crouched beside the opening in the floor. He had retrieved their parents' brass trinket and was holding it up for Corrie to take. He shook it at her. "Take it," he demanded.

She wordlessly reached down and took the heavy item.

Pietje scrambled up to his feet and wiped down his pants and scabby knees. He nodded to the brass trinket. "We won't get much for this, and the only other things we have to sell is the rifle and Pappa's accordion."

"No, not the accordion," their mother weakly whispered.

"What about the rifle, Mama?" asked Pietje.

"Yes, the rifle. You can sell the rifle."

Their mother lay buried in the shadows of the bedstead. She had gotten progressively worse. For the moment, miraculously, Hennie was sleeping fitfully beside their mother in the bedstead. Their *Opa*'s brandy had done the trick, but Hennie had a fever, they knew. Corrie hoped that her little sister would sleep right through the night until morning when she would again take her to the hospital.

She was exhausted. She pulled the beat-up kitchen chair close to her and sat down. She bent down toward Pietje, who was searching under the floor for the rifle.

"I wish we had ammunition for this gun. I know what I'd do with it," announced Pietje, half into the hole.

"Pietje, don't talk like that," said Corrie.

"Well, I would. I wouldn't hesitate one second, those *moffen*!"

Suddenly, Beppie burst into the little house. "Look what I've got!" Beppie held up what looked like used nylons. She tenderly rolled them up in her hand and let them unfold again.

Pietje brought up the burlap-covered rifle and laid it on the floor in front of Corrie. "What is it?"

"A nylon." Beppie grinned.

"Where'd you get it?"

"A friend," she said coyly.

"Where'd your friend get it?"

"From a garbage pail behind one of the whores' houses."

Corrie looked at her sister, wide-eyed. "Their garbage cans?"

Beppie motioned behind her. "Yeah, right there. Up the street."

"Only men go there," announced Pietje.

"You don't go into the street, silly," said Beppie, turning to Pietje. "You go through the alley behind their houses."

Corrie blinked. She looked at Pietje, who looked at her. Then he looked back at Beppie.

"What are you going to do with a torn nylon?" asked Pietje.

"I can wear them."

"It's torn," said Corrie.

Beppie shrugged, "I don't care. I'll get another one, and I'll have a pair. I'd rather wear nylons with a run in them than nothing on my legs at all."

Corrie thought the reasoning was brilliant. It was almost time for school, and bare legs didn't do well in the cold, wet Dutch winters. She reached out for the nylon. "Can I see?"

Beppie let her have the nylon and watched as Corrie twisted it, bunched it up, unrolled it. "I can make dolls out of this."

"Don't be so stupid."

"I can. See?" She stuffed her hand into the foot of the nylon, balled up her fist, and twisted the fiber around it. "I could stuff it with things to make a head and a body. I can make it some clothes from tiny pieces of cloth."

"To each his own," said Beppie, as she rudely snatched the nylon back.

"Pietje."

All three children looked over at the bedstead.

"*Ja*, Mama?"

"Bring the accordion here to me, please."

Pietje looked over at his sisters, curious. They shrugged.

"That's a nice idea. I would like to see Pappa's accordion," offered Corrie. She'd been so sad of late, the sight of those rose-patterned bellows would lift her spirit. No one could play it other than their father, but even the groan of flat chords would be music to her ears.

"We should sell it," announced Beppie.

"No!" yelled Corrie.

Hennie stirred in the bedstead.

"Corrie, keep your voice down."

"Sorry, Mama." Corrie turned to Beppie. "That's Pappa's accordion. We have no right to do anything to it."

Pietje stood up, having retrieved the accordion case. He placed it on the table and unlatched the locks. Slowly, tenderly, he lifted the cumbersome instrument out of its case and unlatched the bellows. He put the shoulder straps over his shoulders and opened the bellows. It made a moaning sound.

Corrie's eyes lit up at the appearance of the rose pattern on the bellows and the heavenly sound of haphazard chords and notes that Pietje was creating as he opened and closed the instrument. All three children laughed.

"Bring it here, Pietje," asked their mother, weakly.

Pietje turned and walked to the dark bedstead. Cornelia's hand reached out and touched the polished red surface.

"I can still see your father's fingerprints on it," she weakly said.

Corrie and Beppie hurried closer. Indeed, they saw his fingerprints.

"So long as we keep his accordion safe, he will come back to us."

Corrie looked questioningly at her mother. The thought that he wouldn't come back never occurred to her. Of course. The Allies bombed everywhere in Europe, so if there was a chance that a bomb would fall on their little house, surely the same applied to their father wherever he was. The thought of him dying and never coming back grieved her overwhelmingly. Another form of fear gripped her heart. There seemed little positive left in this world.

Pietje turned away from the bedstead and latched the bellows closed tightly. He slipped off the shoulder straps, and as he put the accordion back into its box, it fell and clattered to the floor.

Shocked awake, Hennie moaned and then wailed, filling the tiny home with her distinct version of a siren.

Corrie sighed. They hadn't eaten, and the others were probably as tired as she was. Corrie stepped over to the bedstead and lifted Hennie. At two years old, she was now continent, so inevitably, she needed to go. She took her to the water closet for her to relieve herself. Once inside, the walls reverberated with frantic cries. As she placed Hennie carefully over the stinking hole, she silently prayed that wherever her father was, nothing would befall him.

"Hennie, I'm going to make you a doll," she whispered into Hennie's ear.

Hennie looked up at her, hiccupping. "Doll?"

"Yes, so if you go wee for me, and try not to cry, I will find you something I can make a doll from for you."

Hennie looked at her curiously. Then her face collapsed as she clutched the side of her head. She wailed in pain again.

Manischewitz thought Corrie. She hated to give the child more alcohol, but there was no way they will remain sane with Hennie's helpless cries of pain all night. She pulled up Hennie's underwear and took her out of the stifling closet. "Let's see what we have that can help you with that pain of yours," she said, hopefully.

The next morning, an exhausted Corrie carried a whimpering Hennie in her arms back over the bridge and onto the main road. She had learned a new word from Pietje the night before. '*Ack-ack*'—slang for anti-aircraft guns because they sounded like ack-ack-ack-ack sounds.

She noticed there was a different set of soldiers at the guns. She also saw a good number of butts around the sandbags and made a mental note to come and collect them later. Suddenly, there was a distinct and familiar heavy drone above their heads. Corrie squinted up into the crisp morning sky. Allied bombers. But they were coming in low. That meant—

The sirens went off, and Hennie cried out in shock. She continued to wail as Corrie, once again, hurried to the same bomb shelter as the day before. Down below, there were fewer people than the day before, but the bombing sounded a little closer. Almost immediately, a very close strike caused the power to go out, and suddenly the world below was immersed in black. Corrie put her hand on Hennie's head for comfort. She could still hear Hennie crying between the explosions. Perhaps more out of fear than pain this time, thought Corrie.

Fear.

Corrie wished she had stayed close to the others. Now in the dark, she felt so alone. Corrie needed the comfort of warm bodies beside her. As she panicked, Corrie lost her composure. She started to cry as well and started to reach out around her and Hennie.

A few moments later, she felt something cold pouring into her *klompen*. Water. Cold water. A water main had broken! Corrie's panic increased as, with one hand, she continued to reach out to the side and in front of her for another warm body. She only felt the stone walls as she shimmied along the plank she was sitting on with Hennie. For some reason, she couldn't sense anyone else.

Corrie lifted her feet onto the edge of the plank. She held Hennie tightly. But very quickly, Corrie felt the same icy cold water reaching the plank, wetting her skirt. She felt the bottom of Hennie's dress. It was soaking wet.

Corrie screamed. Her vibrations were in sync with Hennie's cries. Finally, when she thought she was going to lose her mind entirely, the bombing completely stopped, and the siren wailed it was safe to come out.

Someone finally opened the heavy door, and a cloud of light and dust swooshed into the shelter.

Corrie looked around wildly, still wailing, and saw where the other people were. One woman looked over, and her mouth dropped open. She rushed toward Corrie and Hennie and held them tightly.

"*Ach, meisje. Ach*," she cooed, trying to calm both girls. "You could've drowned in here!"

Corrie saw that the water had risen thigh high on the woman. She looked down at her wet clothes and that of Hennie's. The woman took a wailing Hennie into her one arm from Corrie and then, with her other arm, picked Corrie up by her underarms. Awkwardly, she waded through the water to the stairs and let go of Corrie so that she could climb out of the shelter herself.

Still sobbing, Corrie reached out and took Hennie from her.

As a bit of the dust settled in the direction of the hospital, Corrie carefully stepped around bits of brick and wood, plaster, and dirt. Eventually, Corrie reached the doors of the hospital, where others had already started to line up with injuries. She shivered in her wet clothes as she joined the fray, grateful for the proximity of so many people. Many looked at her wet clothes curiously, but only for a moment. As the smallest in line, she was sandwiched between two warm bodies. Finally, her shaking subsided and she was able to relax and feel thankful for the fact they had finally reached their destination.

The nights were cold in the train car. Henk sat on straw amongst other men. Some remained standing, leaning against the rocking walls. The clickety-clack of the train put everyone in a hypnotic state. Men smoked, and though, at the beginning of their journey, some men got upset at the thought of straw burning in their mobile prison, they eventually gave up and let things be. There was always the full latrine bucket to put out a fire.

Slowly it dawned on Henk that the train started to slow down. Almost imperceptibly.

He stood up and rocked helplessly as he tried to find his sea legs. He reached the opposite wall where there was a space between men. During daylight, they saw through the crack around the large sliding door, but now, in the middle of the night, all he could spy were some lights in the distance. Wherever they were going, it sure looked like they were in the middle of nowhere.

After some minutes, the train slowed considerably, and suddenly they were able to hear voices and dogs barking over the creaks, groans, and screeching of the trains' brakes.

"I can hear dogs barking," announced a man near him.

"German Shephards. The Nazis train them. They're terrible animals, ready to bite your arm off," offered another bedraggled soul

"*Nou zeg*," said one. "It sounds like we're deeper in the cesspool here."

Henk worked his sore jaw as he stood in the dark, waiting for the full stop. It didn't take long until they came to a complete halt with loud hisses and clacks.

"We're here," he whispered to no one in particular.

"Where the heck are we?" asked another formless voice in the dark.

"Poland, I think," said another.

"You mean, Nazi Poland."

Suddenly, with a clatter of chains and locks, the big heavy door slid open. Arc lights immediately flooded the interior of the car. Henk quickly looked around the interior at the men who were with him. He wondered if he looked as bad as they did.

"*Geh raus! Schnell!*" yelled an armed guard. There were several, two of whom held taut chains attached to very large German Shephards, drooling at the mouths, baring their teeth. They snapped at the men making their way down the ramp of the car.

Henk covered his eyes against the lights as he stayed behind. He wanted to study the surroundings. Where were they exactly?

A guard motioned him to keep up. One of the last ones off the car, he slowly made his way down the ramp to gravel. One soldier jabbed at him with a rifle butt.

Henk swung to face him. He held up his hands. "I'm not a prisoner. I am here to work!"

The guard motioned he would hit him again if he didn't move on.

"All right!" yelled Henk. As he turned to face where he was going, he spied a large, wrought-iron sign attached to a gate through which they were herded. He squinted and read the sign.

"Arbeit Macht Frei"

He whispered it to himself. *Work sets you free.*

Like hell it does, he thought. As he looked down to watch where he was going, he suddenly heard a woman's voice. Looking up past the heads in front of him, he spotted women's heads with coiffed hair. He strained to watch closely. What were women doing here greeting them? Indeed, the women at Camp Vught and Oranienburg did not look so purposely made up.

But as he came closer, something sinister started forming in his awareness. He realized the women were exposing their naked bodies from under long coats. As they stood showing themselves to the men, one of the guards laughed.

"As workers, you have perks! See? Free sex! The prisoners don't get this. You should be pleased here," he laughed. He pointed at the red brick building to the left. "We call them *Sonderbauten*. Or Puff!" He touched the side of his nose and grinned.

Henk looked away, astonished, and humiliated. This place was another form of Hell, he thought. Surely.

Henk was close to tears. He had never actually seen a fully naked woman in his life—not even his wife. It just wouldn't do. He had heard of the pornographic photos that were very popular, especially during the First World War, but he also heard of the horror stories of syphilis, how it could eat away one's brain. Rumor had it that Hitler was crazy because he had caught syphilis during the Great War. Suddenly, Henk moved to the side and vomited. Not that there was anything in his stomach to vomit. The sight simply made him ill.

Intuitively, he knew the women were prisoners, fighting to stay alive and to eat. All the more, he felt overwhelmed by shame. For them, for him having seen them, for the whole nightmare. All the more disdain he held for the Nazis.

Fortunately, the guards left him alone to vomit. He looked up, confused as he wiped his mouth with his sleeve. Over the calls of the women, the guards, and the barking dogs, he was sure he heard music. Beautiful music. He frowned. Amid this nightmare, there was music so beautiful it must be coming from Heaven.

He re-joined the end of the group of men and made his way to a row of wooden tables and men with striped pajamas sitting behind them. They were gaunt. More skeletal then he. Grey in the face. Their skin. With ID patches on their pajamas. And numbers on their forearms. In the harsh arc lights further to his right, there was an even stranger sight: men in the same striped pajamas, arranged in a half-circle. They formed an orchestra that played beautiful angelic music; happy music, modern and flowing, heart-rending, and warming. Was that an accordion he heard in the background?

He moved along the outer edge of the group of men to get closer to the orchestra. He spotted the accordion. It was a red accordion. Excitedly, he moved closer to see what the pattern was in the bellows. The lights were so bright that the brass of the buttons looked coppery, and the red looked purple, but he knew it was red.

As the bellows pulled apart, his heart leaped. It was a rose-patterned bellow. Was it his accordion? Did Cornelia sell it?

Something tapped on his shoulder.

He spun around to see a somewhat squat soldier holding the butt of his rifle on his shoulder.

Henk stepped back. "Sorry. So sorry." He went to go, but the soldier stopped him and stepped closer, leaning in close enough for Henk to know he'd had garlic sausage not too long ago.

"Anyone who cries at an orchestra playing has the heart of a true German!"

Henk was startled. "I am crying?" He touched his cheek.

"Like a baby," said the soldier. "A true German."

"What are you saying? I'm not German. I'm Dutch!"

The soldier smiled and shook his head. "No, you have the heart of a true Aryan. But, unfortunately, you are here to do a job, so I advise you to stand with the others for registration." He struck Henk on the shoulder with the rifle butt. "*Geh raus und schnell!*"

Chapter 16
October 1943

Corrie carefully braided her long blonde hair into two pigtails as she absentmindedly watched her sick mother sitting at the table rolling rough-looking cigarettes from the pile of tobacco extracted from butts.

Her mother picked up one rolled cigarette and lit it with a wooden match. She flicked it and dropped it into a can full of thoroughly-smoked butts—bits of brown and burnt ends. Then she gathered together a bunch of rolled cigarettes and put them carefully into a used cigarette package. It was orange, slightly wrinkled with the logo '*Nederlandsche Jack Vliegers.*'

"Here," said her mother, as she clenched her own cigarette between her brown teeth. Smoke curled into her eyes. "Pietje!"

Pietje was tightening his belt to the last notch. He looked over, finished doing up his belt, and reached out for the package. He blew at bits of tobacco on the outside of the cover and tucked it into a leather school bag.

"Sell the cigarettes individually or, if you can, the whole package. Get whatever you can for them."

"*Ja*, Mama."

Corrie didn't want to go to school. She looked over at Beppie, who was ready and standing by the door.

"And stay with your sisters! If the sirens go off, you stick together!"

"*Ja*, Mama," Pietje answered once again.

"Beppie?"

"*Ja*, Mama. We will."

"Mama," began Corrie, as she lifted her flimsy book bag. She had already put her *klompen* on and had put more bits of rabbit fur inside than usual. The mornings were crisp, as late autumn was about to set in. "I don't want to leave you alone. You still look sick."

Cornelia pushed herself from the little table and brushed the surface for bits of tobacco. She cupped them into her palm and stepped to the kitchen corner. She wiped her hands of the debris, into a pail. "I'll be fine," Cornelia said, facing the corner. She turned, bit down on the cigarette and brushed her hair back behind her ears with both hands. Her hair was greasy and flat and had grown quite a bit. She was pale, and the bags under her eyes were charcoal grey. She took a drag and held the cigarette away from her running eyes.

Corrie blinked. She stepped forward and hugged her mother. Then, on the way to the front door, Corrie bent down in the playpen and kissed Hennie on the head. She allowed Pietje to open the door for her and Beppie, and they embarked on their long walk to school.

"Corrie, come up to the front of the class and do the arithmetic. You will remember from last year, I'm sure."

Corrie gripped the front edge of her battered desk and stared woefully at the teacher standing by the blackboard. He had just put on a formula: $6 + 7 = ?$

She took a deep breath and looked around. The children in her class were no more than seven years of age. She was about to turn nine. One or two of the boys in her class bullied her relentlessly. She towered above them all.

Slowly, she came forward in her bare feet, and took the chalk from the teacher. She approached the blackboard and looked at the formula. She started counting on her fingers, quietly counting them in a whisper. She thought it was 13 but wasn't sure. She couldn't focus clearly. She would start, and then she would lose where she was in her figuring.

"She doesn't know, she doesn't know, Corrie is stupid, Corrie is stupid."

"Quiet! We will have none of that." The teacher turned to Corrie. "Corrie, you know the answer. Just write it on the board."

Corrie's hand trembled as she raised the chalk to the chalkboard. She suddenly knew it was 13. Well, she was pretty sure. But she was almost afraid to be right. She scratched on the board, "12."

A few of the children laughed.

"Are you sure about that?" asked the teacher, looking at her intently.

Corrie nodded wordlessly, her big blue eyes darting from the blackboard to the teacher's face.

"You may sit down now, Corrie."

Corrie sensed her teacher's disappointment and silently shuffled to the back of the class and sat. She felt ridiculously big for the small desks.

It didn't matter what happened after that. Of course, another student knew the right answer, even though she knew it as well.

She looked to her left out the window at the street. The window there was still in one piece with bars on the front, and was taped on the inside. She crossed her feet at the ankles. They were cold. She had somehow picked up a small piece of glass and hadn't had the time as yet to dig it out of her calloused feet.

She realized that her brain wasn't working correctly. She was unable to think very long about anything. Burning tears welled up in the back of her eyes as she envisioned Rebecca, her baby brother, and her brother Joshua. She remembered *Mevrouw Aaronson*, the *moffen*, and the fire. She thought of people who died every time a bomb dropped. Every time a plane was shot down. Maybe that's why her brain wasn't working. It was still working on other problems in the back of her head.

She shifted in her seat, picked up her pencil, and traced the graffiti on the top of the desk.

She was sure she was a lost cause. She felt better at home, taking care of Hennie, her mother, the cooking, the cleaning. She wished she didn't have to go to school. At age nine, you could get away with that during a war, surely. She suddenly had to scratch at her head, something that happened incessantly these days. One of the children started laughing. She looked and saw a girl pointing at her and laughing.

"Corrie's got lice, Corrie's got lice," sang the girl.

Corrie looked down at her shoulder and saw lice squiggling. With a squeel she brushed them off. Then with both hands she scratched at her head.

"Quiet class! Focus on the blackboard!" The teacher, evidently used to lice on her students, continued with the lesson.

Corrie shook with emotion and humiliation. She made up her mind. She was going to devise as many reasons as possible for not coming back. She was done with being humiliated every single day. She was wasting her valuable time.

She knew where she would best serve: At home.

Corrie stood aghast. Not again. Her heart pounded in her ears. Her *klompen* had disappeared with its beautiful rabbit fur liners. She stood until she was the last in the cloakroom. She secretly hoped that once everyone left, someone may have left a pair of shoes behind. Though she knew her feet were probably the largest in that class, save those of the teacher.

She remembered how Rebecca had helped her the last time. For a moment, she stood, grieving.

"Why are you still here, Corrie?"

Corrie turned around to see the teacher standing with his briefcase in his hand.

"Someone stole my *klompen*."

The teacher looked down at her feet. He put down his briefcase and bent down on one knee. Corrie quietly watched as he untied his laces, took off his shoes, and then his socks. Then he put his shoes back on, stood up, and straightened his pants. He picked up the socks and handed them over to Corrie.

"They're not clean, but they'll protect you somewhat."

Corrie quietly took the socks and awkwardly slipped them onto her dirty feet. She looked down at them. Too big, but warm. Better than bare feet.

"I'll wash them when—"

"No need. My mother knitted them, and I know she has another pair almost ready. Go home. We'll see you tomorrow."

But 'tomorrow' came, and Corrie couldn't get herself out of bed. She had planned something the night before and was ready to give in to her misery and stay in bed all day. Well, half the day. She needed to help her mother.

"Corrie, you're going to be late!" Pietje called up the spiral staircase. "Corrie!"

"I'm sick!"

She quietly took a little flour and put it in the middle of her handkerchief the night before. Now, using it like a powder puff, she patted her face. She wanted to look pale and as ill as possible. She quickly patted more a second time and put the handkerchief back under the pillow.

Pietje came marching in from the top of the stairs. He could not stand up entirely straight in the attic anymore. He looked down at her. He studied her. "What did you put on your face?"

"Nothing."

"Yes, you did. You put something on your face. You're cheating."

Corrie broke down and cried. She buried her face in the pillow.

Pietje sat down at the end of the bed. He reached out and patted her back.

"Corrie, Pappa said I am the man of the house. So, as the man of the house, I will let you stay home. Maybe it's better. Mama doesn't look very good."

Corrie suddenly twisted to look at him. "No, I know." She wiped away tears. The cover of flour on her face now streaked.

Pietje laughed. "I'll tell Mama. I think she will be relieved."

Corrie had just washed little Hennie's face when the postwoman slipped a letter through the slot of the old door. Corrie hurried over and picked it up.

"Mama! Finally, a letter from *Tante* Dina!"

Cornelia stirred in the bedstead. "Bring it here, if you don't mind," she asked, hoarsely.

Corrie went to the bedstead and leaned over the edge of the straw mattress and watched her mother open the letter. When her mother took the letter out of the envelope, Corrie grabbed it to look at the elegant handwriting. She loved seeing stamps. This one was a five-cent stamp with two white horses on their hind legs.

"Mama, can I keep the stamp?" she asked as she fingered the edges of the stamp. She looked up when she didn't receive an immediate answer. She frowned. Her mother's eyes had turned red as they drilled into the paper she was holding.

Her mother dropped the letter and let out one big racking sob, covering her mouth.

Corrie picked it up. The handwriting was more difficult to decipher than block letters, but as she carefully whispered the words to herself, she was able to understand it all.

Tante Dina wrote that her mother had made her bed when she had to marry their father because of being with child. She had sinned in the face of God and, therefore, would have to face the consequences.

Corrie dropped the letter. She couldn't quite understand the affairs of men and women, but she did get the gist that somehow Pietje made her parents get married.

But wasn't that good?

Why did it deserve punishment?

She reached out and shook her mother gently. "Mama, does that mean *Tante* Dina isn't going to help us?" They had been relying on any kind of help they could get from her—more ration books, perhaps. Yes, material for clothing. Or money.

Nothing.

"At least we have *Opa*, Mama."

Her mother sniffed. From the pillow, she sounded congested. "No," she said, "Your *Opa* has a big family. We're not the only Gelaufs needing help. It's not fair to him to rely on him for everything. He's starting to show the stress. And he's not eating enough. He's much older. He has to be careful."

Corrie pursed her lips.

By the time Pietje and Beppie returned home from school, her mother had taken a turn for the worse. She'd been moaning and curling up into a ball in bed. Once, she went to relieve herself, and the smell reminded Corrie of her father's horse.

Pietje barged through the door with Beppie close behind. They had been arguing, so Beppie slapped her bag onto the table and stomped straight to the attic. No hello or hug for their mother.

"How's Mama?" asked Pietje.

Corrie handed him the letter and envelope. "*Tante* Dina finally wrote back. She said it was Mama's fault for being in this mess, and there was nothing she would do to help. I think she hurt Mama's heart very much."

Pietje lowered the letter to look at her askance. He then lifted the note closer to his eyes. He stepped to the window to read. His lips silently moved as he read very carefully. He pointed at the latter and turned to Corrie. "What does she mean they married because Mama was with child. That's me, right?"

Corrie looked at him with wide eyes.

Pietje, disgusted, bunched up both letter and envelope and stepped to the little coal stove. He opened the grate and tossed them into the cold ashes. He returned to the kitchen corner, got the box of matches, and lit one. He threw it into the stove and watched the letter burn. He closed the grate once the flames died and walked over to the bedstead. He fingered one of the curtains. "Mama?"

Cornelia, did not answer. She was deep asleep, snoring softly with a wheeze.

He turned to Corrie. "I'm going to stop going to school as well. No one's going to help us, Corrie. No money is coming in, and the rations are starving Mama because she keeps giving us her portions."

"So, what are we going to do?" whispered Corrie.

Pietje straightened up. "We're going to go out at night and start finding things we need."

Corrie's mouth dropped. The soldiers shot at those they found outside after curfew. "But they'll kill us!"

"Not if they don't see us," Pietje answered.

Corrie thought of the stories she had heard of how the German soldiers walked in groups so that they could spread right across the street as they strolled along. They checked to make sure black-out curtains kept all light hidden. If they found someone out and about, they either beat them to a pulp or shot them on the spot. They considered everyone out after curfew members of the Dutch Resistance, or they were looters, and there was no mercy for either.

Also, they heard of people smuggling Jews out of their houses to other places after curfew. One woman who was being transported, had a baby, and the baby started to cry. She had to quickly hide in bushes along the road when they heard soldiers coming. The lady had to cover her baby's face but it took so long for the soldiers to pass that she had accidentally suffocated her own child.

Corrie's stomach turned. She was going to throw up. She was cold and miserable and they didn't have anything to burn in the stove for heat. The house was already cooling down as they spoke, and the one burner she used to cook on wasn't enough to heat their home.

"Is Beppie coming with us?"

"No, she has to go to bed and go to school in the morning. From now on, Corrie," he said, as he gently put his hand on her shoulder, "You and I are going to be the breadwinners."

"Corrie, wake up."

Corrie was running through a field of daisies toward a forest. A beautiful dark green forest. As she ran, she looked up and saw a blanket of planes rumbling above. She hurried, quickened her pace. She was sure her father was hiding in the forest. She had to get there in time before the bombs fell on him. Suddenly, something grabbed her and stopped her from running. The ground shook. She looked up to see bombs dropping from the sky—"

"Wake up!"

Corrie shook awake. She blinked in the darkness and could smell Pietje's breath.

"It's time."

"Wha—?"

Pietje put a finger to her lips. "Shh. We can't wake Beppie up. Come with me."

Pietje lifted the blankets from her side of the bed and stood by as Corrie climbed out of bed. Corrie looked over at little Hennie.

"What about Hennie. What if she wakes up?"

"She's with Beppie. It wouldn't hurt Beppie to help out sometime."

Corrie, fully-clothed as was their war-time habit, followed Pietje down the rickety spiral staircase.

Pietje gave her a pair of thick woolen socks she recognized as her teacher's. She put them on and turned to look at the dark bedstead. She heard her mother snoring loudly. She looked at Pietje.

"Ready?" Pietje looked at her pointedly.

"What are we going to do?"

"We are going to look for pieces of coal along the railroad tracks, and then, if we have time, we're going to the Groene Weg, to the whores."

Corrie thought of the nylons that Beppie found. They didn't match, and they were both ruined, but she had put them on and pinned them to her woolen underwear. It was far warmer than going barelegged. Corrie could have nylons, too. Maybe enough to be able to make a doll, too. Her stomach rumbled.

"Okay, here we go."

Pietje got his empty book bag from under the coat hooks and slowly opened the heavy door. As Corrie watched her brother's profile, in the soft moonlight, lean out of the door and look around the alley, she started shaking. Somehow, her feet obeyed, and she stayed close to Pietje. He slowly closed the door behind her. Quietly, they walked along the wall of the house to the end of the alley. He held up a hand. They stood listening to the sounds of the night. They could hear German spoken not too far off.

Pietje leaned into Corrie and whispered, "Those are not the soldiers on patrol. The patrol will be very quiet, just like us, so we have to be careful."

"Who is talking then?" she whispered into his ear.

"Drunken soldiers, probably."

Pietje stood in the gateway, looked around one more time, and waved Corrie to follow. They scurried from the cobblestone alley to the other side of Spinozastraat. There, they hid in the shadows of the moonlight. Then he led her further along the wall, went past the entrance to the red-light district, and hiked over to the train tracks just southwest of them. Every noise they made sounded like a bomb exploding and echoed far and wide in Corrie's imagination. Surely, their footsteps, however careful they were, could be heard a mile away!

They reached the gravel shoulders of the train tracks. Sometimes, coal bounced out of open cars, or people tried to steal bits of coal from the cars themselves and spilled some while running away. Doing work like that in the light of day was far too dangerous, Corrie understood. She saw the wisdom of doing it under cover of darkness, however frightening and uncertain it was. But it was so very dark.

Pietje moved to look between the rails of the tracks when Corrie grabbed his woolen vest. She pulled him back. "No, you'll get run over!" She visualized him sliced in half. She had heard of people losing limbs, their heads, being smashed by an oncoming train. In her mind, as soon as you stood on the tracks, the train would immediately pounce.

"You could hear them coming, Corrie. It's okay."

Corrie wouldn't let him go.

"Okay, guess what? I'll show you something."

Corrie let him go and watched as he went to the tracks and knelt beside them. He put the side of his face on the metal track.

She inched closer desperately looking up and down the tracks. She was sure a dark monster of steel would come out of the distance and slice off Pietje's head.

He motioned her to come closer. She allowed him to put her head to the track. It was strikingly cold against her face, but she now understood what Pietje was saying.

"When a train comes, we can hear it twenty minutes before it gets here, Corrie. See? There's nothing there."

Corrie quickly got to her feet and quietly watched as Pietje slowly walked bent over along the tracks, looking closely at the ground. Occasionally, he bent to pick something up and calmly placed it into the bag. Corrie looked around one more time and then went on her hands and knees. Soon, she was able to feel and see the difference between gravel and charcoal pieces. Corrie saw the wisdom in their dangerous quest. Already, she knew that tomorrow the house would be warmer for some time. She willed herself to keep searching, to keep crawling, and occasionally rest in the shadows of the bushes.

When they returned home to offload the charcoal, Pietje patted her shoulder. "Now we can go to bed, Corrie. That was good work."

"But we didn't go to the whores," she said, sadly. She thought of nylons. She wanted to find things for free, finding something of interest. There was a feeling of excitement at the thought of finding a treasure that another had thrown out.

"Aren't you tired, Corrie?"

She shook her head in the dark. "No, I want to go."

Pietje opened the door and poked his head out.

Corrie didn't hear any sounds.

Pietje took the bag over to the stove and started to unpack the bits and pieces of coal they managed to scrape together into a bin. The handle squeaked when he opened the grate. He scrunched up paper and put it in first. Then he put a handful of coal on top. He lit a match and lit the paper. The flame billowed.

"Who is that?" asked their mother, sleepily from the bedstead.

"It's Pietje, Mama. We just found some coal."

They both waited for a reply, but their mother had fallen asleep once again.

Corrie sensed her mother was iller than they thought.

"Would they have leftover food in their garbage?" whispered Corrie.

She could see Pietje shrug in the near darkness. "The whores? I guess."

"I want to find out," she announced, as she turned and picked up Pietje's bag. This time the nine-year-old led the thirteen-year-old out into the dangerous night.

Henk stood in the hallway while people of all descriptions hurried by. Some were prisoners with particular jobs assigned to them, wearing their striped prison garb. Some had the letter J on them, others P. He saw purple badges and pink. Some had various colored upside-down triangles with numbers above them. There were soldiers in grey, doctors in white, and women both in civilian clothes and prison rags.

They had finally allowed him to leave, from where he was helping build more barracks, to go and have his rotten tooth checked. He was nursing the right side of his face, swollen under the jawline. The pain made it difficult to breathe. He was marched by a guard to the main building and told to stand and wait in the hallway.

He waited for over an hour. There were no chairs. He missed the lunch break, and his stomach growled. He reminded himself he was still better off than the prisoners. Many prisoners died of overwork. He sensed the guards had no intention of working him to death. His daily calorie intake was far more than a prisoner's. Yet, he knew it was just a slower form of starvation.

He tried to lean back against a wall, but a soldier marched by and demanded he stand straight. There was no arguing. So, he kept his eyes closed and focused on standing on his feet, wavering considerably.

"*Herr* Gelauf!"

Henk jumped awake. "*Ja!*" He stood up straighter.

The man who yelled looked like a Russian in a doctor's garb. He looked down at a clipboard he had in his hands. The hands were hairy. Not exceptionally clean.

"Hmm," he grunted. He turned and waved for Henk to follow.

They made their way through hallways. Henk noticed that every single person in the hall, whether it was a woman prisoner on her hands and knees scrubbing floors, or a man prisoner carrying boxes, no one looked up at the Russian or him. It made him feel quite odd.

Finally, Henk ended up in a small room with an examination table and a wooden chair. There were various tools, surgical of some sort. Also, the type found in any shop.

The Russian motioned him to sit.

Henk sat with feverish eyes clamped on the tools.

The Russian bent over his face, motioning him to open his mouth.

Henk opened his mouth and groaned. He felt a tear run down his cheek.

The Russian turned to the table of instruments. He chose a pair of pliers and turned to put the pliers into Henk's mouth.

Henk put his hand on the Russian's. The Russian looked at him, surprised he touched him.

"Do I not get any pain killer?" asked Henk.

"*Nyet*. No painkillers. *Nyet obezbolivayushchikh*."

The man continued talking while he struggled to get a grip on a tooth.

Henk again stopped the Russian's hands from working.

The man glared at him.

"That is not the bad tooth," Henk mumbled.

The man shook his head. "No matter. One tooth is rotten. Others will rot."

Henk screamed as the man yanked out a functional tooth.

To prevent further inconveniences caused by Henk's teeth, he pulled out every single one.

Good. Or bad.

Henk left the room, holding a bloody rag against his swollen face. Tears streamed down his face in response to the traumatic assault on his body. He could barely see through the pain. He held a note to give to one of the guards allowing him to return to the barracks to recuperate. But just for the afternoon. He was to report to work the next day.

As he slowly made his way through the hallway to the front doors of the building, he saw the back of a short man come out of another office, holding a box overflowing with paper. He blinked at the sight. The man was looking at his feet as he walked.

Henk went to speak, but nothing came out. He quickened his steps and reached out his quivering fingers. He leaned forward, closed his eyes against the pain of the movement, and finally felt his middle finger brush the back of the man's back.

Henk stopped and slowly opened his eyes to look at the man.

The man had stopped and faced him, his eyes staring behind thick glasses.

"Henk," whispered Frans. Frans grabbed both of Henk's upper arms. His eyes filled with tears as his face crumpled into a cross between crying and grinning. He looked closely at the bloody rag against his mouth. Frans looked around the hallway before he looked back at Henk. "What happened?"

Henk, tears streaming, slowly pulled the bloody rag away and tried very hard to open his mouth.

Frans covered his mouth in shock and stepped back. Suddenly, they heard someone march up the hallway toward them from around the corner. Frans immediately picked up the box and nodded. "I know now you are here. May God keep you, Henk. We will see each other soon. My brother-in-law. My brother." Frans turned and walked quickly forward just in time to pass a soldier stepping around the corner.

The soldier eyed Henk's bloody rag. Then he realized Henk was looking directly at him. The man took his baton and slammed it on the back of Henk's shoulders, pushing him roughly forward.

He slammed into the wall, leaving a smudge of blood. *"Du sollst mich nicht ansehen!"*

For the first time in months, the bullying did not affect him. He straightened out and turned, to follow where Frans had disappeared around the corner. Suddenly, despite his bloody, swollen mouth and having lost every single tooth, he felt strengthened. He felt the old confident and secure Henk coming back.

He felt sure that if Providence put Frans in the same general area as Henk, against such astronomical odds which he couldn't even comprehend, then surely their families were protected, as well.

He returned to his barracks and slept the sleep of angels. He missed the evening meal, but the encounter with Frans earlier in the day nourished him as if he'd eaten a feast.

CHAPTER 17
APRIL 1944

Corrie sat on her haunches and leaned back against the wall of the back alley behind the red-light district, a series of tightly-built little townhouses near the Groeneweg just off Spinozastraat. The area was as calm as any bright Sunday morning in spring. For a moment, she basked in the warmth of the sun's rays. While she felt heat emanating from the brick wall at her back, she leisurely reached up to the lid of a battered, stinking garbage bin beside her. It was a treasure hunt each time. The smell was unbearable, especially as it stood cooking in the morning sunshine, but she had become accustomed to the scent. It had acquired a positive meaning in its pungency. It meant spoils. Free spoils.

All was at peace. As if the war, exhausted, had taken a much-needed sleep that morning. People were either at church or still asleep, as were the unique residents of this particular neighborhood. They were sleeping after a long night of employment.

Carefully, she pushed up at the edge of the lid and lifted it, intruding on the Sunday morning ablution of flies. A cloud of them suddenly rose, leaving behind hundreds of grubs. She shifted her body and used two hands to remove the cover, keeping its scraping and soft clattering sounds to a minimum. The larvae inched their way back into the depths of the bin. She took no notice and lowered the lid onto the cobblestones, and went on her scuffed and scratched knees to raise herself to eye level with the opening of the bin.

She peered in. There were newspapers, cardboard, food scraps, but nothing else that looked immediately useful or edible. She lifted a leg carefully and stood up. There was something shiny along the inside wall of the filthy bin. Carefully, she reached past the grubs and grease and pulled out what was a small perfume bottle. She looked at it in awe. She quickly unscrewed the cap and lifted it to her nostrils. She never had in almost ten years—her entire life—smelled anything so beautiful. She lifted it to the sun's rays to see if there was any liquid left.

A tiny amount! She quickly screwed the little metal top back on and put the bottle into the pocket of her awkward, homemade skirt.

Ah, nylon! She fished out the gauzy material, gingerly pulling at it so that it slithered out from the garbage. It had grease and bits of old boiled potato smeared on it. She didn't even look at it closely. She knew she wanted it. She was going to wash it and make another doll for Hennie and herself.

She balled it up and put it in the same pocket as the perfume bottle.

Suddenly, a little swallow flew down from somewhere and landed on the opposite edge of the bin.

Corrie froze.

The little bird tweeted and jerked its head this way and that. It studied her, then the sky, then the contents of the bin, the grubs, and then her again.

"*Dag vogeltje,*" she whispered.

She watched as it pecked at the grubs and let them fall. It bit at a morsel of something unrecognizable and swallowed it. It shook its wings.

Corrie slowly reached out with a finger to see if it would allow her to rub its tummy. But it flew before she could get very close. She watched it fly into the eaves of the house behind her.

She looked into the bin and saw what looked like a bundle of something wrapped in newspaper. She reached in with both hands, and as she did, some *patates frites* fell out.

"Oh," she gasped. She quickly bundled the leftover *frites*, turned, and promptly left through the back gate.

Rations had become so minimal that everyone's health was at stake. Anything extra made the difference between sickness, health, and death. Corrie imagined herself placing the *frites* onto the surface of the stove to heat and crispen. But first, she would have to make a fire. They had gathered together some wood from one of the bombed buildings in town, but she would be using all of the wood available if she did.

Not to worry, she thought, because the meal was going to make Mama very happy. And Pietje would be over the moon.

She hurried down the cobblestone street and slipped through their gate to the alley, the little bird following above her head.

Henk lay awake on the bunk and fretted. The early morning light kissed the edge of the filthy upper windows above where he lay with a few other men. Henk tried to imagine what his children and wife were doing. He frowned and stared past the edge of the bunk above him.

He received no letters in this camp, Birkenau. He closed his eyes tightly against the image of his loved ones crushed by bricks and mortar. The not-knowing was the most challenging part of life in the camp. He raised a rough hand to his forehead and covered his eyes for comfort.

"Oh, please. Keep my family safe," he whispered.

He rubbed his forehead with his fingers. His hands were fully calloused from the work he did; it was a daily trek to a forest where he helped chop down trees to clear land. They marched past fields of planted cabbages, still in their small bulbous leafy state. As a city dweller, even he could see they were healthy plants. The cleared land used to be a marsh, and he always thought the moist dirt was responsible for the healthy bounty. But someone whispered something in his ear that caused his blood to turn cold.

There was a troubling presence in the camp. The atrocities he witnessed almost drove him crazy. However, this new concept stretched his mind virtually to a new breaking point. He had learned that most newcomers to the camp went straight into gas chambers. Mostly women, children, and old men died in those chambers; their bodies hauled to the large crematoriums at the edge of the camp where they burned in the ovens. The flakes drifting down from putrid smokestacks were human ashes. The cremated ashes were taken out of the ovens, gathered together, and spread over the fields as fertilizer.

His mind couldn't think straight. It couldn't think, period. He had gone through the motions of work, of shoving, of carrying, and pulling, and loading wood onto trucks. And he returned as a zombie would, uncertain step after uncertain step. All he could do was follow the man in front of him, step for step, leaning on him, depending on him, for direction, speed, destination.

He welcomed sleep that night. And just before merciful blackness embraced him, he realized the significance of a painting he had seen once in his youth. A Dutch Master—Hieronymus Bosch. He recalled the flames, the hanging bodies, the gaping mouth of a monster devouring naked people. How did the artist know? He died in the 1500s. How did he see the future? Was this evil always amongst us?

The night before, he heard through the whispering grapevine amongst the few Dutch and Belgian workers he toiled with, that there had been a tragedy at Camp Vught. It was the first camp he worked at before transferring to Germany, and then on to Poland. Conditions were adverse there. But the people were kind and supported each other. The women gathered together to help the men and vice-versa. But someone told him about a gruesome incident in which 74 of the women, almost the entire group of female workers, rebelled against unfair treatment of one of their own. As punishment, the camp commander Adam Grunewald ordered all 74 women into bunkers, sixty of them in one twelve-foot-square cell with its small ventilation window shut. By seven in the morning, after standing room only all night, twenty-four women were comatose. Only fourteen of them revived. Ten were dead. No one knew names, but he was confident that at least one, if not more, of the women friends he made and appreciated, had died.

The beastliness of it all.

He ran his tongue along his gums while deep in thought. There were tiny craters where the roots of the teeth were. Many of the holes healed, but his tongue never tired of exploring them. It comforted him, a strange form of distraction from the Hell around him. But this vile piece of news overwhelmed him, eclipsing all distractions, including his gums.

He closed his eyes to the lightening of the world outside the narrow window overhead and inhaled the stuffiness of the room. It was Sunday, a much-needed day of rest, and though there were chores laborers still had to do on their Sundays off, for the most part, he had some leisure time. He was, again, going to focus his time and energy on finding his brother-in-law. Frans was working somewhere in the massive development, and he was intent on finding him.

Corrie bent over her mother in the bedstead. She waved the mouth of the perfume bottle back and forth under her mother's nose. Her mother kept her eyes shut but smiled slightly.

"Beautiful, isn't it, Mama?" Corrie grinned. Her mother's smile broadened.

Suddenly, there was a knock at the door. Corrie swiveled her head to look out the little window. She could see the back of a black coat—a man.

She quickly ran past Hennie, who was on the floor playing with two nylon dolls Corrie had made. Rarely did people come to their door, and on a Sunday, it might mean someone was coming bearing gifts.

It was a very tall man. He didn't ask to be let in but stepped through anyway, first having to lower his head to come through the tiny door. He took off his cap.

"Is your mother around?" He looked around.

"Mama is sick," Corrie offered, staring at him.

"Is Pietje Gelauf your brother?" He peered at her blonde braids.

"*Ja*," Corrie said, shyly.

"Can I speak to him? Is Pietje home?"

Corrie looked over at the stairs leading to the attic. There was suddenly a bang and shuffle, and Pietje, hair in his eyes, came racing down the steps.

He stopped midway and stared at the man.

"Pietje, you haven't been to school again, this time for over a month. I'm worried you will miss another year."

"I'm not going to school. Our mother is very sick, and our father was taken away as slave labor. I'm the man of the house now. I have to take care of everyone."

The man frowned. "You have another sister, yes?" He eyed Hennie on the floor, who watched everything that was going on.

"Beppie. She's still in bed."

The man nodded.

Corrie looked up at Pietje, curious.

Pietje pointed sideways at the man. "This is my teacher, *Meneer* van de Kolk. Well, he was my teacher."

"Where is your mother?"

Corrie turned to look at the bedstead in the wall. She couldn't see her mother's face but saw her chest rise and fall with each breath.

As *Meneer* van de Kolk stepped forward to the bedstead, Pietje and Corrie noticed a little wagon at the door covered in a black cloth. Pietje immediately stepped through the door and lifted the black fabric. There were two massive heads of cabbage.

Pietje looked back at her, surprised and joyful.

Corrie's eyes widened. She shook her head.

Pietje put his finger to his lips and smiled.

Corrie nodded silently, then turned and walked to the bedstead.

"*Mevrouw* Gelauf? I am *Meneer* van de Kolk, Pietje's teacher. I came to see why Pietje hasn't been at school, but I see that you are very ill."

Corrie stood beside the man and looked on as her mother tried to turn to face the teacher. The teacher put out a hand and held her mother's slender, pale hand, giving her some support as she turned on her side and then onto her back.

"*Mevrouw* Gelauf, have you been eating?"

Cornelia's hand pointed into the room past Corrie's head.

The teacher and Corrie turned to see where she was pointing. Pietje stood at the door facing them.

"I want to make sure he has enough. He's a growing boy, and he takes care of us. If he dies, we are lost," Cornelia whispered hoarsely.

"You need a doctor," announced the teacher. He stood up and gently put Cornelia's hand down. He put on his cap and stood in front of Pietje. "Pietje, I'm going to get a doctor." He put his hand on Pietje's shoulder. "We'll get her better. I'll be back later this afternoon, hopefully."

Pietje wordlessly nodded.

Corrie walked over and closed the door. They watched the teacher pick up the handle of the little wagon and trundle away.

Corrie looked over as Pietje bent down. From under a dropped coat under the coat hooks, he withdrew one giant cabbage.

"Accordion man!"

Henk heard it the first time but didn't take notice. The second time it was more urgent.

"Accordion man! *Halt*!"

He and the people around him stopped. Everyone stopped when they heard a German yell, *halt*.

Henk half expected a gun raised in his direction. Instead, he saw the same stocky German guard from that first night of his arrival. The man marched toward him.

"You are the accordion man. The one who cried at the music."

"*Ja*, I am."

The soldier looked at his mouth.

"I see you saw the dentist," he announced.

"*Ja*," Henk said, nodding sadly.

"You lost your handsome smile, I see."

"It's a good thing there isn't a lot to smile about here."

The German laughed. "You have a good sense of humor, crying Dutchman." He slapped a gloved hand on Henk's shoulder. "We try to avoid that dentist like the plague," he grimaced. "Come with me."

Wordlessly, Henk walked beside the guard, wondering where they were going. They followed along doubled metal fencing with reams and reams of barbwire. They walked under one of the watchtowers. Henk looked up as he passed underneath, half expecting the tip of the rifle that stuck out to point down at him. He gulped and moved on. Eventually, the guard led him into barracks he had never seen before. Inside, the air was fresh, with the top windows opened to circulate air. He panicked and stopped. He saw he was in the soldier's barracks, and the soldiers were everywhere. Some relaxed on their cots. Some stood. One shaving at a small mirror on a support beam. Every single one of them turned to look at him.

One was upset and yelled at the soldier. He yelled back, grabbed Henk's arm, and dragged him further into the barracks. There, he made him sit on a bench in the center of the large room. He went over to one of the walls between the bunks and came back with the accordion Henk had seen that first night.

The soldier helped Henk with the shoulder straps. Henk wordlessly allowed him. The guard patted him on the back. He stepped back and motioned to him. A few of the men in the barracks had gotten up and moved forward. "*Abspielen!*" He motioned Henk to play.

Henk shakily looked down at the smudged surface of the red accordion, searching to see if it was his. There was no nick. No scratches. Just dirt and smudges. He gently touched the piano keys and was suddenly aware of how dirty and roughened his hands and nails had become. He stared at them for a moment until tears welled in his eyes. He wished he did see a dent in the instrument. It would be his connection to home. His wife. His children. He suddenly remembered poor Pietje. How badly he treated Pietje. Beautiful Pietje with his huge thirst for life. Why did Pietje aggravate him so much? How could such a good boy, a good heart, have been so irritating to him? What was wrong with him, his father, that he couldn't love his only son. If only he could relive his life and do it right.

"See?" blurted the soldier. Henk opened his eyes to see the soldier motioning to all the others who gathered around. "He cries because he loves music. He cries just because he holds an accordion!"

"*Abspielen*! Play!" demanded one of the men, who held a cigarette and motioned toward him with a smile.

A Nazi smiling at him.

Slowly, he felt his fingers find their places, and as he relaxed into the instrument, he lay his head down, his right ear over the bellows, and began to play.

First, he played Tchaikovsky's 'Waltz of the Flowers.' As he lost himself in the music, he played better than he ever had in his entire life. He was transported back to happiness, safety, love, and comfort. He could see his children and his wife and imagined they sat in front of him, listening.

He did not pause after he finished. He kept his eyes closed and he immediately dove into Franz Liszt's 'Hungarian Rhapsody' No.2.

The soldiers stood with their eyes closed, smoking, motioning with their hands to the beat of the beautiful, mournful piece. As the notes swayed and jerked down, the men took on serious expressions. One had tears run down his cheeks.

When he finished, Henk could not breathe.

The men clapped. Someone slapped him on the shoulder.

"Dutchman, now you play, 'You're Too Fat for Me!" said a soldier excitedly. The men laughed.

Without a nod or wink, Henk immediately played the comical polka. Two of the younger men did a quick polka, and all sung the chorus with glee. Henk broke out in a sweat. It was just another part of the Bosch painting of a strange Hell.

The doctor stood up after examining Cornelia. He looked around at *Meneer* van de Kolk, Pietje, Beppie, and Corrie holding Hennie.

"I understand your father was taken as a worker to a slave camp," said the doctor sadly.

Pietje, Beppie, and Corrie nodded.

The doctor took out a pocket watch, looked at it, then slung it back in, just like their *Opa* did to his.

"Your mother has a kidney infection, a bladder infection, and is severely malnourished and anemic. I will send someone over with some medicine for your mother. You won't have to pay." He looked up at *Meneer* van der Kolk. "I'm glad you brought me here." He looked back at Cornelia before turning to Pietje. He continued, but with his voice lowered. "Your mother is not well; you know that."

They all nodded.

"I can see by looking around that you have all pitched in to help your mother."

"Not all of us," snapped Pietje.

Beppie pushed at him, then looked at the doctor apologetically.

"No matter, I'm sure you are all doing what you can."

"See," said Beppie, pushing at him once more. She looked over apologetically again and lowered her eyes to look at her feet. "Sorry."

"She needs to eat. You must feed her." He held up a plump, soft, and clean hand. "I realize the rations are barely enough to subsist on."

"*Meneer* brought over some eggs and gave her cognac earlier today," offered Pietje.

Meneer van de Kolk looked at Pietje and then at the doctor. He shrugged. "It's all I can do. I have some chickens."

"Whipped raw egg with a good dose of Cognac would certainly do anyone good," smiled the doctor. "Give her an egg and cognac, or any kind of alcohol, once a day for the next week.

Along with the medication, you should see a big improvement." He turned and stepped to the bedstead. "*Mevrouw* Gelauf, you will have medication, and *Meneer* van de Kolk will come with a whipped egg and cognac every day for the next week."

"*Heel erg bedankt, dokter*," croaked Cornelia.

"You're very welcome, *Mevrouw* Gelauf. You have good children." He patted her hand softly and turned. "Your mother needs to be given a soft, warm sponge bath every day." He looked down at Beppie. "I understand you take care of her? You have also stopped going to school?"

"No," offered Pietje. "She still goes to school. When it's open."

"*Ja*, it's difficult when there are always sirens going off," he said, sucking in his lips.

"*Ja*," said Beppie, shyly.

"Do you think you can do that for your mother?"

Beppie looked at him with wide, frightened eyes.

"I'll do it," offered Corrie.

The doctor looked at her closely. "How old are you?"

"I'm ten."

"What is your name?"

"She's Corrie," offered Pietje.

"Well, Corrie. You will make an excellent nurse one day."

Corrie squirmed with happiness at the compliment.

The doctor looked around. "My hat?"

Pietje, who had been holding the expensive hat, looked like he didn't want to let it go.

The doctor let *Meneer* van de Kolk open the door for him and stepped through as he put his hat back on. He, too, had to lower his head to clear the door frame.

Meneer van de Kolk turned and nodded. "I'll be back tomorrow with your mother's egg and cognac." He turned to go but stopped. "By the way, I came by with a wagon earlier and left it outside your door. You didn't happen to see anyone in the alley while I was here? Maybe one of the neighbors?"

Corrie's eyes widened, and she shook her head. She looked over at Pietje, who shrugged.

"I didn't see anybody," said Pietje, very innocently.

Meneer van de Kolk sighed. "A cabbage must have rolled off, or someone stole it while I was in town for a chore." He sighed again. "*Ja*, it's the times." With that, he continued down the alley. "I will be back tomorrow in the afternoon," he yelled back, as he started to walk away.

The sirens went off, and a familiar drone filled the air. Pietje and Corrie ran out in the alley to look up. *Meneer* van de Kolk hadn't left the lane as yet and ran back to them.

"You can't stay here. Come with me, to the bunker, over the bridge!"

Corrie could hardly hear Pietje even though he yelled as loud as he could as a bomb dropped with a massive 'oomph.' "We can't leave Mama! We're okay!"

Meneer van de Kolk stood wavering for a moment. He looked over at the roof of their little house. "If a bomb drops on your house, you will be obliterated to nothing!"

Pietje shrugged. Corrie reached over and held Pietje's hand.

Meneer van de Kolk waved them away with impatience. He hurried through the gate into the street.

Amid the blackness of sleep, he was shaken awake. He opened his eyes to see a young, skinny boy, his eyes wide and startled.

He frowned. "*Ja?*"

"You take things and come," he said, in a staccato voice in German.

Henk leaned onto his elbows. "What is it?"

The boy shook his head. It seemed to barely be supported on his long thin neck. "Come."

Henk got out of his bunk. He gathered what little things he had together and stood looking at the two blankets on the cot. The men around them coughed dryly. One hacked, and another farted. Henk looked around and then at the blankets again. "Do I take these?"

The pallid boy shook his head.

Along the way, Henk needed to stop at the general urinals. As he slowly awakened, he wondered if this new development was good or bad. He had aggravated his gums too much, and blood had gone down into his throat during his sleep. It made him nauseous. He felt miserable. Afterward, as he walked, he looked down at the poor child, who also looked sad. Henk used what little German he knew. "What's your name?"

"Lothar," he said.

"Where are you from, Lothar?"

"We lived in Cologne."

"Are your parents alive?" Henk needed to know.

The boy shook his head and lowered it as they continued walking. They passed one of the long double sets of barbed wire fencing, passing several guard towers. He happened to look up at one of them and was shocked to see that this time one of the guards did aim a gun at them as they passed. He couldn't take his eyes off the soldier. As they walked further, the guard put down the rifle and looked directly at him. Henk shivered as he continued to walk.

In the distance, he saw someone had hung wash on the fence. But that couldn't be true. The electrified barbed wire barrier meant certain death surely. As they walked further, they walked on dirt so worn that there was no sign of life, no weed, no grass, just hard, dried mud. Dust. Dirt. Death.

Henk's eyes stayed trained on the drying laundry. He focused harder on the rags as they neared and suddenly to his shock realized it was a human being hanging from the barbs. The man was skeletal, hanging upside down, his death-gaze down to the dust below him, his mouth agape.

Henk's empty stomach rebelled. He walked as far as he could toward one of the barracks but didn't make it. He retched, but nothing came out. There was nothing to come out. Just bile. Spittle. He wiped his mouth with his frayed sleeve and straightened up. The young boy stood watching sadly.

It was then that he realized the boy had a badge with a 'J.' He went over to him and shook his head as an apology. He looked back in the distance at large chimneys, spewing smoke and ash into the air. There was the smell of death around these barracks. Worse than where he stayed with the workers.

"The Nazis are starving you." He said softly, sadly, in Dutch. He stepped closer and held the boy. A lonely son with no father and mother. Without love. He landed in this Hell of Hells. He patted his bony back softly and stepped away. He wiped tears from his own eyes. "I have a son at home."

The boy looked at him. Then he looked over at the administration buildings in the distance.

Henk nodded and continued to walk. "Where are your barracks?"

The boy looked at him blankly.

"Where?" he asked in German.

The boy pointed to a series of barracks to the side.

Henk looked at them and nodded.

Suddenly, the skies above reverberated with a massive drone. Henk looked up and, in the distance, a large group of planes headed straight for the camp.

He and the boy stopped as did many in the camp. Henk's heart almost jumped out of his chest. He squinted at the sight. "Those are American bombers."

Lothar looked up at him, startled, perplexed. "American?" He scurried closer to Henk.

A prisoner ran past them and screamed in French. "We are saved. We are saved. They've come to bomb us!"

Hordes of people ran in every direction, all looking hopeful and excited.

Without any effect, the guards in the towers shot at the high-flying intruders. Then they shot randomly at the prisoners on the ground. Henk had to grab Lothar and drag him to one of the barracks when bullets started spraying around them.

No bombs fell. As everyone watched, the planes continued flying in formation to somewhere else in Poland or beyond.

Now, all knew that the Allies were undoubtedly gaining ground. A spirit of hope prevailed. But just for a little while.

Because hope in the camp was like a child born in the camp; it was immediately killed and gotten rid of amidst the horrors of this Hell.

Henk and Lothar entered the administration building and passed cubicles along a main hallway. The boy led him to a large office with an open door. Henk stepped in. There was a desk covered in papers and file folders. A portrait of Hitler hung on the wall behind the back cupboard. The chair looked battered. A Nazi flag sat resting in a vase. A large black glass ashtray had cigarette butts crammed into it, ash spilling over the corner of the desk.

Suddenly, boots marched down the hall, and the soldier who had demanded he play accordion walked in leading an officer.

"You are Hendricus Gelauf," announced the officer.

Henk watched as the officer took off his gloves and reached for his ashtray. He walked into the corner of the room and also grabbed a large brown wastebasket. He handed them to the guard, who left after nodding at Henk.

Henk opened his mouth, realizing he hadn't answered. "Yes, I am Hendricus Gelauf."

The officer sat in his chair and pulled it closer to the desk. "I understand you are a brilliant accordion player."

"Well, I play." Henk kept his eyes on the swastika on the officer's upper sleeve.

"Your talent is of value to us. We have decided to move you to another department. You will be driving dump trucks. Easier on your hands. Do you think you can do that?" He leaned back in his chair and took a cigarette out of a gold cigarette case in the middle drawer.

Henk saw a little box of matches. Intuitively, he reached over, lit a match, and bent over to light the officer's cigarette.

The officer looked at him, and then the match. He sat up straighter, leaning forward into the match slowly, keeping his grey eyes on Henk. He inhaled the smoke and slowly sat back.

"I understand you have a brother-in-law here in Birkenau. A Franciscus Riep."

Henk's heart skipped a beat. Two beats. His legs trembled.

"Yes," said Henk in surprise, his eyes burning.

"Well, this is what we are going to do. You are to move into the same barracks as your brother-in-law. You will work as a team. I will have the messenger take you to the other barracks. Your brother's partner dared to try and escape, you see. No one ever gets very far. Unfortunately," he said, as he swiveled in his chair, "we now lost a worker who was of benefit to us. We are overworked and do not have enough labor, both prisoner and volunteer, to carry the great weight of our work given to us by the Fuhrer."

Henk looked at Hitler's portrait before answering. "I am not a—," Henk began. And then remembered technically, he volunteered. He had offered himself up so as not to be shot through a floor.

"*Jongen!*" The officer barked.

Lothar hurried into the office, a frightened and startled look on his gaunt face.

"Take this man to the oven barracks."

Henk didn't understand the remainder of what he said.

The officer looked at him. "And you will play accordion for us at least two times a week for precisely one hour."

Henk shook. "Yes, sir." What could he say?

"Go!"

Henk turned and followed Lothar. He wanted so much to know more of the boy, of what he knew, of where they were going. But his understanding of German was not extensive, and this child knew no other language. As they traveled the length of the complex, they finally arrived at the furthest barracks. It was the first time Henk came so close to the ovens.

The ovens. The smell was almost unbearable.

Pushing the terror and smell aside, he focused on the joy of seeing and working with his brother-in-law. He was still alive, and that was the most crucial part. Intuitively, he knew that whatever happened from then on, they would either survive together or die together, he just couldn't foresee which.

Pietje ran in breathless. Corrie looked back. She was washing down her mother's arms with a cloth of warm water. Corrie heard the droning in the sky earlier, a droning that only increased as time ticked by, going on seemingly forever. The light coming through the little windows darkened as the sky filled with more and more planes overhead. The 'ack-ack-ack' of the anti-aircraft guns fired endlessly, and she had heard the odd plane's props squeal as one dropped down in the distance. Sirens had started to wail their warning, but everyone had by now learned to read whether bombs targeted them or just nearby. It was a gamble everyone was willing to take. The odds against a plane dropping on your house were pretty good.

Besides, Corrie couldn't go to a shelter. Not with her mother bedridden and having her little sister in her care.

"You should see this!" yelled Pietje.

"I don't have to. I know," said Corrie, her tone that of one wiser than her years. "They've been flying over us for over an hour."

"Yes, but guess what? I heard there are about seven thousand planes, and they're all bombing Germany."

"Did you get the bread?" asked Corrie. Pietje had been standing in line at the bakers for their ration of bread for the week.

"No, couldn't. The sirens went off."

Corrie panicked. "But we need our bread!"

Pietje held up his hand. "Wait. I have something even better," he said, smiling. From a big bag he was carrying, he pulled out a tart.

Her heart stopped. A tart! Corrie dropped the cloth in the bowl of water and rushed to Pietje. She put her nose to the tart and inhaled. "Mama, Pietje got us a tart!"

There was no answer from the bedstead.

Corrie ran back to the bedstead, and Pietje followed to show his mother. "Mama, Pietje got us a tart."

Cornelia stirred and looked from underneath her heavy lids. She seemed to have lost more weight. She tried to smile. "Pietje."

Corrie looked up at Pietje.

"Don't ask," he grinned sheepishly.

Henk climbed up into the truck and got behind the wheel. As Frans climbed up into the passenger seat, Henk saw thick white, grey dust all over the dash. Henk reached out and wiped some of it away. It was greasy between his fingers.

"There's no sense in cleaning that. It just gets covered again."

"You breathe this stuff in?" asked Henk. "All this dust?"

"That's not just dust," Frans said quietly.

Henk looked at the dash. Like a sloth, he slowly raised his hand to put the key into the ignition, but his hand shook far too much to be able to get it in. *Not just dust.*

Frans leaned over and put a hand over his. "Brother, hold fast."

Henk looked at him, suddenly feeling sick. Grievous.

"I hate to say it, Henk. But you'll get used to it and not think about it most of the time."

"I don't see how you can."

"You have to. Otherwise, you'll end up killing yourself. That's what the last guy did who drove this truck. He couldn't stand it anymore. It drove him crazy. Damaged. Lost. He ran off. They shot him. He wasn't trying to escape. He wanted to die." Frans' voice trailed off.

The sunshine increased in brightness through the dirty window. Henk turned and looked up into the morning sky. The sun was rising. *How does the planet keep turning, and the sun keep returning?*

Frans padded Henk's trembling leg. "Brace yourself, dear brother. Stay strong." He pointed behind him with his thumb.

Henk put the truck into reverse and backed up. Then, he creaked into first gear. Slowly they trundled over the beaten earth, scarred by the ravages of rain and snow. Ruts as deep as his knees dug by various vehicles. He steered around the worst of the pits and grooves. He saw another truck coming from a different direction going their way. "Where are we going?"

"I will show you. When we get there, you stay in the truck. Drivers stay. I will work with another to load the truck."

Henk didn't ask. He didn't dare because the answer may be what he feared. "Okay," he said, as he continued following a beaten road toward the back of one of the large crematoriums. The closer they got, the more ash fell on the vehicle. Henk made sure his window was tightly shut. Then he gripped at the wheel as it shivered and shook with the rest of the truck. Henk's journey was now heavy with endless horror hugging the edges of his awareness as they drove. He looked over at Frans and studied his profile as much as he could. There were new lines in Frans' face. He looked gaunt, and his eyes were weary. What kept him going? What has he seen? Henk tore his eyes away and looked at the road ahead of them. He wondered if God was looking down at what they were doing. Henk wondered if God had left them in disgust. Tears ran down his cheeks. He thought, perhaps they were not his usual tears.

The tears were his soul grieving for all humanity.

Chapter 18
June 1944

Fewer civilians filled the streets. But more soldiers, SS, officers, officials, trucks, jeeps, motorcycles, and anti-aircraft guns took their place. Nazi collaborators and soldiers rounded up all gypsies and the homeless, including those who escaped devastation and destruction and had nowhere else to go. Lord knew what their fate was. Most able men were gone. Women and old men were left to protect each other and the few children left behind as best they could. Sometimes, the other way around, children protected their loved ones as best they could.

Corrie and Pietje Gelauf became adept at their nightly rounds of scrounging. Dark walls and deep ditches offered cover. They hid in bushes and behind cars and trucks.

On this particular night, they took Beppie along. For a change, Pietje took along an ax. They needed fuel for the stove to cook what little food they had. The burner was of no use to them anymore. There was no money for petroleum. So Pietje decided they should walk along the canal up Koningskade past Bezuidenhout to the Haagse Bos, where they would surely find more wood than they could carry between the three of them.

Haagse Bos was a perfect little forest in the center of The Hague, but it had been heavily mined by the Nazis, who used it as a hiding spot for some of their anti-aircraft guns. But it offered branches and bark to burn and they were determined to grab what they could safely find. Pietje hid the ax under his arm while Corrie carried a burlap bag. School had finished for the summer, so Pietje insisted that Beppie come along. She argued and resisted, but a weak plea from their mother made her realize that the more hands available, the better the results.

The night was darker than usual but, once they were out, their eyes adjusted, and they could make out the different hues of the cobblestoned streets, the surface of the water in the canals, and the edges of the roads. Corrie was concerned that Beppie would not be able to be quiet, and felt more on edge than usual. Corrie jumped at each stone Beppie accidentally kicked, or each loud footstep that echoed through the night. At one point, Corrie grabbed Beppie and pinched her hard on her arm. Beppie squealed. Pietje had to stop and take Beppie to the side. He had a long-whispered conversation with her before they continued further. After the talk, Beppie was a little more careful.

"What did you say to her?" whispered Corrie.

Pietje leaned over. "I told her if the *moffen* caught her, they would beat her to a pulp."

"But she knew that already."

"Yes, but I also said, if they didn't, I would."

Corrie looked back at Beppie and saw her sulk. She sighed, then focused on their journey from bush to bush, wall to wall, shadow to shadow.

As they approached the side of the Haagse Bos, Corrie could make out the sign that warned trespassers not to enter. Corrie knew there were mines, but they also learned there were safe spots to tread. There were areas in the center of the forest reserved for where the *moffen* hid anti-aircraft guns.

They made their way along a dirt track created by constant traffic by Nazi soldiers and their vehicles. They carefully walked within the tire marks. Corrie kept her eye on Pietje's back as well as where her feet landed. When she saw a branch, she picked it up and tried very hard not to snap it as she put it in the bag.

Pietje stopped and held up his hand. Corrie had to look at him with her eyes as open as possible to see him. Their clothing was dark-colored, and she could only see Pietje's blond head and the movement of his hands. Especially if she looked just to the side of him. She found she could see more in her peripheral vision.

Corrie stopped and raised her hand to Beppie.

They watched Pietje step into the dark bushes. They heard him rustling in the leaves. Slowly, Corrie saw Pietje climbing from one mature limb to the other on one of the closest trees. He started to chop at the branch, making a racket.

Corrie looked around like a frightened little bird.

Pietje stopped chopping, to listen. He motioned them to come closer. Beppie had read the warning sign about mines and refused to move from where she was. Corrie swallowed and remembered the path he took. Carefully, in her bare feet, she stepped onto dry flat earth. If Corrie felt taller grass against her feet, she would move her feet until she felt flat surface again. She stopped ten steps away from Pietje, looked around, and listened carefully.

"It's okay. Just pick up the small branches that I'm chopping off." He whispered.

"What about the noise you're making?" Corrie whispered back.

"It will take a while for them to figure out where the noise is coming from." Pietje chopped again, and more branches fell.

As she picked up large pieces of dry bark first, Corrie felt the earth rumble through her bare feet. She straightened up and listened. She heard heavy machinery approaching. Corrie jumped up and down, waving her arms to get Pietje's attention. He didn't look up to see. She rushed to the tree and started to climb the branches. She tore a long branch off a limb and slapped it on Pietje's feet. He suddenly stopped chopping. She didn't have to say a thing. He heard it right away.

Quickly he scrambled down, leaving the ax embedded into the wood, and waited for Corrie to jump down the last stretch before he did. They ran to the edge of the forest and grabbed Beppie. They threw her down into the thicket, and hid by covering themselves with branches.

They lay on their stomachs and watched, staring into the darkness. They heard the engines come closer and closer.

Finally, around a bend, they saw a faint light approach, followed by a line of military vehicles. One crawled along on massive caterpillar wheels towing a large bed with the largest mysterious object they had ever seen. It looked more like a giant rocket ship painted with a large checkerboard pattern.

"That's a missile!" Pietje whispered. "I bet it can shoot to England!"

Corrie looked closer at the missile. Her heart pounded against the ground beneath her.

The vehicles and missile finally passed, and the last to approach were soldiers on foot. Corrie could see the burning tips of cigarettes they were smoking. She watched the polished jackboots pass. Her eyes followed the journey a tossed cigarette made, flipping into the air, landing on the road, then bouncing into the edge of the grass. Her eyes were glued to the cigarette until all passed and disappeared into the darker depth of the forest.

Corrie heard Beppie cry. She put her hand out and patted her on the back.

Finally, Pietje scrambled from out of the thicket and helped his sisters to their feet.

Corrie bent down and picked up the smoldering cigarette. She pinched its burning end and stuck it in her pocket. She followed Pietje back to the tree and collected more harvested branches and bark. Once they filled all three bags, they headed home.

Corrie realized they had left the ax behind in the tree. "Pietje," she whispered earnestly, "the ax!"

Pietje froze. Corrie knew they needed that ax. All three stood still listening to the ongoing activity further up the track.

Pietje dropped his bag and took two steps back when suddenly the land rocked beneath them, and something exploded further in the woods. Above them, a fiery heavy rocket shot up and up into the blackness of the night. Its mighty burning tail lit its way high into the night sky, painting the low-hanging clouds a fiery red and orange. Its tail was ferocious, gaining speed as it climbed.

Pietje, Corrie, and Beppie huddled together and watched the mighty V2 rocket cut its course to London, England. Corrie suddenly wanted to leave.

It was much too dangerous in the Haagse Bos. They eagerly hurried back home.

They forgot all about the ax in the tree.

"The Allies have landed in Normandy," Frans excitedly told Henk.

Henk, quietly distraught, looked up from where he was brooding in his bunk. Frans had left to use the lavatory and on the way back picked up more news from the gossip chain.

"You're kidding!" Henk couldn't believe it. "Is that possible?"

Normandy was still a very long distance from Auschwitz, but it was closer to The Hague. The Allies had crossed the North Channel!

"What else did you hear?" Henk distractedly picked at a scab on his elbow.

"The Germans have created a missile that can cross the North Sea. The V2 Rocket can clear reach London. They're beating the Brits on the head with more force than ever."

Henk felt dizzy with emotion. The last month had been especially hard. The Nazis reassigned him to driving a dump truck as part of a massive excavation at the end of Birkenau. It wasn't until they completed an elongated and enormous crater in the surrounding land that he discovered its significance. He was one of several truck drivers assigned to cart the dead directly from the gas chambers and deliver them to this newly-allocated mass gravesite.

When he realized what he had dumped into the massive crevice that first time, he almost lost his mind. They gassed up to 4,000 people a day. They had more than that coming, and the Wehrmacht killing machine had hit a bottleneck. As a result, their new assignment was to take away many of the gassed bodies to mass graves, to offset the growing mountain of bodies waiting for cremation at the ovens.

Henk sat sobbing behind the wheel many times after backing up against the edge of the dug crevices so others could unload his cargo. He was not to help unload. His orders were to stay in the truck at all times. In the side mirror, he would occasionally see Frans and the assigned prison slaves pull off and throw bodies into the gaping wound in the earth.

Frans had kept him sane. "They will shoot you, Henk. It doesn't matter that you're not a prisoner. As soon as you're of no use to them, they're finished with you."

Henk rubbed his face hard. *How many times did I cry silently to Heaven? Where was God in all of this? Did the Devil completely take over?*

At times, he looked over at a guard, who stood with his rifle ready, always pointing down. The guard might be smoking a cigarette or have his hands clasped in front of him as he stood and watched. Once he saw him smile and take photographs.

And the smell.

The smell was unbearable. The entire camp was marinated with the scent of death. It was in his nostrils, his sinuses, his ear canals. His clothing. His gums. It was everywhere he went.

Eventually, he learned it helped to close his eyes and imagine playing the accordion. Note for note he would play, the lyrics echoing in his head along with the memory of voices sung by his family. He tried to remember every celebration he'd played at over the years. He relived them over and over again until he finally lost sense of which world was real.

One day, while playing for the soldiers at their barracks, without thinking, he played a sad and brooding version of Toccata and Fugue in D Minor. It reflected the blackness of the death camp and the ongoing nightmare torturing his soul. He was shocked back to reality when a soldier tapped him roughly on the shoulder, telling him to stop playing depressing music. The soldier pronounced they worked far too hard in this godforsaken place to have to listen to such garbage in their free time. "Play the Happy Wanderer," he demanded.

Henk had trouble shaking himself out of his trance.

The soldier started singing the lyrics.

> *"I love to go a-wandering,*
> *Along the mountain track.*
> *And as I go, I love to sing,*
> *My knapsack on my back.*

A few of the other soldiers joined in.

> *Val-deri, val-dera,*
> *Val-deri, val-dera,*
> *Ha, ha, ha, ha, ha, ha,*
> *Val-deri, val-dera,*
> *My knapsack on my back."*

The soldier stood and pushed Henk's shoulder, almost making him lose his balance and fall backward. Then he reached out to take the accordion from Henk, and without thinking, Henk violently knocked his hand back. For a moment, he forgot it wasn't his accordion.

The soldier sneered at him, then looked over at the squat one who had arranged the twice-weekly entertainment, for an explanation. He held his arms out in surprise.

The squat one stood up and walked up to Henk. "Gelauf, you must play what we want. It is one of the main reasons we appreciate your presence here."

Henk slowly turned and looked at the guard's eyes with red-hot eyes. He couldn't see through the tears. But the guard kept a steely lock on his gaze. Henk knew he had to give in. If he continued like this, he could end up imprisoned, or worse, dead.

Slowly, Henk forced himself to the surface, adjusted the accordion straps, gathered his head together for a moment longer, and took a deep breath. He smiled wanly at the soldier who had complained. "*Entshuldigen Sie mich,*" Henk whispered with trembling lips. Bravely, he played the Happy Wanderer. Eventually, the soldiers relaxed, and Henk sensed they were able to shake off his brief inability to maintain decorum. Relieved, they began to enjoy themselves. But Henk knew that everyone was aware of the fact that he was very close to an emotional and mental breakdown.

It was just a matter of time.

Henk rocked back and forth, and played with his eyes closed. He saw Cornelia in his mind's eye. He also saw little Corrie's beautiful smile. Beppie's serious but adorable face. Hennie, who must surely be walking and talking by now, and finally, his beloved, precious son. Pietje. Before he knew it, he was smiling at their images. His smile made him feel good. It took root in his soul, and it thirsted to remain, regardless of what was going on. The act of smiling became both a form of medicine and an act of rebellion at the same time. It helped to fool his body and soul that all was tolerable. All was just a figment of his imagination. Everything wasn't real anyway. So why fuss? And the soldiers? They didn't question the smile.

From that day forward, the smile never left his face in the presence of the Nazis. Henk had finally discovered a form of a shield, a mask that helped protect him. It kept his soul separated from 'them' and their reality.

He grinned whenever he played, and that smile lulled the soldiers into only hearing and enjoying the music. They no longer judged him, studied him, saw him as a possible threat. They no longer needed to feel uncomfortable when reminded of their victim's discomfort. His smile made them think Henk enjoyed playing for them. The thought eased their minds. Without them realizing, they allowed Henk full control over their emotions. The magic of his music pulled them this way and that in their hearts. They, too, felt sadness at being away from loved ones. They also felt transported through his heavenly chords and notes. They, too, forgot the Hell they had a personal role in making. They didn't even realize he chose the mood they would experience. He decided the sad and happy, the raucous, and the transcending. They lapped it up.

He played God.

For one hour, twice a week.

Corrie looked down at the greasy surface of the rainbow oily waters of the canal. She was thinking of her birthday coming up in a couple of months. A brand-new ribbon for her hair was her most ardent wish. She surely was too old for the massive bows she used to wear, but it would be nice to have a more slender, lavender satin ribbon to tie at the end of each braid. She leaned over the edge of the canal to see if she could see her reflection. She could just see the top of her head before feeling dangerously close to falling in. She looked down around her bare feet at the stones and picked up a pebble. It was a brilliantly, sunny day, and the waters sparkled happily in the reflection of the afternoon sun. She felt the weight of the stone in her hand and aimed it into the middle of thousands of tiny bursts of light. For the hundredth time, her stomach cramped terribly. She ignored it. As she was about to toss another stone, she heard a shattering of glass behind her.

She twisted around in time to see boys, a little older than her, climbing through a broken storefront window. Propelled by the need for excitement, distraction, and, most importantly of all, hunger, children from all directions quickly migrated toward the store. Approximately fifteen children climbed over the broken glass to steal whatever their hands could touch.

Corrie choked and shrieked in surprise. She raced barefoot toward the manic crowd without a thought of danger.

She scrambled over others to get into the store. She wasn't aware of a store-keeper or guard, for it did not matter to her in the least. As soon as she landed inside the store, she eyed a large round, heavy wheel of Gouda cheese. With all her might, she grabbed it and scrambled out before anyone could take it away from her. On the way out, she spied rolls of grey toilet paper scattered on the pavement in front of the store and scooped one up into her other arm. As she ran to the canal's edge toward the bridge, shots rang out.

The sound of guns quickened her pace, and her legs carried her as fast as humanly possible. A bullet hit a boy next to her in the back. Corrie jumped sideways in horror, and the wheel of cheese suddenly slipped from her grasp. As she continued to run for her life, the Gouda cheese rolled ahead of her. It wobbled and bounced over the cobblestones heading straight for the edge of the canal. With a heavy plop, it fell into the waters of the canal.

She cried. She cried all the way home, back to the alley off Spinozastraat.

She bawled as she ran through the gate and into the house.

Cornelia was sitting up with a blanket over her shoulders, rolling cigarettes as a cigarette dangled from between her brown teeth.

"Mama, someone broke the window at the *moffen's* storage depot, and we all went in to get stuff," she cried, "And they shot at me!

Her mother looked at her quizzically, then held out her arms.

Corrie ran into them and cried on her bony shoulder. Her body shook violently from shock and painful disappointment. After a moment, Cornelia pushed her away slightly to look at what she was carrying in her hands. "What do you have there?"

Corrie held up the toilet paper. "But I had a whole wheel of Gouda cheese. I dropped it when they shot at me, and it fell and rolled into the canal."

"Ach, what a waste. Corrie, why didn't you drop the toilet paper instead of the cheese?"

Corrie wiped her eyes and nose with her frayed sleeve. She stared at her mother.

"And what is that?" her mother asked.

Corrie looked at the floor to where her mother pointed. She saw a trail of blood leading from the door to the table. Corrie lifted a foot and looked at the bottom of her sole. She saw that she'd cut her feet with glass.

"I didn't feel it."

"Better glass than a bullet, *ja*?" said her mother, weakly. She let go of Corrie, put her cigarette in an overflowing ashtray, and stood up. She shuffled to the kitchen corner in her bare feet. She stopped to catch her breath. Corrie looked on, holding her one foot so as not to bleed on the floor. They had sold the rug long ago, so it was just the wood that would stain, and she wasn't anxious about it. There were far more critical things to consider. But then she did a double-take. Looking down, she realized blood was pooling and dripping through the cracks of the hole in the floor.

The accordion case!

She got down on her hands and knees and tried to get a hold of the hatch cover.

Her mother came back with an enamel wash bin and a cloth. "Corrie, what are you doing?"

"Mama, I think the blood is dripping on the accordion case under the floor. I can't get the hatch cover loose. It's too heavy!"

Pietje suddenly burst through the door. "Mama, kids, took over a store, and the *moffen* shot at them!" He stopped suddenly, seeing his sister with bloody feet and on her knees under the table.

"I can't get the top up!" Corrie cried. "I think I'm bleeding on the accordion!"

Pietje ran forward and lifted the lid with a grunt. He pushed the table aside for more room. They both looked down onto the top of the accordion case. Indeed. There was blood.

"Oh, no!" With a gasp, Corrie grabbed a cloth on the table and leaned down to rub the blood off the cover. It spread the stain even more. She began to cry.

"Don't worry, Corrie. It couldn't be helped." Pietje pulled her back gently and replaced the hatchway cover.

"*Ja*, but I don't want anything to happen to Pappa. It would be my fault!" She cried anew.

"No, Corrie. It doesn't mean that at all. We still have it, do we not? Pappa will come back."

Corrie stopped crying and wiped her face with her sleeve. "*Ja*, but maybe it means he'll be hurt. He'll be bleeding."

"Come, sit on the chair and put your feet in the basin." Pietje helped her sit. "Swish your foot around a little," he added.

Corrie swished the foot around. The blood swirled and mixed in with the water.

"Your sister was there at that store," said Cornelia, holding up the toilet paper.

Pietje's eyes widened before sitting down on the other battered kitchen chair. He looked at Corrie's foot in the rosy red water.

"They could've killed you!" He sadly eyed his sister.

Corrie looked down. "I almost had a wheel of Gouda cheese."

Pietje sat for a moment, looking from her face to her foot. "Well, the *moffen* got one of you—a boy my age. I don't know him. The *moffen* made him write on the wall with his own blood. He had to write that he was a thief."

Corrie looked up, shocked.

"Then the *moffen* shot him dead. He's there now, lying on the pavement. They're leaving him there to teach us all a lesson." He looked at her foot again. He motioned for the rag and carefully lifted Corrie's foot. He placed it on his knee. It was still bleeding slightly. He wiped off her foot, making her wince. Then he looked up at her. "You want to come and see?" He was sad. Remorseful.

Childlike curiosity always wins out. Corrie nodded.

Pietje tied the cloth around her foot with a knot, then stood up and motioned her to climb up on his back. He bounced her to adjust her weight more comfortably, then he carried her to the door. Corrie leaned forward to open it for them.

"Don't go, children." Cornelia slowly lowered herself into a chair, reaching out with an emaciated arm. "It's too dangerous."

"It's okay, Mama. Lots of people are there. We'll be right back."

Pietje took Corrie back to where the boy lay in his blood, surrounded by a sizeable curious crowd. They made their way through the crowd and abruptly stopped. Pietje didn't want to be so close as to stand in the boy's pool of blood. They almost stepped in it. He stood back a few inches and remained standing with Corrie on his back, both staring at the lifeless boy who lay on his side with his eyes slightly open.

"They're coming!" yelled Beppie breathless as she ran into the house. "Mama! Mama! The war is over!"

Corrie was shredding sugar beets into a bowl. She looked up. "Who's coming?"

"The Allies! Someone said they freed Belgium! Next, they'll free us! We're going to be free of the *moffen*!"

Corrie looked back at the bedstead. Her mother had a turn for the worse, and Corrie had lain Hennie beside her for her afternoon nap, hoping it would keep her mother's state of mind buoyed somewhat. Corrie was excited but confused. Is it possible that all of this was over? She got up out of her chair and wiped the front of her clothes, which hung on her skinny frame. She had found a hemp rope and tied it around her middle to help stave off the pangs of hunger.

Outside, somewhere on the streets, people cheered.

Corrie ran to the door and out into the alley. She stopped. Yes, happy sounds. Freedom! She ran out of the gate and into the street. Toward the bridge, she saw people waving little orange flags. Someone had hung a red, white, and blue flag out their window in one of the tall ancient town homes.

She ran back to her mother's side. She shook her mother and noticed her eyes were open. She shook her again, hoping to get her mother's attention, but her mother remained mute. Corrie stood back a few inches, observing, willing her mother to breathe. Yes, there was movement. She again leaned over her mother. "Mama, the war is over!"

Without blinking, her mother raised one quivering arm. Crepe skin hung off the bone as she pointed to the low ceiling of the bedstead. "Look." Her voice was nothing but a raspy whisper. "I see angels. I see them."

"Don't die, Mama! No more war!"

"No more war," her mother whispered.

Corrie left her mother and little sister and ran back out. She and Beppie excitedly raced out of the alley toward the city center. They wanted to be there when the Allies finally marched down the streets.

As they approached one of the main squares, they witnessed an exodus of officials, some *moffen*, and Dutch and German Nazis in their uniforms and badges. They were running away like rats from a sinking ship, Corrie thought.

Suddenly, a machine gun fired into the crowds. Then a rifle shot ripped the air. Corrie saw people falling, some dead, some wounded. People screamed.

They looked from behind one of the few cars left on the street. They saw people, young and old, firing with guns at the *moffen*. "The Resistance!" yelled Beppie over the tumultuous concerto of gunshots.

Corrie looked at the bridge. "Let's go back!" Without another thought, they jumped up and headed for the bridge.

It wasn't until later they learned that the Allies had indeed liberated part of Belgium and Holland, but something went wrong, and they stopped and retreated across the Rhine.

And there they stayed.

No one had liberated them. In the course of the battle, the *moffen* destroyed the dikes and flooded the lower parts of the country to slow down the Allies.

Pietje later told them that the *Koningin* encouraged the Dutch to rise and strike. No more trains, buses, deliveries, utilities. Squeeze the *moffen* out of Holland! And they did. Over 25,000 people went on strike, according to Pietje. As a result, the *moffen* dug in again, bombed the city of Eindhoven as punishment, and blew up all remaining bridges and railways into The Hague.

They shut off the gas, and very soon, there was no water. All shipments of food and what meager supplies the general folk relied on for survival were blocked.

Absolutely and thoroughly blocked.

Corrie was about to face the worse part of the entire war because the Germans had no intention of ever letting anything come into The Hague. The Nazis were starving the people to a slow death as punishment for their insubordination.

The woman who moved into the Aaronsons' home discovered that her husband had died at a work camp in Germany. They heard her crying and moaning for days.

Suddenly, there was a real possibility that the reason they hadn't heard from their father in over a year was that he, too, had been dead all this time.

Corrie's grief was unbearable. In her childlike, superstitious way, she blamed it on the stain of blood she caused on the accordion case. But there was also the possibility they angered God by not going to church. As well, Pietje did that unforgivable sin of pouring ink into holy water. Everywhere she looked, everything she thought about, pointed to reasons why it was their fault that her father was dead. It seemed that between she and Pietje, they did a bang-up job of guaranteeing the end of their father's life

Ironically, within a few weeks, the local churches combined their resources to provide relief to the children from starving in this Hell. They arranged for a mass exodus of children from the city to temporary foster homes and shelters where food and a safe roof could be provided. But Corrie, little Hennie, Pietje, and Beppie could not leave their mother behind, for she would undoubtedly die without them. For once, the church could help. But they were in no position to accept it.

They had no choice. While many children left the city, the Gelauf siblings stayed behind.

They were left to face a slow but sure death.

Chapter 19
November 1944

It had been two and a half months since all food and supplies were cut off from the rest of the world. The Hague became an isolated, besieged city. Hunger, already a constant companion to its long-suffering citizens, became an obsession that regulated their days and nights. Many suffered to the same extent as their neighbors, but there were small little back neighborhoods where, without men and money, its citizens were hit the worst.

Just off Spinozastraat, three children—three shapeless forms—shifted between garbage bins behind the whores' houses in the pitch black of night. Like quiet skinny rats, they foraged bent over banged-up, metal garbage bins, or on their haunches, desperately searching for anything to consume on the ground. Cold, filthy fingers stretched out and caressed potato peels, carrot scrapings, wilted beet greens, a bone perhaps for soup, a greasy newspaper for the fire.

Water was also hard to come by. It was a precious commodity they could never find in garbage bins. Every castaway pot or tin potentially held little pools of precious water. Drips collected here and there in an old milk bottle offered hope for surviving these strange, horrific times. For a city slashed by canals and snuggled against the North Sea, people were dying of thirst and dehydration.

Corrie, her thin, delicate face covered in grime, lifted her sunken eyes and listened intently. She froze. She looked over at

Beppie, wearing a torn oversized man's coat. Corrie clicked her tongue, and Beppie looked back. Beppie reached out to touch Pietje's back to gain his attention. Pietje shifted on his haunches to look at Corrie. Corrie lifted a grimy finger and widened her eyes. All three froze and listened.

Jackboots marched nearby. The echo of their heels sounded muffled, and Corrie could tell the patrolling *moffen* were crossing over the rebuilt bridge. Unfortunately, toward Spinozastraat. It meant they'd have to stay where they were for a little longer.

Corrie had turned ten. Beppie was twelve and Pietje, fourteen. Together they kept their mother alive by coaxing her to share roasted peels, a morsel of old bread. But Cornelia, though bedridden for the most part, still smoked, claiming it staved off the feelings of hunger. The harvest of cigarette butts was always more abundant than any food they could scrounge or steal for their stomachs.

Corrie fiddled with a large black button that hung by a thread off her coat. It was her mother's coat. Her mother lay in the house for a year, and it would be a while before she was well enough to go outside. The weather had turned for the worst, and they expected a frigid winter. Corrie had no other option but to wear her mother's things to keep warm.

The sound of jackboots passed them along Spinozastraat and sounded as if they turned off at Van der Duynstraat before reaching their laneway. Corrie relaxed. It meant that they wouldn't be coming back this way for the rest of the night.

She shivered in her coat. Her dirty and sore bare legs froze, and her toes felt like ice despite the torn material she had wrapped around them. Even these pieces of cloth were tattered and worn from walking the cobblestones.

Corrie had managed to gather together enough little treasures to wrap into a rag she brought along. She stuffed the bundle into her coat. She wiped her runny nose with her coat sleeve and shuffled to the end of the back lane. She stood up and leaned against the end back wall of the series of red light courtyards.

She rubbed her hands together for warmth and listened to the rustlings of her brother and sister coming closer. As she shivered and looked into the darkness, she thought of Rebecca. She missed her terribly. The memory of her startled face and the wave goodbye was consistently at the forefront of her mind.

She scrunched up her toes and wished Beppie and Pietje would hurry. They had an early morning the next day. They planned to be one of the first in line at the new mobile central soup kitchen opening the following day near one of the hospitals. It was a twenty-block walk. Rumor had it that it was going to be a sweet meaty broth with vegetables and maybe even some vermicelli noodles. Lovely black crusty bread would surely be an addition to the meal. Corrie's stomach rumbled and hurt acutely. She bent over the pain and panted.

She looked up at the sound of bullets firing in the distance. Dutch Resistance had stepped up their activities by murdering *moffen* or sabotaging their *ack-acks*. But there was always gruesome retribution. The SS had recently shot 29 people dead because the Resistance had attacked and destroyed one of their facilities.

Something else caught her attention. She turned and saw a bright orange, red glow over the housetops. Something caught fire, and she wondered what that was. She sniffed the air and felt the acrid smoke through her nostrils.

She jumped when Pietje and Beppie suddenly appeared around the corner.

Pietje put a finger to his lips and nodded. All three looked around before they quickly crossed Spinozastraat and slipped back into their lane.

Quietly, Pietje opened the door into the house. Only candlelight softly glowed through the closed curtains of the bedstead. Electricity had stopped running in their city a while ago, so they now relied heavily on candles: another scarce commodity and something to forage.

Corrie took off her coat and hung it over the back of one of the chairs at the little table. There no longer were coat hooks.

Pietje had torn down two walls to burn including the one with the hooks.

Corrie hurried to the stove and held her dirty hands close to its warm surface. She shivered and dreamed of the soup they would be getting in the morning.

She turned at the sight of reflected flickering on the wall over the stove.

Pietje had pulled back the bedstead curtain. "*Dag*, Mama, how are you?"

Corrie only heard indecipherable whispered words from her mother. She watched as Pietje leaned in and helped their mother out.

Cornelia had lost more weight if that were possible. She was a grey skeleton with a mop of brown hair on top, her nightgown so loose that her breastplate was exposed. Cornelia slowly moved her legs, which were sticks with bony knees. Slowly she slid off the side of the mattress and seemed to calculate the strength she needed to find her balance before standing up with the help of Pietje.

Pietje looked over at Corrie, and she knew right away what to do. She walked over, smiled at her mother, and held her by the middle. Corrie was still small, but she noticed her mother kept shrinking in size. She was like a little bird in Corrie's hands. Carefully Corrie helped her to the dark water closet and helped her mother to find the hole in the dark. Corrie stepped out and looked around the room as she waited.

In addition to the missing two inner walls, they had burned the trim around the door and windows. The wind whistled through the cracks during bad early winter nights, so Pietje stuffed more newspaper and bits of rabbit fur into the holes along the edges of the windows and door. Corrie seriously wondered if they had enough house to burn to survive the winter. She took inventory, two walls, a kitchen counter, and shelves. She looked down at the scuffed floor. The floor could burn if needed. But surely, by next spring, they would have collected enough branches, garbage, wood to help stretch what wood the house provided.

Her eyes filled with tears. She wavered as she stood, watching Pietje take his bundle, Beppie's and hers, and place them on the little table. Beppie eagerly moved beside Pietje and cast her hungry eyes on the booty. Corrie stayed put near the water closet but watched, expectantly, as Pietje unrolled the bundles. He organized the found bounty in separate piles. He placed potato peel with potato peel, the newspaper with newspaper on the floor, a green crust of hard bread off to the side.

Her mother stirred behind her. She turned and rearranged her mother's nightgown and allowed her to lean on her shoulder back to the bedstead. When they reached it, three-year-old Hennie popped her little head from the depths of the bedstead. Hennie, her long messy blonde curls in disarray, pushed herself to a sitting position and watched with dewy eyes as her mother struggled to get back into the bedstead with Corrie's help.

Cornelia stopped and coughed weakly. Twice. Raspy. Then she settled under the woolen blanket. Corrie straightened out the bedclothes and padded the edge of the mattress. Little Hennie climbed over her mother's body and allowed Corrie to lift her out of the bedstead. Corrie hugged her tightly.

The eggs and cognac stopped a while ago. Their mother had improved enough to sit at the table, rolling cigarettes again. She even mended the odd piece of clothing. But then, one day, *Meneer* van der Kolk no longer came. Strafing from a plane blew his head off.

"*WC,*" Hennie demanded, squirming in Corrie's arms.

Corrie took little Hennie to the water closet for her last pee before going up to the attic to sleep. Wordlessly, she took one final look at the spoils and hesitated close to the table.

Pietje held up the crust of bread and gave it to Corrie.

"What are you giving that to Corrie for?" demanded Beppie. Beppie reached out and took it from Corrie's hand.

"That's for Hennie," retorted Piet. He went to take it from her, but she popped it into her mouth. Pietje slapped her across the head.

Beppie squealed, spitting bits of bread. As she cowered, she pushed the food back into her mouth and frantically chewed. She had trouble swallowing the dry bread. She coughed while her mouth remained clamped shut.

Hennie began to cry. Corrie hummed in her ear until she stopped. She watched as Beppie suddenly ran past and stomped up the stairs. She heard her pounding on the floor above their heads as she plopped herself onto the shared bed up in the attic. Dust trickled down from the ceiling. Corrie looked back to see what Pietje was doing.

Pietje had taken another little morsel of green bread. He held it up to her. She took it and eyed it carefully in the flickering light of the stove. She put Hennie down and carefully crumbled bits away from the green part, breaking off a tiny piece. She gave it to Hennie. Then she swallowed the other little lump. She had trouble swallowing it down, choked a little, and coughed.

They badly needed water. The laundry tub sat outside, ready to catch rain and dew that ran off the clay shingles of the roof. But they used the last of the water just before they left to forage. They would have to wait until morning when the sun rose and water in the air condensed on the clay shingles again. That is, if the temperature was right.

Before going upstairs, she turned to see Pietje put a ball of newspaper into the stove. She watched the flames briefly grow and flicker. Paper made such beautiful flames but little lasting heat. Ah, well, watching a warm glow, however long or short, was comforting to the soul.

Pietje turned and saw Corrie. He held up a finger to stop her, pulled his sleeves over his hands, and took a brick off the stove. Pietje motioned for her to go up, and he'd follow.

Wordlessly, they slowly climbed the rickety winding staircase. The boards under their feet creaked and popped loudly. Beppie had fallen asleep on top of the covers, keeping the oversized coat on.

Pietje pulled at the blankets, causing Beppie to stir.

"Bep, get up. Get under the blanket."

Beppie, upset, kept her eyes closed and rolled off the edge of the mattress. She waited for Pietje to throw back the cover, then she climbed back in at the farthest end.

Pietje put the brick down at the foot of the bed under the blanket and helped Corrie put Hennie to bed. Hennie faced Beppie's back lying on her side. She dutifully waited for Corrie to climb in. Corrie allowed Pietje to cover her.

"I'll wake you up at five." Pietje went back down the staircase. He no longer slept in the attic. He preferred to be near his mother and keep the furnace burning. He slept on the floor on another blanket and a pile of what clothing they had.

In the dark, Cornelia heard a neighbor softly call for her cat. Corrie knew that the cat would never come back. Even the butchers were selling cat carcasses under the guise as rabbits. Without the head, and fully skinned, the corpses were identical.

Corrie thought that cat had been gutted and skinned for someone else's supper already.

Corrie woke up. Something tickled her face. She opened her eyes just as a snowflake landed softly on her eyelid through a crack in the roof.

She sat up. It was still pitch black. She looked toward the top of the stairs and saw the glow of the furnace. As her eyes adjusted, she looked up at the cracks in the ceiling. The cracks had always been there, but worsened due to the constant shaking during bombing raids and the occasional rain of heavy debris and shrapnel.

She settled down once more. If it continued to snow, perhaps there would be enough in the tub and on the ground to melt to water. She closed her eyes, knowing Pietje would wake her far too soon.

It seemed only two minutes later, Pietje shook her awake.

"It's time. We'll go in five minutes." He turned and slowly went back down the stairs.

Corrie squirmed around to look at Hennie and Beppie. She reached out to wake Beppie but thought better. There was always an argument with Beppie. She needed to be forced to help. But perhaps, this time, it was better to leave her sleeping along with Hennie.

She lifted the blanket off and put her bare feet onto the ice-cold floor by the bed. Her clothing was warm enough from her sleep to fend off the icy morning air emanating from the walls, floors, and ceiling as she went down the creaky stairs.

She saw Pietje standing at the stove poking at the fire. She noticed that their pile of branches and bark was meager. Perhaps there will be some wayward paper or branches along the way to the soup kitchen.

She used the water closet briefly, then tiptoed to the table to sit down. She lifted a hand and touched one of her unruly braids. She decided to do her hair quickly and unraveled one of them.

"What are you doing?" Pietje asked, turning around. "We have to get going."

"I don't think many, if any, will come to wait for soup right now, Pietje. It's still curfew. We'll still be the first."

"I truly doubt that, Corrie," Pietje said quietly. He pulled out the other chair covered in coats and sat down. He had a full head of blonde hair—long, uncombed.

"We should comb your hair, too," whispered Corrie.

Pietje shook his head. "I doubt there's anyone to impress waiting in line at a soup kitchen. You expect the *Koningin*?"

Corrie smiled and combed her blonde tendrils with her dirty fingers. She began braiding her greasy hair anew as her eyes rested on the glow of the stove. She visualized the soup they were going to collect. Sometime that day, they will all have a beautiful bowl of hot vegetable soup. Maybe some bread. Corrie started on the second braid and smiled, "Did you know it was snowing outside? Snow came in through the roof."

Pietje looked up, hopeful. He got out of his chair and pulled back one of the black-out curtains. The light of the stove was enough for him to see slow, lazy snowflakes floating by the window pane. He let go of the curtain, turned, and nodded.

Finished braiding, she got up and went to the corner and picked up their pail. She turned and watched Pietje close the shutter on the stove, which threw the tiny house in darkness save for the flickering light from the vents in the back of the stove. In the dark, she put on her mother's coat, and then she followed Pietje with her hands outstretched to touch table, chair, and wall before finding Pietje's back. Together, they stepped out the door into the freezing air.

As they made their way down the alley to the street, snow settled gently on Corrie's forehead, nose and cheeks. She turned her face to the sky and stuck out her tongue and caught a snowflake or two. Once at the entrance to the alley, she waited for Pietje to check that the coast was clear. He pulled at her coat to continue down the street, sticking close to the buildings on the right. They faced a dangerous journey of about twenty city blocks during curfew—the longest they had ever traveled in secret. There were two *ack-acks* along the way which they had to circumvent. *Ack-acks* had round the clock guards. Most likely, they would be dozing, snuggled for warmth amid sandbags. But still, the children were placing their lives on the line.

They were not the small frightened children they once were. They had grown into experienced clandestine troopers capable of calculating the odds of taking dangerous risks. In this high risk scenario, the gains far outweighed the possibility of being caught. Their slow starvation turned priorities upside down because by now, this night, the unspoken question was: Is it worth risking one's precious life and those of others for a small bowl of soup?

Yes.

Irrevocably and absolutely, yes.

Henk checked the state of his gums with his tongue as he sat and shivered, waiting behind the wheel of the truck. He watched as the cold prisoners in their striped pajamas, hauled wheelbarrows full of ash and bone out of the crematorium. It was still dark, which made them look like ghosts spewing plumes of moisture from their lungs, appearing and disappearing, as they struggled in and out of the security spotlights that shone up, down, and across the walls and his truck.

He saw Frans walking out of the crematorium. A guard followed Frans and spoke to him. Frans carried a large cardboard box with large lettering on it. In the dusk and the waltz of the searchlights, Henk could not make out the markings. He observed Frans turning slowly to face the guard. The guard poked Frans' chest with his baton, forcing him to step back to keep his balance.

Henk stiffened as he went into high alert. The question was always, was he ready to risk his life to attack a soldier who was too aggressive with his brother-in-law? For that matter, with any human being in the camp? Deep down inside, he knew what the answer would be, yes. But one only had one life, and there were so many different gallant reasons why one should put their life on the line. Each option had to be based on meticulous and calculated study of the reasons why. Would it benefit one? Many? A strange form of camp philosophy.

This was not one of those times to put his life at stake, however. Frans was just harassed by the German, not used as a shooting target.

He continued to watch as the soldier motioned to the truck. Frans looked over at Henk. Henk saw Frans' breath in the cold air as he breathed heavily. Then Frans spewed two columns of mist from of his nostrils. Like a dragon out of a fairy tale, thought Henk. Frans had the same deep inner strength and courage as a dragon, and now he breathed smoke and fire. Henk couldn't help but smile to himself.

Finally, Henk heard, "*Geh raus!*"

Henk knew how to read his brother-in-law. Frans was upset though he didn't show it. Frans was very good at pretending that nothing bothered him. For the hundredth time, Henk was grateful Frans was with him. Without his strength and leadership, Henk knew he would've taken his life by now or he'd gone crazy.

This time, however, from the look in Fran's eyes, he sensed that perhaps Frans would need his emotional support.

Henk sat up straighter as Frans finally walked toward the truck. He disappeared for a moment at the back of the vehicle. Henk turned and looked through the little window behind the front bench and watched Frans shove the box in and drop the canvas tarp to cover the opening. Almost immediately, Frans opened the passenger door and climbed in.

He shut the door and stayed leaning over toward Henk.

After a moment, Henk looked closer at Frans's face. "Everything alright?"

Frans didn't respond. He sat frozen in his leaning position, looking as if he was deep in thought.

"Frans? What are the orders? What are we doing today?"

Frans sat up with a long sigh. He looked away from Henk and looked out his window and watched the prisoners working in the dark, occasionally slashed by security searchlights. "I don't know how much longer I can take this," he whispered as he fogged up the window in front of him.

Henk waited, wondered. He shivered in the cold.

Frans turned to face the front and covered his face.

"What is it?"

Frans turned to Henk. In the darkness, he could just make out the tears welling in Frans' eyes. "I can't tell you, brother. Secret."

Henk nodded. As much as possible, the workers were not to divulge anything of what the Nazis ordered them to do individually. "So, where do you want me to go?"

Frans sucked in his breath and sat up straighter. The temperature had dropped, and Jack Frost waltzed over the windows. "The usual. To the gas chambers."

"Henk turned the key in the ignition and shifted it into a crunchy reverse. He backed up slowly, then in first gear, and gently drove by the prisoners. He waved and tried to smile at a few of them. Each one waved back. One smiled. He was forever amazed at the resiliency of people. One smiled. He put the truck into second gear, then third.

The usual.

Again, he was to sit and wait while the dead were loaded for another run to the mass grave.

Corrie cuddled up to Pietje and shivered uncontrollably. She ignored the cold as much as possible. She'd already licked the snow off the surrounding leaves and branches and had gathered the odd little handful of snow and melted it in her mouth. The cold meant snow, and that was okay.

From their hiding places under bushes, Pietje and Corrie watched as six Dutch NSBers took out tables and massive steaming pots from the back of a truck. They set up a few barrels and had fires going with grates on top, and one of the soup kettles already sat on top of one. They were in the process of lighting the fourth barrel. Long, banged-up ladles stood inside the pots at ready. Once they set everything in place, they each took a spoon full of soup and poured it into coffee mugs. Then the cigarettes and matches came out of pockets. The siblings watched them draw on their cigarettes and exhale the plumes of steam into the black sky above them in between sips of steaming soup.

Corrie salivated. She went to get out from under the bush. The pail handle clinked down and made a sharp noise. Frightened, she watched as the NSBers turned and looked in their direction. One lifted a ladle and nodded at them.

Corrie looked over at Pietje, who nodded. But he thought better and held her back before she could go. "I'll meet you back on the street and walk home with you. Then we'll do a second run back with the pail and other pots with Beppie. They won't know we're from the same household, and we'll have double, maybe triple, the soup."

"What if they ask for our address, and we've already given ours?" she asked.

"I'll give them another address."

"But then the people who live at that address can't get their soup."

Pietje shook his head. "All's fair in love and war, go!"

Corrie scrambled out. As she bent over to get the pail, she looked up and saw a group of people coming up the road with their own containers. Many pairs of *klompen* marched toward them on the cobblestones and pavement. She hurried and rushed over to the table.

She was the very first to get soup. She watched expectantly as the spoon dipped into the steaming pot. She didn't take her eyes off that spoon. It came around and emptied into her pail.

It looked like clear hot water with a few bits of something floating in the broth.

"What kind of soup is this?"

"Take it and stop complaining."

"But someone told me it would be a nice vegetable soup, and we'd get bread, too."

The man stood back, took the cigarette out of his mouth, and shook his head, grinning. "It is what it is, *meisje*. Take it or leave it."

Sadly, she lowered her head. "I'll take it." She stood, holding the pail for more.

"Go. You've had your share."

Corrie panicked. She looked into the pail. One ladle-full. "But—"

The man ignored her and motioned the next person forward.

Corrie again looked into the pail. There was so little that it might even freeze by the time they got home. She quickened her pace to meet Pietje back at the road. They were going to be in real trouble if this was all they received at this soup kitchen!

Henk reversed the truck to the backloading doors of the gas chamber. He took the cigarette out of his mouth and flicked the ash out the window before rolling the window back up. He got out of the truck and stretched his legs.

His orders were never to get out of the truck while waiting to be loaded. He wasn't to witness any of the work they did in and around the gas chamber. But it was dark, and, unlike at the ovens and mass grave, no one had ever bothered him so long as he walked away from what they were doing and stayed behind the truck.

As if he couldn't smell. As if he couldn't hear. As if he didn't see in the rearview mirrors.

As if the hundreds of naked people he saw were not being herded to their death into the building as he passed.

As if he didn't know what they dumped from his truck into the very pit, he helped dig.

As if.

He took another drag of his cigarette. Flakes of ash fell mixed with snowflakes. He held out his palm, and in the dawning light, watched a couple of the snowflakes melt on his palm. But there was also a different kind of flake that didn't melt. Grimly, he put his cold hand into his pocket. He took the cigarette out of his mouth with the other. Without his teeth, the cigarettes got mushy much quicker when clenched between his gums. They weren't a pleasure smoking once they were wet. His stomach growled, and he looked at the smoke in his hand. *Funny that I get all the cigarettes I want for playing for moffen,* he thought grimly. *Food would be helpful for a change.* He patted his stomach, then rubbed it. His clothes hung on him as if he were a stick. He could feel how his face had tightened; the skin stretched over his cheekbones and forehead, how gravity pulled at the loose skin from off his frame. And yet he looked beefy compared to most of the starving prisoners. He took one last drag and flicked the cigarette through the icy air. He watched its tip brighten momentarily and marked its trajectory before it fell to the hard ground and disappeared.

He turned to go back into the truck, but from the corner of his eye something caught his attention. He looked up at the roof of the gas chamber and stepped away from the truck as much as he dared, for a better view. In the dawning light, he saw Frans, his breath floating up into the air. He had a canister in his hands. With a fright, Henk looked away. He kept his eyes downcast as he hurried back to the truck and climbed back inside. He felt his blood pounding in his ears.

It was never Frans that went up there! It was always one of the *moffen*.

Always one of the *moffen*.

Always one of the *moffen*.

Corrie and Pietje hurried through the lazy falling snowflakes along the cold morning streets. They headed back to the temporary soup kitchen to see what more they could get. The little that Corrie had brought back home earlier wasn't enough for five teacups. Corrie had watched Pietje carefully ladle equal amounts into five cups, making sure each cup had some of the little pieces of cabbage that floated in the pail. The children had insisted their mother eat her share, but Cornelia refused more than just a spoonful when she saw how little there was.

That disturbed them greatly. "We have to get more," Corrie said tearfully. It was frightening to look at their mother. As Pietje heated the soup, their mother sat at the table, shivering and smoking a cigarette. She watched over them as they slurped their little bit.

"Slowly," she had warned. "You don't want stomach cramps."

So, they slowly sipped the soup that quickly cooled in the cold house. They had also used up the last of the debris gathered along the way to burn. As Corrie swallowed the last bit of broth, Pietje was at another wall with a hammer, pulling out nails and cracking wood into splintered pieces. She watched him throw these pieces into the dying embers of the little stove. Slowly the bits of wood smoked from underneath and flames licked at the edges. It would take a lot more wood than this to get the house warm, but these few pieces would have to do.

"We better go before they run out of the soup." Pietje got the pail from the table.

Corrie dipped her dirty finger into the cup to wipe off the liquid clinging to the inside of her teacup. She sucked at the finger. But the soup seemed to make her hungrier than before. Her stomach growled for more.

Pietje pulled out one of their father's sweaters from the pile of clothes Pietje had been sleeping under and handed it to Corrie. "Take that coat off, Corrie, and wear this. Let's cover your braids. No, better still, brush them out."

He handed the pail to Beppie. "Bep, you take the pail. Corrie and I will bring cooking pots. When we get there, we split. I'll give you guys addresses."

Beppie looked curiously at Corrie.

"They go by addresses," Corrie pointed out.

"What if people from those addresses already came?" Beppie asked.

"We'll take that chance," said Pietje, shrugging. He took in a deep breath. Then he got up and went to the door.

The day turned crisp with plenty of sunshine over an otherworldly white mist hanging just above the ground. Some snow had accumulated in the alley, and lazy flakes still flitted around.

Pietje opened the door and waited for his sisters. "Let's go."

Henk shook awake when Frans suddenly jumped into the cab of the truck. His body shook violently; his face was ghostly white.

"Frans?" Henk asked softly.

Henk hadn't seen Frans since seeing him on the roof before sunrise. Since then, they had processed a gas chamber and cleared it out. The truck was now fully loaded. Henk tried not to think about what they stuffed into the back. But that stench. Those poor souls.

Henk forced it out of his mind. Instead, Henk studied Frans. Something had happened to him that was different from other horrific days. He reached out to pat him on the shoulder.

Frans suddenly hit his hand away, threw the door open, and retched. He heaved and heaved, croaked, heaved, and then pulled himself into the truck and slammed the door. He opened his mouth, covered in drool, and silently cried to the roof of the car. His eyes widened, his eyebrows knitted together tightly. His palms slowly lifted to the ceiling. He shook his head slowly as if in agony.

Henk was worried. Frans wasn't breathing. He patted Frans on the back a little harder. "Frans, breathe!"

Frans didn't breathe. Instead, a primal, deep-throated moan erupted from the depths as if from his soul. It continued until the last bit of breath from the bottom of his lungs was squeezed out.

Henk pounded his back. "Frans! Breathe!" Henk shook him hard.

Frans immediately twisted and grabbed Henk's shoulders, scrunching up the material with his worn hands. He buried his face into Henk's chest, shaking his head. "May God forgive me, Henk! May God forgive me!"

Henk didn't have to ask why. He held Frans as he shuddered in grief and bawled like a woman. Henk looked up and spotted one of the *moffen* looking over their way. The soldier started walking toward them, motioning with his rifle for Frans to get out. To keep working.

Henk sat up and patted his brother-in-law. "Frans, one of them is coming. We have to keep working."

Frans couldn't move.

Henk bent over and took out a cigarette and lit one. "Here, take this. Pretend you came in to get a cigarette. Go! Keep moving!"

Frans shakily took the cigarette, opened the passenger door, and climbed out. He held up the smoke at the soldier, then walked along the length of the truck to the back entrance of the building.

Henk watched in the rearview mirror until Frans disappeared out of sight. He looked over at the soldier, smiled, and waved.

The soldier didn't respond. He turned and walked back to where he stood watching over the work around the building.

Henk kept watching him. Over time, he watched snow slowly fall and cover the ground around the soldier's feet. The snow was whiter than the ash falling from the distant chimneys. The ash was greyer. But soon, the grey was covered completely. By morning light, it was all white.

Henk felt the truck shoved this way and that as people loaded more cargo they had just removed from the chambers.

Cargo. That's the term Henk decided to use to keep his sanity. He thought of that as he watched the soldier earlier. The soldier stood and watched dead bodies all day, but he might as well have been waiting in a deserted field of grass, that's how unmoved the young man was.

Henk crossed another dangerous line drawn in the proverbial sand. He had to harden his heart. For as long as he had to be the driver, he did not see the bodies as people. But deep down inside, a voice whispered that one day he would pay with remorse and agony for crossing that line. But Henk knew if he didn't do something to distance himself from the truth now, he would lose his mind, and he wasn't ready to give it up.

It was the lesser of the two evils: sanity versus paying for it later. Well, sanity won out. For now.

Corrie looked back along the long line of bedraggled sad-looking women and children. One or two older men stood in the line, unshaven, wrinkled, hunchbacked and bent into their coats against the cold air. Then she looked over at the hospital just off the clearing. In the dark, earlier that day, they took no notice, but in the light, she could see partially into the windows. Some patients looked out and watched them. She waved, and one person waved back.

She looked to her left and looked at three soldiers standing with their rifles. They weren't there before dawn. Corrie turned to face the front again and stamped her foot for circulation in her numb toes. With one hand, she lifted her long blonde hair and covered her mouth, breathing into it to create warmth against the bottom of her chin. Though being squeezed between other people in line generated some heat for her, it wasn't enough to warm her bare legs, feet, and hands. She wished she still had her rabbit fur muff, but the fur had crumbled and deteriorated. Now the bits were used as stuffing around one of the windows. And there were no more rabbits to make another. The demand for their meat weighed far more than what the rabbits could provide by propagating. Rabbits are famous for how quickly they multiply, but it wasn't fast enough to keep up with the need to fill the demands of empty stomachs.

Corrie fidgeted. She wasn't comfortable. She had been up since before dawn, and had drank a bit of broth with one or two little pieces of cabbage. She also had a tiny morsel of bread during the night. She quickly grew weary standing in line, shuffling forward, and standing still again. She suddenly dropped and sat cross-legged on the ground and crawled forward to keep in line.

Beautiful red hair caught her attention and she looked up to see a very pregnant woman. Her hair hung down to her waist. Even from where she rested on the ground, she could see that the woman was starving to death with a baby inside of her. Suddenly, the woman collapsed. Corrie scrambled to her feet as others in front of her gathered around the woman. Corrie stepped over to look.

The woman, though thin, looked as if her stomach was going to burst. Someone bent over and patted her cheek. Another lifted her head, but the head moved like that of a rag doll.

"*S'jonge*, she's dead!" said one of the women.

An old man put his ear to her stomach. He lifted his face and looked closely at the woman's stomach. Everyone could see movement.

"That's the baby!" one yelled.

"No, not baby. Babies! She's big enough for twins," yelled another.

Two of the soldiers hurried over and pushed everyone to the side. One knelt down and lifted her frail-looking wrist. He dropped it, shaking his head. The two soldiers lifted her and took her to the back of the truck.

Everyone looked on. After a moment, someone spoke up. "What happens when the mother dies but the babies are still alive?"

People around Corrie looked at each other with pained expressions. Birds chirped in the nearby forest and there was no chatter for a few more moments. Then, as if of one mind, everyone formed their line once again.

Corrie took her place in line. She wasn't sure, but the sun appeared to be brighter. Beautiful snowflakes, never heavy, continued to float in and about, swirling up and down at the whim of breezes coming in from the frigid North Sea.

She closed her eyes. She felt faint. All she could think about was food. As the line moved closer to the tables, Corrie's eyes clamped onto every pail and pot that passed by her face. She craned her neck to see how much they had in their buckets as they passed. She saw that every person either shook their heads or cried as they left. But they had something. Better than nothing.

As she crawled further along, she saw she was finally three people deep and stood up. Now she could watch the ladle going into the pot and out again. *God, let there be enough for us.*

The person ladling out the soup looked very cold and tired. She recognized him. He'd been standing there since they set up the tables in the pre-dawn, and he looked weary. As he filled a ladle of broth, he accidentally let the spoon bounce off against the rim of the pot, and the ladle spilled its contents onto the table and ground. Suddenly, without thinking, Corrie sprang forward and was able to beat the other two people to licking the broth off the tabletop. She missed out, however, on the bits of cabbage that had fallen on the ground below. She looked down at a woman's back, who picked up every single little bit of cabbage and tossed them into her mouth, dirt and all.

She scrambled back in line, but the woman behind her wouldn't let her back in.

"This is my spot," argued Corrie, looking up at the cross face.

The woman pushed her away. "Too bad. You got out of line."

A woman behind the cross one overheard. "Let the poor child back in, *mevrouw*."

The cross woman sneered at her, then down at Corrie. She stepped back slightly to let Corrie back in. As she squeezed in, the cross woman bounced her from behind. Corrie stubbornly stood straight and firm against the struggle.

Suddenly, from everywhere sirens whined and blared through the cold air. People grumbled, and stood considering whether they should run for cover or not. After a few moments of the sirens blaring, some finally ran off to flatten against the side of a truck, or flatten against the ground, anything that would protect them against shrapnel. Many ran to the hospital and huddled between ground-floor windows.

"Corrie!"

She could hear Pietje calling her. She ignored him and kept her eyes on the pot of soup. The one person left in front of her didn't move either.

Three people from the soup kitchen ran and slid under the truck. The tired one stood alone with the ladle. He had dark circles under his eyes. He looked sadly at the next woman in line, and then at Corrie.

Suddenly, they heard the ear-shattering scream of a massive bomb falling their way. Corrie knew that so long as she heard that scream, she was safe. If it stopped screaming, it meant you had to run for cover. Everyone froze as they listened. When the scream of the bomb stopped, the man with the ladle yelled, "Run!"

Corrie refused to run. So long as that pot was on that barrel, she was not going anywhere. As she stood, the woman in front of her ducked under the table with the man.

In an instant, the world kicked into slow motion. A mighty blinding flash of light outshone the daylight itself and white-washed what she was looking at while an ear-shattering explosion burst in the hospital next to them. She swiveled her head slowly to see people and beds flying through shattered windows. She saw a mattress, and a patient still under a blanket soar gracefully toward her. When it landed about a hundred feet away, the body on the bed flew up into the air, then crumpled headfirst into the clearing behind her.

Someone suddenly grabbed her and toppled her onto the ground. She fell into the cold hard dirt. It was Pietje.

Then she fainted.

Henk took over caring for Frans. It was his turn to be strong. Frans saved his sanity long enough to survive the Hell in camp, and now he had to step up to the plate. He looked over to where Frans was resting on his bunk. The room was spacious compared to the spaces Henk had been in since being taken away from home. He got up and took a sheet off of his upper bunk and placed it over Frans. Frans stirred slightly, but he could see the path of tears that had streaked his dirty face earlier.

Henk placed a gentle hand on the suffering man's shoulder. He was breathing, but every once in a while, Frans' body shuddered violently. A frown would cross his face, and he'd grimace.

Pneumonia came to mind as Henk went back to the bench he was sitting on with a few other men by the stove. He crossed his legs and kept his eyes on Frans' curled-up form on the cot. He was seriously concerned for him. Frans refused to eat. That haunted look of horror and grief rarely left him now. Henk didn't know what to do precisely, but he sensed that the worst was yet to come and it would take both of them to live through it. He no longer needed Frans to carry him, but he required Frans to grieve and then get over it. It would take two of them to be there for the other if they were both to survive the next few months.

Everyone felt it, and some became giddy at the thought. A hint of hope hung in the air. More planes went overhead to bomb German-run factories and plants further into Poland. The *moffen* now didn't hesitate to shoot any prisoners jumping and waving their hands at the bombers, hoping they bombed Birkenau instead. Nobody cared anymore if they were going to be shot. Someone had whispered in his ear that the Allies had destroyed one of the Wehrmacht headquarters in Amsterdam. And that there was a partial liberation of Holland. But it was the northern parts. The Hague was still in the grips of the evil Fuhrer.

Henk thirsted for the information whispered to him by others. Especially when he had to bring his weekly report to the front offices. There he noted the changes in the way Nazi soldiers and guards walked and talked. When safe, a prisoner or worker would pass him in the hall and quickly whisper an update. He would do the same with the next person he passed. Thus, there was a whispered communication network that never stopped whispering;

their echoes reflected off the barrack's ceilings, the latrines' walls, in the clearings. Information was like food; it offered sustenance of another kind. They seemed to know that no longer was there a quiet, efficient killing system running amid all the horrors the system created with pride. Quiet panic resided in the eyes of those who traumatized the prisoners.

It reflected on how things were run outside the offices as well. There was a different type of frenzy in the soldiers' barracks. Trains had stopped coming and spewing new bedraggled people. Instead, the massive killing machine turned on itself, devouring its inhabitants. The Nazis were frantically cleaning house, ridding themselves of the evidence of atrocities, before the war inevitably ended. Gassing still didn't work fast enough for them. People were executed on the spot or herded off to a nearby forest. Henk heard the cracking of guns and knew it had everything to do with the new pits dug in the woods.

There were other disturbing changes: There were significant oversights in the regular feeding of the prisoners. Sometimes the prisoners did not get their *ersatz* coffee in the mornings or their ration of watery soup during the day. Henk saw prisoners, some with their pajamas falling off their frames, others naked, lying out in the cold air against the outside walls waiting for death. Without the few calories, they received each day, the deaths piled up quickly. Also, the powers that were did not take away the dead as quickly as they used to, and bodies were now left a day or two.

As foreign slave workers, Henk hoped they were a separate class. He panicked at the thought of either one of them losing their usefulness to the Nazis. For now, the Nazis still needed their labor, their time, their energy, and it was important Frans pushed himself to hang on to dear life.

But the *moffen* felt the pressure, too, and they could almost taste the change in the winds. The day before, one of the *moffen* he performed for, half-joked about catching two of the prisoners cooking a piece of flesh they cut from a dead prisoner in their barracks. The two souls were dragged out and shot immediately. Henk saw the pained expression on the soldier's face even as he laughed it off. Drinking wasn't allowed by prisoner, worker, or soldier, but there was an increasing presence of beer and alcohol among the soldiers. Henk figured, for self-medicating.

Henk threw his cigarette into the stove and got up. He wished he had the accordion in his hands. He wanted to pray more fervently but knew not how, except through the sound of those bellows.

Suddenly, the ground trembled. Everyone stiffened. Some stood up, alert. Then, as one, the men raced to the doors to look out on dusk.

Black smoke billowed from the gas chambers. Sirens wailed, and there was action in other areas of the camp. Trucks of soldiers, still buttoning up their uniforms, raced out of their doors clutching their rifles.

Henk looked toward the main buildings and saw soldiers on foot walking from barrack to barrack, threatening they would shoot anyone who left the barracks and buildings.

Henk hurried back in, as did the others.

As they huddled at the stove, they heard gunfire and bombs exploding. Then another deep rumble.

The atmosphere turned from shock and curiosity to quiet optimism.

Henk looked over at Frans' bunk. He awoke finally and leaning on one hand, watched them curiously.

Henk hurried over and sat on the edge of the bunk. He grinned.

"What was that?" Frans croaked.

"That, brother, sounds like a rebellion."

Frans stared at him as they both continued to listen to the fighting in the distance. Then he struggled to sit up, shaking. He scratched at his stubble with his dirty finger nails and slowly focused his eyes on Henk's face. A tiny smile formed along his thin lips.

"Well, well, well," he whispered. "There is hope for us yet, Henk."

Chapter 20
December 1944

The attempted rebellion failed, but not without offering more hope to the imprisoned inhabitants of Birkenau. Frans recuperated, and his mental alertness and fighting spirit returned, just in time. They were two of many ordered to clear up the aftermath of the fighting. The rebels had fought tooth and nail against the SS troops and their superior ammunition. No one knew what the rebels fought with, but as Henk and Frans cleared things, they found knives, home-made grenades, and chains. The rebels also managed to smuggle bales of human hair destined for market, to the top floor of the crematorium and set them on fire.

Henk was surprised to hear there were more than 600 members in the group they called the *Sonderkommandos*. No one escaped. The dead were taken to the crematoriums and burned to ash.

The whole affair was started by the women who worked in Kanada House, where they sorted all the belongings confiscated from prisoners on their way to the chambers. Over time, they had smuggled enough gun powder to make a bomb. Four of these women were captured alive and were tortured, but refused to give names of members of their group left in the camp.

Birkenau now had an informal list of stars and superheroes to inspire them all. Execution of those who dared to fight was the stuff of legends now.

People felt hopeful.

CORRIE AND THE ROSE ACCORDION

As did Henk.

Corrie ambled along the pavement, keeping her eyes looking down. She was harvesting cigarette butts for the day, and whatever other little treasures that lay in her path. The streets seemed very different from before the war. There were large swathes of missing wooden 'plugs' that paved the space between the tram tracks. People had cleared trees of their branches and limbs. Shells of bombed buildings still stood, their debris diligently cleared away long ago.

In her peripheral vision, she saw a large lump in a sewer grate. Her eyes flicked in its direction briefly, but she already knew what it was—the head of a dog recently butchered for food.

She suddenly heard a crowd yell and scream. She froze. Lately, marauding hordes gathered where there might be new sources of food to steal.

Corrie hurled herself from the pavement and raced across the demolished tram tracks. Around the bend, she saw a horde of people assaulting someone at a wagon. Corrie screamed as she flew to the crowd. With all her strength, she pushed at bodies larger than herself. Whatever it was, she needed it.

Hiding her face from sharp bony elbows, she finally ended up front. A man was fighting to stay upright as the horde yanked loaves of bread out of his metal box on the wagon. By the time Corrie could reach the box, many had already taken their share and run away. The man freed himself finally and stood up and slammed the metal lid down. As Corrie's arm was still fishing for a loaf, the top slammed down, and its sharp edges cut into the flesh of her thin forearm.

The scream that left her throat was long and mournful. She felt yanked away. Someone took a stained handkerchief and wrapped it around her slender arm as she cried. She opened her eyes to see the baker under attack, and the box lid was thrown open once again.

Suddenly, she was left to stand alone, crying and holding her throbbing arm. Blood oozed through the wrap quickly, and dripped onto the cobblestones. She wiped her tears and slowly headed home, holding out her dripping arm and eventually losing the soaked handkerchief in the gutter where the dog's head lay. Before moving on, she glanced at its face. The eyes were opaque, and she could see the dog's teeth in mid-snarl. She remembered Poekie and his eye hanging out of its socket and his frozen snarl.

But she only thought of Poekie a brief moment. It was imperative she get home and have Pietje help stop the bleeding.

Somewhere else in the city, she heard the crack of guns firing. Its noise was a common occurrence and no longer something of concern. The world was falling apart around them.

She finally arrived at her gate and slowly walked to the door. No longer crying, she glanced behind her and saw a trail of blood following her in a straight line. She turned slowly and opened the door. They had burned all the floorboards for heat, so there was an immediate drop to the sand below. But she couldn't bend and use a hand in lowering herself the extra foot and a half. She stood, crying, hoping someone would be home who could help her.

She saw the curtain over the bedstead move slightly. Her mother looked out with one eye. She whimpered and let the curtain drop. Corrie could hear her mother knocking at the ceiling over her head with a stick. That usually meant Beppie was hiding in bed.

"What!" yelled Beppie.

A shuffling noise signified someone was getting out of bed. A second later, Beppie's head popped around the corner at the top of the stairs.

Corrie looked towards the stairs, still silently holding out her arms, dripping blood into the sand below.

Beppie gasped and ran down as fast as she could barefoot.

Corrie collapsed and fell the distance from the threshold to the sand below before Beppie got to her. She bent over and dragged Corrie to a chair, creating two deep cuts in the sand from Corrie's bare feet.

Corrie revived enough to feel lowered into a chair. She opened her eyes and saw the curtain at the bedstead move, and a stick of an arm came out and pointed toward the stove.

There was a rag hanging off the side of the stove pipe. Beppie took it off, shook the dust and ash off of it, and ran through the sand to Corrie. Quickly she wrapped the arm. Corrie winced and cried.

Their mother's arm motioned for Beppie to come over to the bedstead. Corrie tearfully watched as Beppie leaned in to listen to their mother's whisperings. Beppie then immediately scrambled to the kitchen corner and took a tiny brown glass vial and hurried back to Corrie. Beppie carefully took off the bloody towel, dabbed at the gash to rid it of blood, and then unscrewed the bottle and pulled out a small stick with a sponge on its end. Iodine.

"Close your eyes," said Beppie.

Corrie screwed her eyes shut as Beppie dabbed the pungent yellow-brown liquid onto the gash.

Corrie yowled and then looked down. She watched as Beppie painted the whole arm with the iodine. She whimpered as Beppie rewrapped the now gold and brown-stained arm.

"Mama says to squeeze it tight to stop the bleeding," Beppie said, as she took the vial back to the shelf.

Corrie dug her toes into the sand as she squeezed against the pain of her throbbing arm.

"You should lie down with something under your arm. You look awful," offered Beppie. "Did you find anything on the streets?" she asked, hopefully.

Corrie nodded and shook her head. "Cigarettes," she said quietly.

"Oh," said Beppie, disappointment oozing out of her pores. Beppie eyed Corrie's arm. Then she looked over into the far corner, to the side of the stove. They had left a small portion of the original floorboards next to the furnace, acting as a low shelf. Standing safely in the corner on top of that make-shift shelf was their father's accordion case.

Connie saw her staring. She looked over at the accordion herself. "No, Beppie, we can't," Corrie said quietly.

Beppie took a step toward the accordion case, but Corrie reached out with her unharmed arm and grabbed her skirt. "Don't touch it," she begged.

Beppie threw off Corrie's arm and went straight to the case. She took it down and laid it on the sand.

"Don't! Leave it alone!" cried Corrie tearfully.

Beppie sat in the sand and proceeded to unlock the latches on the case. As she was about to take the accordion out, Pietje opened the front door. He stood with a bundle of newspapers in his arms. For a moment, he looked from Corrie and her bleeding arm covered in brown iodine to Beppie, who sat in the sand holding the accordion. He blinked. Then stepped inside and closed the door.

"What happened?" He looked from Corrie to Beppie. "And what are you doing? Leave the accordion alone."

"No, Pietje. We should sell this stupid thing because Mama is dying from hunger. We all are dying from hunger. And we have this thing," she slapped the polished surface of the accordion, "sitting here. We've sold everything else, why can't we sell this for food?"

Pietje took the newspapers to the stove and dropped them on the sand. He stepped toward Beppie, grabbed her by the braid, and pulled her up and away from the accordion.

She squealed and fought him. He ignored her slaps and threw her on the sand away from the accordion and case. Corrie watched as Pietje brushed the accordion clean of any wayward sand, and carefully put it back into its case.

"I hate you!" yelled Beppie. She scrambled up on her hands and knees and stumbled to an upright position. She scurried over to the bottom of the stairs, the bottom step of which was a foot and a half higher. She yanked herself up and scrambled up the creaking stairs. They heard the bed groan as she flew onto it. She began to howl, her cries muffled by blankets.

Corrie looked at Pietje. He pointed at her arm.

Corrie sniffed and lowered her head.

He came over and looked at her iodine and blood-soaked wrapping. He lifted a hand and fingered the edges of the rag. "We need water. We should be washing that wound."

Corrie nodded. "There's been no rain."

"I know," whispered Pietje.

Corrie swayed in her seat as she closed her eyes. She felt faint.

"Corrie, you're not going out tonight. Beppie and I will go without you. You can't go like this."

Corrie nodded and allowed him to take her to the edge of the floor below the bedstead. There the clothes had been piled up underneath a blanket. She laid down on the soft pile, curled up in a ball, and immediately fell fast asleep, exhausted.

Something woke her. Someone stepped on her head. She shook awake in time to see the back of her mother stumbling in the sand toward the door. She sat up and watched as her mother opened the door.

Corrie was shocked to see a thick wall of falling snow through the opening. SNOW.

She got up, winced when she put pressure on her wounded arm and continued across the cold sand in her bare feet. As she reached the door, her mother stepped through it out into the snow still in her bare feet.

"Mama!" yelled Corrie. She pulled herself up onto the threshold and looked out. Her mother bent over the snow on the ground, gathering a snowball together. "Mama! You have to come back inside!"

"Water," said her mother in a raspy voice. The thick snow lightened the night skies, and she could see her mother's chest moving in and out under the strain of physical exertion. She was only in her worn thin nightgown, steam rising up from her body.

Corrie saw her mother put a bit of the gathered snow in her mouth with a shaking hand. Then she continued to make a bigger ball. Corrie turned and looked back into the house. She didn't see Pietje anywhere. Hoping he was upstairs, she yelled. "Piet! Pietje! Help!"

Pietje appeared and stumbled down the stairs, Beppie running close behind him.

"Mama is out here in the snow!"

"Snow?" Pietje frowned and peered past her. He gasped. "Snow!" He jumped into the sand, scrambled to the kitchen corner, and grabbed what pots he could. He dragged them to the door and tossed them out in the snow. He looked for his *klompen*, found them, and then put them on quickly. He then pulled himself up over the threshold and squeezed past Corrie. She watched him clomp through the deepening snow to his mother. He grabbed the giant ball of snow she had formed and threw it toward Corrie at the door.

Corrie fumbled with the snowy missile with one hand and let it fall onto the threshold of the door. She quickly scooped it up in her good arm and jumped back into the house. She dumped the ball on the table and immediately ate some of the snow. It didn't matter that the ice-cold temperature hurt her fingers, her mouth, her throat. She let it melt in her mouth only for an instant before swallowing it. With nothing in her stomach, she could feel the icy cold lump go all the way down the esophagus. It hurt, and her guts cramped.

"Put it in a bowl, Corrie!" yelled Pietje from outside as he gingerly lifted his skeleton of a mother into his arms.

Corrie retrieved a used chipped bowl off the table and put the snowball into it. She looked up as little Hennie poked her head out of the bedstead and looked at what Corrie was doing. Corrie got up with the bowl and walked to Hennie. She tipped the bowl against Hennie's chapped lips. Hennie put a hand on the bowl and let the water slip into her mouth. Her eyes widened and softened. She smacked her lips. "Water," said Hennie.

"You're right, Hennie. We'll have lots of water to drink."

"Corrie, put that down. Mama's hands look hurt."

Corrie twirled around to see Pietje lowering their mother onto the sand from the front door threshold. Her mother's legs trembled as she stood, her nightgown hiked up on one side, showing white flabby flesh and sores. By having held so much snow against her thin nightgown, she was soaked and chilled to the bone. She feebly stood with her hands straight out toward the children. They were beet red. She moaned and cried, staring at her hands.

Corrie, with a start, rushed to her mother and helped her to a chair.

Her mother winced, as her bony rear landed on the hard surface. Her hands shook violently.

"What do I do?" she screamed at Pietje.

"Cover her!"

Corrie grabbed the old winter coat from the clothing pile by the bedstead and put it over her mother's bony shoulders.

She looked up to see Pietje grab a pot and fill it with snow from the pile nearest the front door. Then he hurried it to the stove. With a sizzle and pop, the pot danced on the hot surface. He tipped it to one side and then the other, watching the snow melt. He turned. "The water's already melting. As soon as we have enough, we put Mama's hands in it."

"Don't' we need hot water?" asked Beppie, watching everything from the bottom of the stairs.

"No, hot water would hurt more. Just water."

As the snow melted in the big pot, Pietje went to the door and leaned outside to get the other containers. He filled each one. He turned and held one out to Beppie. "Beppie, take this and put them near the stove. And get me the bin."

"Corrie can help, too."

"No, Corrie cannot help, too. She has a bad arm."

Corrie looked up at Beppie from where she was standing with her moaning mother.

Beppie pouted as she fetched the bin from the little kitchen sink.

Soon, Pietje had filled all the pots with snow, then emptied their contents into the big pot on the stove. He lifted and tipped the pot to pour melted water out into the bin. He put the big pot back and took the bin to his mother.

"Here, Mama. Put those hands in the water." He gently took their mother's shaking frostbitten hands and placed them in the bin. His mother winced, moaned, then relaxed, tears streaming down her face.

Pietje looked over at Corrie, standing on the other side of her mother. He grinned and mouthed the words, "WE HAVE WATER."

Corrie wiped Hennie's dirty face with a cloth of warmed water. She looked over at Beppie, who stood in a ray of sunlight over the bin, washing her forearms and hands. Pietje was at the stove, plopping more snow into the pot for melting. She looked over at the little window. Daylight had finally come, and it was a grand day. Snowflakes were still floating down, and the snow had fallen into beautiful, sparkling large drifts. After washing up for the first time in months, they were going to get the laundry tub and fill it up. They were also going to boil potato peels for supper.

Corrie squeezed the water from the cloth and refreshed it in the warm water. She dabbed the cloth against Hennie's button nose. She giggled. Corrie grinned, but her grin didn't last. She suddenly felt very faint, and her stomach churned. Corrie dropped the cloth and stood up. She untied the rope she had around her middle and attempted to tighten it but couldn't because of her bad arm. Pietje looked over and saw what she was trying to do. He came over quickly and tightened the rope for her against the pain of hunger.

Eating snow didn't fool her body. She looked forward to lying down. If they were to go out this night, she would need her sleep. But her body was so weak with hunger that it craved sleep anyhow.

They planned to each have a cup of hot water with some chicory after their sponge baths before crawling into bed to sleep the day away. As they focused quietly on their little chores, a large shape suddenly blocked the sun coming through the window.

Beppie gasped loudly.

Pietje scrambled to the front door. He looked wide-eyed back at Corrie.

A substantial piece of equipment hit the door, and then the door flew open, throwing Pietje against the bottom of the stairs.

In the opening of the doorway stood two SS troopers.

Corrie's heart went ice cold.

The soldiers looked down at the sand floor and the damage of the interior of the house. They stepped inside, their outfits making all sorts of noise, metal on metal, heavy coat on pants, the rustling of armaments in their holsters. They both turned to Pietje. One held out his gloved hand.

"Your identification papers."

Pietje turned to look at the table, then up the stairs. Quickly, he scrambled up the stairs to the attic.

"Corrie," whispered her mother from behind the curtains in the bedstead.

Corrie turned and went to the curtains, pulling one back. She had brushed her mother's hair after a sponge bath, and she looked a little more refreshed. But certainly not any better. "*Ja*, Mama?"

"Bring that soldier to me."

Corrie turned wide-eyed. Her heart jumped into her throat. The men were so frightening, so big, so mean. She'd seen them do such horrific things, that to have to address one and tell him what to do was something she would rather not contemplate. But her dying mother asked.

She shyly moved toward the soldiers. She saw Pietje return with his identification papers and shakily hand it over to the soldier.

The soldier read the paper and looked at Pietje's photo.

"Am I in trouble?" asked Pietje feebly.

"No, but you will be if you resist. The Wehrmacht needs more men. We've lowered the age of men to sixteen to over forty."

"But, I'm only fourteen." Pietje stared at him, shaking.

"You can pass for sixteen," said the soldier, keeping the paper in his hand.

That prompted Corrie to jump forward. She grabbed the hand belonging to the soldier holding the papers and dragged him toward the bedstead. The other soldier took out the gun from his holster, Corrie noticed, as she looked back for an instant. Of course, they probably thought someone was hiding behind the curtain with a gun. Instead, Corrie threw the curtains back to expose her dying mother and her three-year-old sister playing in the corner.

"*Mevrouw*," said the German.

Her mother motioned for the German to bend over closer. He did, amazingly so. She whispered German into his ear. He stood up and stared at her for a moment. In rough Dutch, he spoke as he turned to look at the children.

"My mother is like your mother. Dark hair, blue eyes, and she, too, must be starving in Berlin." He looked over at their mother again and then over at his companion at the door. He stepped toward the front door. "*Scheisse*. To hell with it." He turned suddenly, clicked his boots, and saluted. "Heil, Hitler!" He grabbed his companion, handed Pietje's identification papers back, and they left, closing the door behind them. As they trudged past their window, they conversed angrily in German.

Corrie looked over at Pietje.

Pietje suddenly fell to the sand and leaned back against the threshold of the front door. Every close call left lingering numbness, a form of shock that sapped the body. Pietje looked like, this time, it completely sucked him dry to his core. He lowered his head and cried.

Chapter 21
January 1945

Those who could, silently gathered to watch the *moffen* hang the four tortured women from the gas chamber rebellion. None of the accused cried. These women who withstood torture for months and who never gave any names, stood proudly while nooses dropped around their necks. And as they dropped off the tall wooden structure used as gallows, people gasped, screamed, and cried. Everyone imagined themselves being as courageous as these souls up to the last moments of their lives. They had to tear their eyes away from the four swinging bodies as they were herded back to what they were doing. But not before they felt a fresh surge of empowerment and hope.

The hangings upset Henk terribly. He'd seen men shot, killed, and hounded by German Shephard dogs. But he'd never seen a woman killed in the open. Women stayed in separate barracks in an entirely different part of the camp. But here they were young, intelligent women, and they died for fighting for the freedom that belonged to all of them.

He looked over at Frans with a renewed fire in his loins—that strange feeling that can magically nourish one's soul; it was what helped him continue to find his own strength throughout the ongoing day to day grind of working as a small extension of the Nazi killing machine.

Of late, their job was elevated to cleaning out the crematoriums. The Nazis planned to destroy all the ovens before Christmas.

But first they had to get rid of every bit of evidence within the ovens themselves. Ash, bones and, most gruesome, human fat 18 inches deep had to be carted away. Full and heavy wheelbarrows traveled back and forth, all their contents dumped into more pits dug in the forest or burned in giant open bonfires.

Even after almost all the crematoriums were destroyed and carted away, there was still so much and ash left that the Nazis knew they needed an army of workers larger than the hundreds of people already put to clearing away the evidence. Even so, the evidence did not disappear fast enough. The Nazis' greatest fear happened sooner than they expected: On the morning of January 17, as the prisoners stood in the cold for roll call, great thunderous booms indicated that the Russians were very close.

Henk stood outside the barracks. He looked to his right and could hear the closest roll call echoing in the winter morning air. Henk looked to the left and listened to the oncoming thundering combat. He smoked the last cigarette he had on him and flicked the butt into the trampled, deep snow. He turned back into the barracks.

Frans buttoned the tattered jacket he wore over his rags of clothes. These were clothes allotted to him after his clothes disintegrated from sun, rain, and wear. Henk still had most of his original clothing, but they were quite worn. They had no gloves and no hats, having lost their caps long ago to those who stole in the night.

Henk walked up to Frans and eyed the other men around them. They were slowly getting ready to do their work. "Frans, we have to have a plan for when the Russians come."

"A plan? What kind of plan?" Frans asked, holding out his palms. He looked at Henk, shocked. He looked around and shrugged. "What plans would that be? I mean, we don't know what's going to happen. Everyone's saying the Russians are as bad as the Nazis. Worse! They're cannibals, they say!"

"Come on, Frans. That's just talk."

"Is it? Just talk?" Frans had lost so much weight, there were permanent black hollows under his eyes and cheekbones. You could almost see the rounded bumps under what were his cheeks of the few teeth he had left in his mouth.

Henk absentmindedly put a finger to his gums. "They say the Nazis aren't going to leave a single living soul behind. They'll shoot us all."

Frans stepped closer to Henk. He pointed a finger at Henk's bony breastplate. "They don't have enough bullets to kill all of us here in this camp. Think about it." Frans turned and walked to the stove and touched the surface, hoping for more heat than there was.

"They won't leave any witnesses behind. They're too smart for that." Henk looked out the door. Someone stepped over and shut the door, obliterating the bright light from his eyes. "Well, we'll talk about it. But we have to decide soon."

Frans shook his head and walked past Henk to the door. He opened it again and looked back from the bright sunlight into the dark interior. He squinted at Henk still standing at the stove. "Henk, when it's time to know what's going on, we'll know it soon enough." He stepped into the snow and left the door open for Henk.

Henk looked at the men around him, some were listening quietly. All had carefully tied rags over their feet and up their legs to fight against the cold, deep snow. *All of which would only work for about ten minutes* thought Henk. They were all in the same boat as him. He suddenly felt so tender toward them. He realized how important it was that they all treated each other kindly. They were all frightened, hungry, overworked, and filled with a mixture of dread of the Russians, but also gratitude. He blinked back tears, nodded at them, and led the men out the door. He felt comforted to be with them.

Once again, misery loved company.

Sirens wailed through the encampment. Guards barked harsh commands from towers, from blow horns. Everyone was to gather outside.

Absolutely everyone.

Henk was just giving himself a sponge bath. He quickly dried himself with his shirt and put it back on. He hurried out and fell into line with everyone else outside the barracks. Off in the near distance, the fighting sounded closer than the day before. Smoke was visible on the horizon.

> *"You are all to fall into line.*
> *We are leaving the camp*
> *and marching to a German camp."*

Someone beside Henk gasped.

"What? A German camp? Do you know how many kilometers that is from here? And in the middle of winter? Look at us!" the man yelled, his eyes wide with fear. "We won't last ten minutes out on a march."

Someone hissed at him to stay quiet.

The man squinted at everyone. He was in shock. He was appalled. "People will die by the hundreds. By the thousands!"

> *"If you do not come, we will burn you in your barracks;*
> *we will shoot you on sight. And if we don't kill you, the*
> *Russians will. You have no choice but to follow."*

Pandemonium broke out. Groups of soldiers spread out across the camp to bring together organized crowds. While people were still wondering what it all meant, they were herded into lines six people across.

More commands blared over loudspeakers.

> *"You will march in line. Never fall back. Those who do*
> *will be shot immediately on the spot."*

It was ridiculously below the freezing point, and everyone's breath hung heavy in the still morning air. Suddenly, four soldiers marched toward Henk and Frans standing amongst the other workers.

One soldier pointed at them and then over his shoulder.

"You, and you." He pointed at about a half dozen of the other men. "Come with me."

The four soldiers marched them along the well-trodden route to what remained of the crematorium. They didn't have time to bundle up, and their feet were freezing. Henk thought his toes would end up frostbitten. For some strange reason, he worried he was losing his toes just like he had with his teeth. The pain in his feet painfully twisted his heart. Toothless and toeless. The image was ridiculous, but it terrified him. He felt sick to his stomach suddenly and shook his head. These were silly thoughts, he realized. Then he had another terrible idea. They were going to be shot by these soldiers for the work they had done. They routinely shot the Kapos, those prisoners assigned to watch over fellow prisoners. They received better treatment and had perks, but they were always inevitably replaced by new Kapos. Were they now going to do the same with their foreign slave labor?

Unable to come to any sort of alternative, Henk stupidly trudged along. His heart kept skipping beats. He held his hands in his armpits and felt the freezing air rasp through his lungs. He started to sweat despite the cold. Finally, when they arrived at the one functioning crematorium, the guards pointed at a mound of dead bodies thrown in a massive pile the night before. These were killed prisoners, still in their pajamas, piled up like stacks of firewood.

"You are to burn these bodies. Do not stop until the Russians stop you by bullets or you are finished getting rid of them all." The soldiers trained their guns on them.

Slowly, Henk and the men looked around the ovens. There were still embers in the chamber of the one functioning oven. Henk looked over at the pile of bodies. They could only cremate four or five bodies at a time.

"Get the fires going! *Geh raus!*"

Henk walked over and grabbed a shovel leaning against the back wall and took it to a vast pile of coal. He looked back. Frans also took a spade. As the others fell into line and carried out chores, all but one soldier left, and he kept his rifle on the men.

As time went on, the SS trooper tired and sat on a barrel and kept his rifle handy, its nose pointing down. He nervously munched on nuts, flicking away the shells.

"Frans, what do you think? There's more of us than him."

Frans looked over at the soldier. Then he looked at the other men. Frans shook his head and went back to work.

Henk walked closer to the window to steal a look at where the other soldiers went. He could see in the distance there were groups of them with prisoners, and there were guards still in the tall guard towers. He lowered his head and kept working. His mind raced with how to get out of their situation successfully. At least, the cavernous workspace was warming with the fire in the oven. Henk no longer felt cold. He had to open his shirt against the heat.

Suddenly, the ground rocked beneath them. The German soldier jumped up and scurried outside. After a while, as Henk opened the oven for someone to scrape out the ashes and bones, he realized it had been a very long time, and the soldier hadn't returned. He stood back and looked around.

"Where is he?" he asked no one in particular.

Someone next to him looked over to where the soldier had been. He looked back at Henk and shrugged his bony shoulders. "I don't know!"

Henk dropped what he was doing and ran over to the doors. He looked out and saw that the camp looked deserted. He stepped out onto the trodden snow and looked around. No guard. All vehicles were gone. Over the sound of the oven, they couldn't hear anything outside the building. They were left to die at the hands of the Russians.

Henk ran back in. Frans walked up to him, questioningly.

"He's gone. They're all gone, I think."

"Did you go out to the fence?" Frans asked.

"Fence?"

"To know what's happening everywhere else." Frans immediately walked through the doors, and disappeared. Henk followed, as did the other men.

They followed Frans to the fence.

Henk looked up at the guard's tower. There was no one there. As he came closer to Frans, he too looked along the length of the fence. Most of the towers closest to them had no guards. Henk could also see the back of what appeared to be the last of the prisoners marched out the notorious front gates.

Suddenly, a puff of smoke came out of one of the towers closest to the front. A bullet hit the man next to Henk.

He jumped back. Henk was astounded that the soldier could aim so precisely from that distance. Bullets rained around him and the men. Henk broke into a run and back around the barracks to the safety of the crematorium. A few hundred yards from the building, he looked up and saw the white, grey plume of smoke still billowing from the last remaining chimney.

"A truck full of troopers are coming in our direction," yelled Frans as he caught up.

Henk turned around in time for Frans to grab him and run back into the crematorium building.

They turned and faced the other men following them into the building. Henk counted the men and they were all accounted for except the one who was shot. They barricaded the doors with everything they could find.

"The bodies!" someone yelled.

Henk stepped back in shock and disbelief. He refused to move the bodies in harm's way. He shook his head.

Frans pulled at him. Henk shook his head again, vehemently.

"Come on, Henk!" Frans pulled Henk over. As he followed, he thought he could hear trucks coming closer, but it was hard to tell. Suddenly, explosions rambled against the cement walls. Different kinds of bombs. Somewhere in the camp.

As Henk jumped over the growing barrier at the door, he ran and grabbed a body. He dragged it by its arms toward the door.

It groaned.

Henk dropped the hands and shrieked. He stood and stared intently at the corpse.

Frans went by him with a corpse. "What?" he called over.

Henk pointed at the young man. "This one is still alive."

"They do that; trapped air escapes their lungs. It sounds like they're still alive." Frans yelled as he placed his corpse at the edge of the pile.

Henk looked again at the young man. As he leaned over and looked into the gaunt face, the lids stirred. "*Jezus Christus!*" Henk yelled. Henk immediately pulled the young man to the side out of harm's way. He slapped the pasty white face until a touch of pink showed under the crepey skin. Henk put his ear to his chest and heard a very faint heartbeat. He looked again at the familiar face. The boy looked like someone Henk once knew. Suddenly, he had a flash of the young boy, Lothar, a couple of years before. It was Lothar!

Quickly, as if his entire life depended upon it, he rubbed Lothar's hands. Then his feet. He took off his shirt and put it over his body. Lothar's eyelids fluttered again, and his body began to shake. Slowly the lids opened.

Suddenly, machine guns spewed bullets at the building. Some of them went through the door, the windows. One of the men was shot between the eyes and ricocheted back.

Henk looked up and watched him fall. He hunched over Lothar, covering his face from debris with his hand. Then he took his hand away to look at Lothar's face.

Lothar's eyes rolled in their sockets.

Henk sobbed. "Lothar, I've got you. You hang in there."

The roar of crackling flames and white smoke outside the building caught Henk's attention. Flames licked at the windows and through cracks of doors. Machine gun fire once again puncturing surfaces, this time blowing in the top of the doors. A can of gasoline came through another window, spraying its contents as it flew threw the air. It landed on the bodies by the door. An instant later, flames crept through the front doors and lapped at the gasoline sprinkled surface of the pile, and it whooshed into a monstrous blaze.

Henk's eyes darted around, squinting against the smoke. He could see no way out. As the flames crawled up the walls to the ceiling and along the dirt, it hit the pile of coal.

Henk lifted Lothar, carrying him as far away from the flames as possible.

"Henk!" called Frans.

Henk cupped his mouth. "Frans! Here!" Smoke filled every nook and cranny, and it was difficult to see anything. Henk's eyes burned with the acid-like smoke. He held his arm against his face to breathe. He waited to hear a reply.

There was none.

Henk fell back against the wall, his legs bent, his hands hanging over his knees. He looked down at Lothar, who was now silently watching him from where he lay.

Henk wiped his eyes and squinted at the growing wall of smoke. He lowered his head.

"We're finally leaving this Hell," he said to Lothar, reaching over to touch his bony chest. He frowned. He shook Lothar slightly. "Lothar?" Henk knelt beside him and shook him again. He slapped Lothar's face. "Lothar!" He saw by the lips turning blue and the face pale that Lothar was no more. He held Lothar's hand. He shook, and hot tears stung his eyes more than the acrid smoke. He thought of Pietje. How tall he must be. Of Beppie and little Corrie. Was Cornelia well? Were they dead like Lothar? Were they still alive, or would he be meeting them soon on the other side?"

As he passed out, he was curiously, not afraid. Slowly, he imagined the walls falling all around him. He dreamt a truck drove into the inferno. Henk knew the SS was going to do everything possible to make sure the truth died with them. In his case, he wryly thought they accomplished the job.

Chapter 22
March 1945

Corrie, her feet bound in rags against the spring thaw and mud, trudged toward her *Opa*'s house. Or at least, she trudged the only route the cement Atlantic Wall would allow; she had to first walk to the closest gap in the wall and then double-back along the other side of the wall, back to the canal, then to the house above the pub. Corrie stopped, out of breath and energy, and looked in the distance to the closest opening through the wall. She was weak with hunger, and slid down onto the driest spot in the mud and leaned back against the cement wall. The cobblestones in the road had warmed in the sun causing all the snow to melt. It had been a harsh, cold winter with record-breaking snowfalls. When February hit, the temperatures rose so dramatically, the city became one muddy mess. The snow melted so quickly the waters saturated the top layers of the ground before the frost below could melt.

Consequently, it was a bloody mess, and traveling anywhere was a challenge. At least, the cobblestones in the road were dry. Corrie looked at fresh horse manure steaming in the middle of the road before her. She wondered about the horse. It was a soldier's horse, she knew. All the other horses, people ate long ago.

She looked up the street from where she came. There were far fewer civilians in the city. She, Pietje, Beppie, and Hennie were some of the few children left. She leaned back again. She was starving. She had secretly hoped that perhaps her *Opa* had a stash of food. She passed a stall with sugar beets earlier, but she had no money. Pietje stole some beets the other day, and she cooked and shredded it, making *pannenkoeken*. It burned the throat and the stomach. It occurred to her it was better to eat tulip bulbs than sugar beets. Recently, she had come across a small cook book put together by the *Regeering* on how to cook tulip bulbs, and she tried many of the new recipes. But tulip bulbs, in whatever form, still tasted like tulip bulbs.

She looked across the road to see where she and Pietje had dug up a massive slew of bulbs the previous night. They belonged to the city, but they didn't care one bit. She cooked them for breakfast and had some ready for supper. But it caused her terrible heartburn.

She looked back to where she came from again and spied a tall, gaunt man stumbling toward her. Eventually, he came close enough for her to see sores on the man's skeletal face. As he stopped opposite her, he looked down at her.

Her eyes widened and she struggled to stand up.

He held up his hand to her and his mouth opened, as if to speak. As she stood up straight and pressed back against the cement wall, he stepped back and lowered his arm. He turned and continued walking.

She watched him walk away. He suddenly collapsed onto his knees, then fell face down.

She jumped back in shock. She covered her mouth and stared, not knowing what to do. But he wasn't the first person she saw drop dead from hunger. She knew the term people gave this Hunger Winter:

Honger's noot,
Honger's dood.

Corrie licked her dry, cracked lips. She wondered what the right thing was to do. It was the first time she was alone with a dead person. In the back of her head, she thought it would probably be wise to see what the man had in his pockets. Perhaps he had some food. But that was a silly thought because if he had food, he wouldn't be dying of hunger. Instead, maybe he had some money. That was another silly thought, she realized. He would've used it to buy food. As she stood, quivering with indecision, she noticed another man coming from the opposite direction pulling a wagon with branches piled on top. She could tell he saw both her and the man on the ground.

Corrie wondered where he found the wood, and then she had a thought. What if this man took what belongs to Corrie. After all, the man died right in front of her.

Corrie retreated into her head, as she stared at the dead man's coat pockets. She stood indecisively as her frail body swayed to the beat of her pounding heart. Corrie did not look up at the man when he stopped beside the body. He said something to her, but she didn't hear the words. A storm roared in her brain. She looked up and watched him go through the man's pockets. He stopped when he found the man's identification papers. As he read them, he sadly shook his head. Slowly, he put the papers back into the man's pocket and gently lifted him onto the wood on the wagon. Carefully, he put the hands over top of the other over the man's sunken midriff, and readjusted the head. The dead man's eyes stared up, his last look into a bright early spring sky.

As Corrie quivered, she watched the man bend over to close the dead man's eyes. Then he turned, waved at her feebly, and pulled the man along.

Corrie's eyes watered. She blinked the tears away and felt them rolling over her feverish cheeks. She stared blankly at her surroundings. Then she looked down on the ground where some of the man's branches had fallen. Out of habit, her hands picked up the wood. Then she stood not knowing what to do. She knew nothing. She thought nothing. She felt nothing. She only wanted to lie down, go to sleep and, like that man, never wake up.

She looked at the pavement and then the cobblestones on the street. She slowly turned and watched a truck full of SS Troops race toward her. Her eyes remained glued on the vehicle. As it passed her, she looked up into blue eyes, grey eyes, brown eyes of very young faces. Boys. All were staring back at her. One waved. It was Rebecca.

She held up her hand to wave back. "Rebecca," she whispered. She stood watching Rebecca's face as the truck disappeared around the far corner of the Atlantic Wall.

Corrie sat on a chair and stared at her toes. She had dug them into the sand. She wiggled her dirty toes. They looked like thick worms. People in Africa ate worms, she thought. She bent down and brushed two fleas away from her bare leg. She sat back and rocked.

She had tried to keep Hennie occupied by building sandcastles in the sand, but it didn't work for very long.

Hennie cried. She was crying all the time now. Hennie had a big stomach, and it wasn't food that filled it. Hennie was dying of starvation.

I'm dying of starvation, too, Corrie thought. She put a hand on her own bulging stomach.

She thought of the tall man who fell dead in front of her. She never did get to her *Opa*'s that day. She simply did not have the energy to walk that far. She sat back against the Atlantic Wall for a very long time before Pietje came looking for her. They slowly traced their steps back and it was dark by the time they came into the house.

She looked over to the stairs when she heard someone coming down from the attic. Beppie walked into her view. "What are you doing?" she sneered.

"I'm going to die," announced Corrie. She looked up at the ceiling above her head and looked where Pietje had started to take down the strapping from behind the plaster, exposing the floor from the attic above her. She looked down into the sand and saw the bits of plaster they missed after cleaning up the debris.

There was ample water now. So much so, that all pots, bowls, bins, even the big laundry bin, were filled to the top.

She queerily had a notion that there might be something behind the whore houses she was going to miss. She looked at the window. She continued to listen to Beppie, talking in the background, as she imagined missing out on *patates frites*; perhaps a morsel of cake. Or a small fruit tart.

"This is stupid," sneered Beppie, cutting into Corrie's wandering thoughts.

"WHAT'S STUPID?" yelled Pietje from the water closet. He made a tumbling noise and came out of the stinking nook. He hiked up his pants and tied the hemp rope as tightly as he could around his protruding belly.

"THIS IS STUPID!" yelled Beppie. She lunged at the accordion case in the corner for the second time, and grabbed the handle. She pulled it off the floor shelf beside the stove and lugged it toward the door.

Pietje jumped at her and grabbed the case.

"I'm selling it for food. I'm going to take it to the *markt* and sell it. I'm going to buy bread. Beautiful big loaves of bread. Jam." Her eyes widened. "Butter," she screamed excitedly.

Pietje yanked at the case. He was weakening. They all were.

Beppie yanked the case back. "No!" she screamed.

Pietje jumped on her.

"Leave me alone, ugly animal! I hate this. I hate this house. I hate you!" She grunted as she fought to free herself.

Corrie looked over at the curtains and saw one move aside slowly and then close again. She twisted and looked at Beppie and Pietje. That case. Her father. That case.

"And why do you care about Pappa's accordion? He hates you. Do you think he'll be grateful to you? It won't matter. He thinks it's your fault they had to get married!"

"Beppie," their mother croaked from the depths of the bedstead.

Pietje froze, his nostrils flared.

"And what does it matter anyway! He's dead, and we'll be dead, too, if we don't sell his accordion!"

"Pietje," their mother tried again but with no success.

"He's not dead!" Pietje snarled. "You take that back!"

"He's dead!" screamed Beppie.

Pietje tore the case away from her and let it fly into the soft sand with a thud. He grabbed Beppie by the hair and dragged her screeching to the kitchen corner, knocking over a chair on the way. At the laundry bin, Pietje plunged Beppie's head into the water.

Hennie cried from the bedstead. Corrie looked over at the curtains and saw her mother's shaking hand trying to keep the curtain open.

Corrie felt dizzy. A body, mind, and heart could only take so much pain and confusion. Corrie looked at what was unfolding in the kitchen corner. She saw the back of Pietje. His legs were far apart, straining forward with his feet digging into the sand as he fought to keep Beppie under control. His left hand kept Beppie's head underwater while he kept a grip on the side of the bin with his right hand.

Corrie realized Pietje wasn't letting go of Beppie. Beppie's body, trapped underneath Pietje, jerked and jumped, her arms flailed at Pietje, but they didn't hit their mark. Beppie's head was in the bin longer than Corrie felt comfortable, and slowly she felt panic rise. Finally, fully awake, she realized Pietje wasn't going to let go of Beppie.

Corrie slowly pushed against the table and stood. She opened her mouth to scream but couldn't find her voice. Instead, Corrie stumbled to Pietje and weakly slapped him on the back. Then she pulled at Pietje's shirt. Then at his hair. She slapped his ears and tugged at his collar. She pounded him on his back. She scratched him. She kicked the back of his legs. Finally, she found her voice. "Stop, Pietje, stop! Please! Please stop!" she cried as she fell back, exhausted and helpless.

A flying pot hit Pietje in the head. In shock, Pietje let go of Beppie, who blubbered and coughed, her hair creating a wave of water as she jumped back, splattering the ceiling, walls, everyone's clothing, and spreading the water over the sand.

Corrie looked over and saw her mother quivering outside her bedstead. Hennie's cries cut through the unexpected silence.

"There is no blame, Beppie!"

Corrie looked at Beppie. She was gasping for breath. Her eyes were bloodshot and her face swollen. She pulled wet hair out of her face as she stared at their mother.

"Your father and I love all of you," she whispered. "And Pietje, especially because he is our firstborn, and he has kept us alive." She stumbled and reached out to the chair. She held out an arm to Beppie. "*Kind*, I know what you are going through. You don't say very much, but I know."

Beppie took a step toward her mother, then stopped. Her face collapsed as she jumped into her mother's arms, almost knocking her over.

Corrie jumped to help her mother sit. As she did, Corrie adjusted her nightgown. Her mother's bones protruded against skin. She looked away, as Beppie fell on her knees into the sand at her mother's feet and bawled clinging to her tiny body. Cornelia looked at her son.

"Pietje, Beppie does not mean to be difficult. Everyone has their own way of coping with grief." Cornelia bent her head over Beppie, caressing her sodden hair.

Pietje stood still, breathing deeply, staring, deep in thought.

Suddenly, someone pounded on their door.

No one moved. The intensity of the moment was too deep.

The person pounded on the door again.

Corrie, closest to the door, turned and reached up to the doorknob. Slowly, she opened the door, half expecting to see an SS. Instead, it was *Tante* Antonia.

"*Tante* Antonia!" she whispered, surprised.

Antonia didn't look the same anymore, though Corrie knew it was her. Her brown hair was now grey, and she had lost much weight. There were dark circles under her eyes, eyes that darted at the scene spread out in front of her. She covered her mouth in shock.

Tante Antonia held onto the side of the door to carefully lower herself into the sand. She stood and wrung her hands, looking at the skeleton that was her sister-in-law, Cornelia, leaning over a drenched Beppie at her feet. Antonia eyed the sand floor and the missing walls.

Cornelia slowly looked up at *Tante* Antonia. Beppie, too, raised her swollen face. Beppie moved back and stood up so her mother could reach out to encircle her thin arms around her approaching sister-in-law.

"I'm sorry so much time has gone by since we've seen each other. Pap was ill and I—well, the children went off to a farm a few months ago, and after they left, I became quite sick." She wrung her hands. "I haven't heard from Frans and I—well." She covered her face and broke down in tears.

Corrie watched her mother stand and hold *Tante* Antonia closer. She nodded when she pulled away and sat down again, exhausted.

"I know, Antonia, I know," their mother whispered.

"Oh, of course, you would, too!" *Tante* Antonia sat in the other chair, took out a handkerchief from her coat pocket, and blew her nose. She reached out and patted Cornelia's hand and nodded. *Tante* Antonia sadly looked around, fidgeting. Then she looked over at Pietje. Then she looked at Beppie again. "You look like drowned rats." Her eyes brimmed with tears. She stood up. "I've come to make sure you knew that the Red Cross is giving out a ration of dried milk powder in Oranjeplein." She pointed out the window. "A member from each family has to come, and I can vouch for the five of you. But one of you will have to come with me."

Corrie looked around. Neither Pietje nor Beppie could go, as they were soaking wet. She looked down at her bloody arm. It was throbbing, and she felt feverish. "I'll go, *Tante* Antonia." She got up and slowly walked to the door. *Tante* Antonia stopped her and picked up the old man's coat Beppie had been wearing and put it around Corrie's little shoulders. With her good hand, Corrie pulled it tightly around herself. How fortuitous that the distribution was only kitty-corner from their lane. Because she knew for sure, she didn't have the strength to go much further.

"Do what the nurse instructed you to do," *Tante* Antonia said over Hennie's cries when she and Corrie returned from Oranjeplain. It was getting dark, and Pietje had pulled the black-out curtains shut. One single candle flickered on the table while shards of warm light danced on the torn ceiling from the stove. "Corrie, you tell your brother and sisters what they must do."

Corrie looked up at *Tante* Antonia, remembering the conversation they had with the Red Cross nurse.

"Go ahead," smiled *Tante* Antonia.

"They said to save our energy by resting in bed, and we must only break a little piece off at a time to suck it very slowly. Our stomachs won't be able to handle more than that. It will slowly help give us some strength."

"Yes," nodded *Tante* Antonia. "Do that for me, please?" she said, looking at Beppie and Pietje.

Pietje nodded, as did Beppie.

Corrie put down the package with the Red Cross symbol on the top.

Tante Antonie wiped at the tip of her nose with her handkerchief and then stuffed it, along with her package, into the deep pocket of her coat. "I have to go back to your *Opa* now, and I have a long walk ahead of me, thanks to that stupid Atlantic Wall." *Tante* Antonia held out her hands, begging for a hug from everyone.

"Let me help you, Cornelia," she said, as she helped Cornelia on her feet and walked her back to the bedstead. They spoke softly together before *Tante* Antonia kissed her on the cheek and stood up. She hugged everyone and walked to the door.

She stopped suddenly and looked down at her bare legs. Corrie saw fleas and watched as her *tante* swiped them away. *Tante* Antonia turned to wait while Pietje hid the candle behind his hand before she opened the door. *Tante* Antonia reached up to the door frame and, with a grunt, pulled herself up over the threshold. She turned in the dark, nodded, blew a kiss and waved. She didn't say a word from then on, but Corrie could swear she saw her about to break down and cry again before she closed the door.

Corrie looked down at the package in the soft candle light and opened it. She felt Beppie and Pietje move closer to her, to watch. Corrie unwrapped the chunky dried milk powder and took a tiny morsel. She tried to put it into Hennie's mouth first. She shook her head and refused to take it.

"*Nee. Vies.*" She squirmed away from Corrie's hand.

"Corrie, let me help you," said Pietje. He picked up Hennie and put her on the other chair. As Beppie and Corrie watched, Pietje tried to get a morsel of dried milk into Hennie's mouth by pretending it was a plane. "*Kijk*, Hennie. It's a plane!" He blew through his lips and made a flying noise. Then he aimed it at Hennie's mouth. This time it went past the lips.

Corrie picked up a cup of water, and Pietje held it out to Hennie, and she drank the whole glass. Hennie smacked her lips, giggled, and pulled Pietje's hands closer so that she could drink more water.

Corrie and Pietje laughed. "I have to get you more water, it's empty, Hennie. Just a moment." Pietje got up. Beppie suddenly took the glass. Pietje froze and looked at her.

"I'll get her water," Beppie said softly.

Pietje looked at Corrie. She shrugged slightly. Then they both watched, surprised, as Beppie took the glass of water, put it on the table, and picked Hennie up to put on her lap.

Pietje and Corrie looked at each other in surprise. They smiled and watched Beppie gently hold the glass while Hennie clung to it and drank.

Corrie slowly took a chunk of dried milk powder out from under her pillow and broke a tiny piece off. She put it in her mouth and let it slowly melt. Corrie fell in and out of sleep. At one point, a fly flew through the cracks in the attic ceiling and buzzed around her face, bringing her back to wakefulness. But that didn't last very long and she fell deep asleep, once again.

The next morning, sunshine filtered through the cracks and did a jitterbug on her eyelids. A pigeon, resting on the warm clay shingles above, flapped its wings directly between her and the sun. Slowly, she became aware of sirens wailing and rib-shaking explosions.

It didn't matter what happened; they had to stay in the house. Even if her mother did get better, Corrie did not have the energy to go anywhere. Lying in bed hearing bombers coming closer, was a bit of a wrestling match for her, but soon her stoicism won out. If death happened, it happened.

This time a bomb exploded just a few blocks away.

The impact was deafening. Dirt poured down from the clay shingles above her. She looked over at Hennie and Beppie, sleeping next to her in bed.

Beppie's eyes flew wide open, and a look of terror pinched her face.

"Guys, get down here!" yelled Pietje from downstairs.

Corrie threw the blankets aside. Perhaps the dried milk had helped after all. She felt she had far more energy. She quickly got Hennie off the bed and she awkwardly held her coming down the stairs. Beppie followed. They all crammed into the bedstead and huddled together with their mother.

The house shook violently. They clung to each other, crying, yelping as they heard screaming bombs drop from the sky, and land five, four, or three blocks away. They listened to the mighty V2 Rockets shoot from the Haagse Bos into the air, and Corrie shivered with fright as she remembered the rockets when they failed were known to fall back onto rooftops of surrounding buildings.

Corrie and her family waited helplessly as the bombing continued for ten days straight. One night, Corrie dared herself to crawl up to the attic and look out the small window. Between the buildings, she saw the massive fire and smoke pillar of a V2 rocket launch. The Hague had become a frontline of the war.

Exhaustion must always take its toll, and Corrie fell deeply asleep after sleepless nights amidst the horrific noise and chaos.

She dreamt of blood; the blood of human remains, the blood of German soldiers, blood of fathers, neighbors, friends. Blood of Rebecca and her family. Blood of the chicken half-beheaded. Blood of the rabbits they slaughtered. She dreamt of her father lying in a pit covered in blood and surrounded by the guts of other people.

Even in sleep, she felt heat burning her eyes, the blood having reflected too long and too deeply into their depths of horror. She dreamt of the pilots that never jumped out of their falling planes. She relived visions of soldiers in parachutes shot to death like sitting ducks hanging in mid-air, bodies limp as they continued to drop. She dreamt she would never be normal, crazed instead. She dreamt of her mother's gaunt face, her dying carcass, her starving little sister. She dreamt that a V2 rocket misfired and fell back to earth, and landed on top of their small house. Each time she was about to awaken to awareness of her dreams, she thought she was still in the depths of her nightmare and could no longer recognize what was real. She cried when awake and also in her sleep for the people who were surely smashed, burned, torn to pieces, obliterated just meters away.

And somehow, miraculously, their little house remained whole as did their bodies. But their minds were traumatized.

Pietje opened the black-out curtains and stood for a moment with his eyes squeezed shut against the glare. Corrie watched him from the bedstead, also squinting against the sudden light. Silence roared in her ears, louder than the days of bombing and horrific assault combined. She leaned against the cold back wall. Their bodies warmed the bedstead enclosure while they huddled together, but the rest of the house was frigid in the early spring morning.

Corrie watched her mother stir slightly under the cover. She looked down at her face, partially hidden by a sheet. Beppie was still asleep in the far corner, as was Hennie.

Slowly, she climbed as gently as she could over her mother and slid off the mattress. She closed the curtains behind her. She hurried to the water closet, opened the door, and gingerly sat on the cold wooden seat. Plumes of icy air wafted up from the stinking depths. It made her shiver uncontrollably. She finally pulled up her haggard woolen underwear that had to be safety-pinned to her undershirt to stay up. She stepped out of the water closet and went to splash some water on her face at the laundry bin.

"Corrie, wake up Beppie," said Pietje softly.

"Why?"

"Because we need wood to burn. There will be lots to burn where they bombed."

Cornelia thought, bodies. Blood. She gazed at Pietje.

He looked back. Then he walked over to the bedstead and poked his head into the enclosure. Corrie could hear him whispering to Beppie.

Beppie groaned.

A moment later, Pietje helped Beppie out of the bedstead. Beppie went into the water closet, and Pietje went over to Corrie at the kitchen corner.

"Where's the dried milk powder," asked Pietje.

Corrie walked over to the bedstead and peeked in. She spied the remainder of the Red Cross package next to Hennie and leaned in and took it out. Slowly, she unwrapped it as she went to the table. Beppie came back out of the water closet and, between the three of them, they took a morsel, ate it, and drank as much water as they could hold. "To fill the stomach," Pietje said. Then they dressed warmly and left the house.

A bomb destroyed a water main, and the three children stepped around pools of water and mud in the alley.

They slowly trudged onto Spinozastraat. There, they stopped and looked both ways. The sun shone on a city cruelly painted by a brown and black brush here and there with a heavy sprinkling of ash that looked like icing sugar. Debris, paper, plaster, splinters stuck out of a thin layer of what looked like snow. They had a choice of going along the Groene Wegje or the other way by Oranjelaan.

"Do you think the bridges are still in?" asked Corrie, as Pietje led them to the left along Oranjelaan.

"We'll just have to double back if the bridge is out this way," Pietje said, breathing heavily.

Their noses ran, their eyes teared, and they didn't walk very far before they spent what little energy they could muster. The three stopped a few times to catch their breath before moving on. They clapped their cold hands and kept them under their coats until warm enough to move on. The air was cold in the shadows of the sun but when they walked along a sunny part of the street, they turned their faces up to the cloudless sky. The heat of the sun's rays and light felt good. It warmed Corrie's front, and gave her healing nourishment. She remembered other sunny days. She thought of past days on the beach in Scheveningen and happier days playing beside the canal. Playing on the ground while her father groomed his horse. She remembered the ant and her water bombs. Suffer. She knew what suffer meant now.

As they continued, they saw others slowly making their way through the ash and debris, undoubtedly with the same mission in mind. Foraging, finding treasures that would keep them alive. Perhaps some food. Plumes of smoke rose from behind the last building at the corner.

As they turned and faced the canal at the end of Oranjelaan, they came to a sudden stop. Corrie gasped and looked from right to left. Was she dreaming? Through large clear pockets within the wall of smoke, they saw there was barely nothing left standing on the other side of the canal. Nothing except skeletal remains of the odd structure. Corrie felt her heart beating hard against her ribcage. A whole part of her world was gone—demolished. It all disappeared: people, buildings, parks, streets, sidewalks, bicycles.

"Come," said Pietje, grabbing Corrie's hand.

Corrie let Pietje guide and pull her along. She looked over at Beppie as they walked. Beppie was focusing on the sharp objects on the ground and stepped gingerly over things in her bandaged feet. Corrie noticed that the bottom of Beppie's feet had worn through the layers of material and she could see the skin on the side of one of her feet. She looked down at her own. She hadn't taken the rags off her feet for days and had only wrapped more hemp or string to keep the tattered protective bundle on her feet.

Corrie kept an eye on the ground, too. There was wood with nails, plaster chunks, glass. She slowed down and pulled at Pietje. She was frightened of falling forward and landing on her hands, cutting them. She kept a wary eye on where their feet took them.

As they neared the bridge, people joined them. Wordlessly, grimly, silently, they fell into line and crossed the bridge miraculously left intact. Corrie looked down at the canal. There was a significant amount of indescribable rubble tossed into the water. She thought she saw the back of a body and wanted to make sure it didn't need saving, but Pietje kept pulling her along, and she had to tear her eyes away.

They turned onto Schenkweg. People climbed slowly, slothfully, through the scattered debris, flattened buildings, and misshappen melted metal. Plumes of smoke squirreled out from underneath the rubble and sought the clear blue sky before joining into a more massive cloud of smoke that puffed and gyrated to the heavens. As Pietje looked for a safe place to forage, Corrie saw arms, legs, fingers, bodies with clothing, a headless torso, a baby. They continued trudging ahead. She stood by, stunned, as Pietje and Beppie pulled at wooden planks, handrails, bits of boxes. At one point, Pietje looked at her. She slowly looked at him. He looked down at where she had been staring.

A mangled body, half-covered in plaster dust and ash, the skin blue against the white of the ash, blue lips, one eye searching the clouds above.

"Don't look, Corrie," said Pietje, pulling her away from the gruesome sight. "Come, stand by me."

Corrie silently watched as Pietje yanked out a whole door. He dragged it over to where the road used to be and found a small clearing. She watched as Pietje and Beppie trudged back and forth, back and forth, piling wood onto the door. She looked around and watched other people search through the rubble.

Bricks were toppled here and there, in their efforts to find pieces of wood to burn.

She looked back at Pietje and saw him pull at a rope and free it. He perused it as he held it up in the air. It wriggled and twisted like a hairy snake. Pietje wrapped it around the pile of wood they had made on the door. He tied the rope's ends to the doorknob and tested the strength of the line by yanking it.

Satisfied, they started their way back. Corrie had to walk past the same contorted human remains and metal. Suddenly, she stopped. Corrie could not walk another step. She stood shivering in the warmth of the sun and stared at nothing. Corrie didn't want to see and didn't want to think. She wanted to go back to sleep.

She was startled when Pietje gently took her by the shoulders.

"Here, you sit on this pile, Corrie. Beppie and I will pull you."

Pietje placed her on top of the pile of gathered wood tied to the door. She bent forward and held the rope and watched the landscape slowly fall back as if it was the very same never-ending nightmare in reverse.

Chapter 23
April 1945

Distant rumblings and muffled explosions filled the nights. Bright flashes of light on the horizon masqueraded as lightning bolts promising much-needed rain. But no, this was human-made thunder and lightning—a sad and brutal show of despair, destruction, and continual death. Corrie knew this monster well. It stoked her fears every day and every night. Her worries had become constant companions, dragging her into the depths of blackness that a ten-year-old should not know. What she saw and heard was part of danger's ongoing, never-ending opera. She knew each flash meant people died—a tremendous and tragic extravaganza. The air was there to fuel the fires, consuming human bodies. And she knew well that it was the Nazi monster's last attempts to keeping its hold on her world.

Corrie stood barefoot watching the distant displays of desperate fighting in the black of the night. She had known nothing but war since her fifth year. Now she was ten years old. Wise in the ways of surviving against all odds. Her large, deep-set aqua eyes were wise beyond her years in things that no being so small should see. Yet she suffered with innocent acceptance. Life had become such. She could barely remember when it was not this way. Fear and a sense of foreboding hung over her as she slept fully-clothed, awaiting those sirens, the bearers of coming destruction and possible death, and complete loss. Yet for years now, they had gambled, and remained in their defenseless little home, to stand by their dying mother.

Their little home had become a mere shell. All walls, ceilings, and floors sacrificed as fuel. Now wood was only to be found in recently-bombed areas of the city, at the cost of other people's lives. One day, they took part of a mantle over a dead family's stove from over 'there.' They burned trim taken off a dead old lady's door over 'here.' They burned portions of wooden chairs found 'further on.' And so it went every single day.

The circle of life.

Their circle of life.

They weren't the only ones relying on this macabre exchange of death for such an unfortunate source of heat. Walking skeletons in loose rags infested scenes of tragic destruction. Slow, ponderous steps, their heads down, gaunt faces, and grey. No energy to acknowledge a fellow human life who also treaded softly amongst the torn dead, scrounging through the splintered wood.

Her ear suddenly picked up another familiar sound in the distance. Closer. Immediately more menacing. Jackboots. The sound of an engine. They were moving their ack-acks from one place to another, hoping to confuse allied bombers, helping to increase the collateral damage of the already dying civilians.

More wood.

She looked behind her to where bushes provided cover. Their branches had begun to bear new fragile buds of hope. She pondered on how the green of the earth with the coming spring could not foresee potential danger and destruction and try to stay dormant. New life stubbornly broke through thawing earth, appeared on bare branches and twigs. But there was no room for any form of life, she thought. Just constant worsening, constant dying, spiraling into destruction. There was no use in bearing buds. No use in life.

The sparse bushes and grass ignored her, Corrie thought. They were going to stubbornly grow anyway, taking risks as she did. She thought of the starving woman she saw the day before on her hands and knees in the dirt, desperately stuffing newly-grown grass into her mouth.

    She turned slowly and backed into the bushes, crouching on her haunches. The jackboots were close. Out of habit, she lowered herself onto her stomach. Moments later, a series of jackboots came startlingly close. She watched them pass. Her nose was just feet away. They were so close she could smell the polish on the leather. Dust spewed from their steps and powdered her already filthy face, threatening a sneeze. She quickly pinched her nose, her eyes wide with fear. Then she saw the massive tires, and the gigantic undercarriage of what she knew was an *ack-ack*. After it rumbled past, she wiped her eyes and waited for her heart to stop fighting to get out of her chest, before putting her hands on the ground to push up. Her weak arms trembled with the effort, and she lay back down.

    Everyone slept day and night to conserve energy, to mercifully sleep away the daily fear and the painful pangs of hunger. But it was the agony of starvation that drove her out just after midnight. The whore houses drew her as if by magic. The filthy garbage bins had become her Mecca, her holy shrines. Her promise of life.

    She waited a moment before trying to get up again. She lay her little face on her filthy hands and allowed the darkness to comfort and shelter her for another few moments.

    Tonight, all she found in the usual bins behind the whores' homes were burnt pieces of sugar beets. Not good enough to eat for the whores, who were evidently not doing well themselves, but indeed good enough for little Corrie. There were no potato peels. She could feel the meagre bounty in her skirt pockets. Perhaps there was more food to find around the newly-bombed homes, but one needed the energy to walk that far.

    Energy she did not have.

    Neither did Pietje nor Beppie.

    Her next attempt to raise herself got her onto her hands and knees. She slowly crawled out from under the bushes and stood up. She felt lightheaded, faint—a common occurrence now.

She crossed Spinozastraat and into her alley. The smell of death was strong in the lane, where there was less wind. People died throughout the day, every single day. There was no wood for coffins, so they were laid to rest on tables, in beds, on floors, and in churches. Sometimes they lay where they fell. They died of starving and fell off their bikes in the street. They collapsed from starvation in mid-stride along a sidewalk. A person crossing the street could suddenly crumple into a mound of clothing, hunger finally biting the dust. There they lay for hours, for days, for weeks. Corrie knew that *Meneer* Beek, around the corner on Van der Duynstraat, died two weeks ago, and he was still lying in the front room of his house. Not enough wood for coffins. And not enough hands to help. Everyone was dying.

Numbed to the horrors in life, she still sharply feared the loss of her mother. It seemed to Corrie that her mother had been hanging onto nothing but a silver thread tied to the gates of heaven for a very long time.

Hennie, too, had stopped crying. Too weak to cry. Corrie feared her little sister would not survive.

Crying was what Corrie knew how to do best. Her soul and heart cried throughout the day and night.

She was so very, very tired.

She entered the dark house and was careful to slowly lower herself to the flea-infested sand. The smell of sewage under the water closet overwhelmed her. It added to the smell of death and their endless misery and dismay.

Without taking the burned pieces of sugar beet out of her pocket, she slowly walked through the house. She dragged herself through the cool sand to where Beppie and Pietje slept. Slowly, she felt for the rags they were laying on, found a spot, and collapsed next to them.

A knock. Several knocks. Corrie slowly woke up. Light shone through the crevices around the front door and dark curtains at the window.

"*Ja*, hello?"

Corrie opened one eye and looked over at the doorway. She saw the doorknob turn. The door slowly opened, and an older man in a long overcoat filled the opening, blocking the light. He sniffed at the air. "Is there anyone home? Anyone alive?"

Corrie heard stirring in the bedstead above her and at her feet. She slowly raised her head and squinted at the man. She looked over and saw Pietje weakly raising his head.

"*Ach, onze liefe heertje,*" the man said, gently. "Seyss-Inquart has finally allowed us to bring in some emergency food. Come."

Corrie saw him disappear into the alley but still saw the back of his coat as he bent over something. She got up slowly. Her skirt was in the way of her legs momentarily. Pietje bent down and pulled her up. They walked to the door, leaned together over the threshold, and looked out. The man had a little wagon full of boxes. The Red Cross provided desperately-needed gifts again. One box sat open, and the man stood counting loaves of bread. He turned and saw them at the door.

"How many of you are there?" he asked softly, his eyebrows raised.

"Five," croaked Pietje.

The man took a knife and cut one loaf in half. He then turned bearing two whole loaves of bread and a half of one. He bent down and held them out to Pietje, who gently took them in his arms like newborn babies.

"Are there people living in the other houses?" he asked, pointing across the alley.

Pietje and Corrie nodded, wordlessly but also shrugged. Who knew who had died over the last number of days and nights.

The man turned and pulled his wagon toward the other houses.

Corrie reached over and touched a loaf. She blinked. She couldn't remember the last time they had seen such an abundance of bread.

Pietje went to the table. Corrie followed and saw that their mother had pushed one of the curtains aside from the bedstead. She was trying to get onto an elbow to raise herself.

"What is that?" she whispered.

"*Brood.*"

"*Brood?*" Cornelia struggled to sit up straight. She slowly untangled her excruciatingly-thin legs from the covers. "Bring me a knife and dish," she asked faintly.

Corrie went to the kitchen corner, took a knife out of a wooden drawer, and a plate off the shelf. She brought them over to her mother.

Bread. It slowly dawned on her; they had food. Sustenance. Beautiful, dark bread. She watched as her mother cut the two whole loaves in half and then proceeded to cut one half into cubes. Her mother gave a few cubes to Pietje, Corrie, and then reached down to give some to Beppie, who had sat up and leaned back against the wall below the bedstead.

"Eat one little piece now. Don't eat it all at once. You will get sick."

Corrie looked at her few little pieces and sat in the sand beside little Hennie.

"*Brood*," said little Hennie.

"*Ja*," answered Corrie, smiling feebly. "*Lekker.*"

"*Lekker*," said Beppie, as she put a piece of bread into her little mouth.

Corrie stuffed one piece into her mouth and savored the taste of it. She closed her eyes. Tears started to flow with joy and sensation. She sucked at it once and then began to chew.

"Mmmm," she moaned. She slowly chewed some more and then swallowed. She looked at the two pieces in her hand and held them up to her nose. The bread would make the sugar beet more palatable. They were going to feast that day.

"Hitler is dead!"

Strange shivers spread across Corrie's scalp. She suddenly couldn't breathe. A little boy ran across the bridge toward her. Again, he announced the news. The wicked wizard, the dreaded evil Hitler, the mighty Fuhrer, was dead.

Pietje, beside Corrie, dropped the bowl he had in his hand. They had been foraging through the new grass for crumbs and morsels of anything edible.

Children fighting over a treasure they found nearby stopped and looked, mouths agape.

"Hitler is dead!" the little boy repeated, as he continued to run up the street.

The two boys suddenly jumped with joy and screamed.

Suddenly, the awareness of what the boy was yelling hit Corrie in the diaphragm, and she fell to the ground, feeling nauseous. She wrapped her arms around her middle. Pietje, whooped, and hollered and jumped for joy next to her. He bent down and pulled her up and made her bounce with him, and she felt her blonde braids flapping up and down in the air.

"Hitler's dead, Hitler's dead! The Hun is dead!" Pietje cried as he grinned. "Come, let's tell Mama and Beppie!" Pietje excitedly yanked at Corrie's arm and dragged her over the bridge toward Spinozastraat. As they ran in their bare feet, she kept an eye on the ground racing beneath her. She could feel herself starting to smile. She wondered if Hitler dying meant the end of the war. Or would it be a false hope, once again, like last time they thought the war was over but liberation was not finally theirs? Maybe the war monster had another head and serpent body set to squeeze every last breath of life out of them. It was still Seyss-Inquart who was the ruler in The Hague. He had been the boogie man for half her life, and it was difficult to imagine him not being in charge, even if Hitler was dead. She closed her eyes as she ran and dared herself to hope.

She dared herself to believe.

May 1945

As she feared, nothing changed even though Hitler was dead. Seyss-Inquart was still in charge, as were the NSBers. Hunger. Though their deaths through starvation was slightly staved by the delivery of small Red Cross packages the month before, their cadaverous frames were still dangerously close to giving up, almost welcoming the grave.

Pietje and Corrie struggled out of the city center to the Laakmolen windmill, to where they had heard of endless fields of stinging nettle. They were, amongst many others, foraging the weed to cook and eat.

At midmorning, the sky darkened above their heads. The accompanying roar had become such a familiar sound in their lives, no one stopped harvesting the bitter, stinging weed.

Pietje glanced up, scratching at his red and swollen forearm. He shielded his eyes to get a better look. "Those are Lancaster bombers," he yelled over the roar.

Corrie looked up from where she crouched. She also shielded her eyes against the bright sky.

"Boy, they're coming in low!" Pietje dropped beside her in the nettle. "From England. The RAF!"

The wind whipped hair into Corrie's eyes, and she brushed it aside. "Will they bomb here?"

Pietje looked around them. Clear fields, windmill, only starving people. "No, there's no *ack-acks* here. I think they can see that."

"But they bombed Bezuidenhout. Couldn't they see there were no *ack-acks* there?"

"They were too high and looking for V2's, Corrie. They couldn't see them because the *moffen* hid them in the trees.

Corrie watched the oncoming horde.

"They're flying very low," Pietje added, observing. Suddenly, he pointed. "Look, Corrie! Their bay doors are opening! They're dropping bombs!"

Corrie stood straight up to see better. Her brows knitted together as she ached to see more clearly. She clutched at her breast and started to whimper.

They watched as objects fell through bombers' bay doors. But there were no explosions. It took them a moment to realize what dropped from the planes were not bombs. As the Lancasters passed overhead, Corrie and Pietje excitedly flattened to the ground and watched the underbellies of the magnificent metal birds fly low over their heads. Their eardrums quivered with the massive roar of the engines. Then they squealed and yelled as a couple of bundles fell and bounced nearby. They settled with a hiss as they flattened the nettle beneath them. They saw they were large burlaps bags. Hundreds of them continued to drop everywhere they looked. Slowly, some of the Lancasters, evidently depleted of their loads, turned down the coast.

Pietje shot up and ran to the closest burlap bundle. Corrie got up and ran as fast as she could to join him. They both tackled the closest one.

Corrie, wide-eyed, looked at the best treasure mystery she had ever seen. "Open it!" she screamed.

With shaking hands, Pietje yanked and prodded at the bundle until finally, an end opened, and he retrieved a tin can. They both eyed it carefully. "Spam," read Pietje.

Corrie stuck her hand into the bag and pulled out a package.

Pietje dropped the tin and eyed the package Corrie held. "Dried egg," he read.

Corrie's mouth dropped open. She stuck her hand into the bag and brought out what looked like a chocolate bar. She gasped and stared at it.

Pietje took it and looked at it. "Chocolate!"

They scrambled to their feet. Without another word, Pietje threw the bundle over his back and quickly started for home. But it wasn't long before he weakened and had to stop. Corrie scurried closer and took one end. Together, each holding an end, they trundled home while bombers continued to roar overhead dropping bundles like oversized flakes of snow.

After Corrie and Pietje returned with the bundle of food, they all huddled together and cried. Corrie was so relieved not to have stinging nettle for supper and intended to feast immediately. But as she fingered the tiny metal loop on a can of spam, imagining what the meat looked like inside, her mother warned her not to eat too quickly.

"Corrie, not the meat. Eat something that's gentle for your stomach," her mother whispered.

Corrie picked up a chocolate bar but her mother took it out of her hand. Then she held up a package of dried egg. Her mother nodded as she stood up to head back to the bedstead.

Corrie looked at the package and decided to make dried egg omelets for everyone. Just before serving the food, she noticed everyone eating chocolate at the table, so she grabbed a piece from the opened bar. She crammed the piece into her mouth as fast as she could. Tears of joy streamed down her cheeks. As quickly as she could, she chewed and sucked and chewed, breathing through her nose loudly. She moaned. She closed her eyes to the luxurious smoothness of the melting chocolate. She finished sucking the remnants in her mouth and, finally put the omelets on plates. But as she put a plate in front of everyone, she suddenly felt extremely nauseous. She hurried into the water closet and doubled over in pain.

"Corrie's sick from the chocolate," she heard Beppie say.

Someone knocked on the door. "Corrie?" It was Pietje.

She wiped her mouth with her sleeve in the dark. "What?"

"Are you sick?"

"Yes!" she yelled.

She heard Beppie laugh. As forks clicked against the plates in the kitchen, Corrie let herself slide to the floor and huddled in the dark, stinking corner until she felt well enough to get up.

When she finally got out, still clutching her stomach, Hennie was sitting at the table on her own, swinging her little legs and eating bits of egg on her plate with her fingers.

Corrie took a plate of omelet for her mother to the bedstead.

Her mother could not eat. She barely drank the water that Corrie coaxed into her. She looked closely at her mother. There was no meat on the exposed arm.

"Mama?" whispered Corrie.

She listened to the soft rasp in her mother's chest. But her mother did not stir. She seemed to be okay a moment ago when they looked at the food bundle, but now, it was almost as if she was back on her death bed again.

Planes flew continually overhead, shaking the outside walls of the house. Distant explosions and the crack of *ack-acks* would briefly cease but never for very long. They'd begin again somewhere else in the city. They had heard the SS destroyed what dikes still stood, flooding more of Holland to slow down the Allies advance. There was a tremendous amount of fighting just north of them.

Then, one morning, the sand beneath Corrie's feet trembled. Dishes in the kitchen rattled. Slowly, a roar grew in intensity around the house. It was not the roar of planes approaching. It was a more massive, deeper, and frightening roar.

Apoplectic with fear, Corrie grabbed Hennie and quickly hiked her up and over to her mother who groaned when Hennie's little knee dug into her ribcage.

"Stay there, Hennie," she commanded.

Hennie cried. But there was no time to console her.

Corrie ran out of the house and stood in the alley for a moment, listening. *From where was that noise coming?* She heard the roar of a tank. More *moffen*!

She ran out of the lane and ran toward the bridge. Suddenly, the shaft of a massive gun jutted out from around the corner. Then the body of a gigantic green tank slowly rumbled into sight in the middle of an enormous cloud of dust.

Her heart jumped with fear as she continued to watch. But she saw that the soldiers standing on top were not SS. They were not even in German uniforms.

She slowly walked toward the sight, frowning. She squinted her eyes to see more clearly.

People started to gather along the street. Soldiers started throwing things to people, and the people cheered and scattered like crazy animals as they went on their hands and knees, searching the ground.

She broke into a run, keeping her eyes on the tank. Another tank came into view. And another.

She finally joined the growing crowd of cheering people. People cried, others stared, and some wanted to climb up onto the tanks.

One girl ran past her. "The war is over!" she yelled at Corrie. Corrie watched the girl running away, yelling at others. "It's Canada! The war is over!" she yelled again.

Corrie swung around and raced to the edge of the crowd. Quickly, others joined her. As another tank approached, she watched a soldier smile and throw things in her direction. The soldier yelled in English, "The war is over!"

She looked up at a man cheering next to her. She yanked at his dirty coat until he looked down.

"Who are they?" she yelled.

"They are soldiers from Canada, *meisje*." He grinned and nodded while still waving his hand at the soldiers. "They have come from Canada to save us!"

She didn't know where Canada was. But surely, they were heroes. They beat the *moffen*! Suddenly, she screamed and squealed, jumped, and danced. She scrambled down on the pavement and competed with others in gathering together as much bubble gum and chocolate as she could. She got up and ran home with her bounty.

She burst into the house. Flying to the bedstead, Corrie laid the bubble gum and chocolate onto her mother's stomach.

"Mama, mama, the war is over!" she yelled above the roar.

Her mother groaned and moved her head.

Corrie shook her. "Mama, *kijk*. Bubble gum and chocolate!"

"*Nee*, the war isn't over, Corrie," her mother muttered.

Corrie held up the bubble gum and chocolate over her face. "*Kijk*, mama. I have bubble gum and chocolate again. Soldiers from Canada threw them at us."

Cornelia opened her eyes slowly. She looked at the bedstead's low ceiling above her.

"Mama?"

Cornelia reached out to the ceiling. Then she looked at the wall next to her, behind little Hennie. "Corrie, I see angels."

"Mama!"

"I see angels. They've come for me."

Corrie shook her mother hard. "*Nee*, Mama. The soldier from Canada said that the war is over."

Cornelia slowly looked over at Corrie. Her eyes moistened. She blinked once. Slowly. She shook her head. "No, *schatje*. The war is never over and your Pappa will never come home."

"No, Mama, don't say that! Look!" Corrie held up the chocolate bar. She opened it and took a bite. She broke off a piece and handed it to Hennie, who looked at it and then stuck it in her mouth. Hennie smiled and laughed.

Her mother craned her neck to look over at her toddler. She saw Hennie's mouth slowly oozing dribbles of chocolate. She looked over at Corrie, wide-eyed. "*Meer chocolat?*"

Corrie broke off a piece of chocolate and put it into her mother's hand. Slowly, her mother moved her hand. It wavered and shook on its way to her lips. Gently she put the piece in her mouth and closed her eyes. Under her breath, she moaned ever so slightly.

Corrie left the bubble gum where it lay and slowly lowered herself down the bottom wall of the bedstead. She slipped off the edge of the torn floor and dropped onto the rags in the sand. She unwrapped more of the chocolate and devoured it, thinking it would be funny if she died from overeating chocolate from a Canadian hero instead of being shot, bombed, or starved to death by the *moffen*.

She wiped her mouth with her sleeve, shot up, and ran out. She wanted to see more smiling Canadian heroes. Her heart burst as she joined the crowd again to wave, laugh, and cry at the passing vehicles and soldiers.

She thought the Canadian soldiers were the most beautiful people she had ever seen in her entire life.

Chapter 24
May 1945

Corrie felt shoved in all directions as she clung to Pietje's neck. He had given her a piggy-back so she could see what was going on. Squirming bodies pressed hard against them as they all cheered and cried. It was the victory parade, and they were on Koningstraat watching their heroes, the Canadian soldiers, slowly roll past them. The soldiers waved, and laughed, threw bubble gum and chocolate bars again. Everyone was deliriously happy. She watched as girls and boys tried to climb and ride on the tanks or in the trucks. She saw flowers tossed from the crowd at the vehicles as they passed. Some people quickly tucked the flowers into the radiators of the vehicles. Orange ribbons, flags, and tri-colored coronets were everywhere. Wherever she looked she saw red-white-and-blue flags of The Netherlands hang on the buildings and out windows. Old men cheered, and women cried and laughed. Children called out to the new heroes in their hearts.

Then, as the parade dwindled to civilian cars and trucks, there was a shift in the way people moved and yelled, and it no longer felt festive.

Pietje turned and carried her from the road to the safety of the sidewalk.

"What's happening?" asked Corrie.

"My back hurts," said Pietje. He stuck his hands in his pockets and looked around as he flicked his long blond locks out of his eyes. Pietje finally spied the storefront window of Albert Heijn's grocery store behind them. He walked her to it and turned to face her. "Here, let me lift you on the sill. Maybe you can see what's going on from there."

Pietje lifted Corrie on the sill. Corrie held onto his shoulders as she strained to see over the sea of heads again. A horse and wagon slowly rolled past their crowd. People jeered and spat at two women in the cart, their heads shaved, and their clothing disheveled. They looked frightened and miserable. Men stood beside them, carefully watching the crowd.

"They shaved women's heads," she said.

Suddenly, she recognized the young woman who had bullied her and given her cigarettes—the one who hung around the *ack-ack* in town. She was holding a baby and looked miserable and humiliated.

Corrie stared at the painful sight and wondered what that young woman was going to do. Was she alone with the baby? How can that girl go on and live as if nothing had happened? She watched as the horde pushed and shoved the wagon as it continued down the street.

"*Moffen meiden!*" screamed one angry woman nearby, "*Moffen hoer!*" The crowd was quickly becoming ugly.

Pietje took Corrie down and pulled her away. "Let's go home. We've seen the best, and this isn't something for you to watch."

Pietje took off his vest and shirt as he and Corrie entered the gate into their alley. They were ecstatic. They had spent a bit of time with a few Canadian soldiers who showed them how they cleaned their guns. They also shared some of their rations in their kits. Showed them how they cooked in a little tin tray. One of them taught Pietje how to throw a knife into the trunk of a tree. They taught them how to say some words in English. Nose, eyes, mouth, chin. It all sounded so exotic. They finally left bearing a few little gifts of cigarettes and chocolate for their mother. As they walked into the house, Pietje, jovial and happy, aimed his clothes at one of the chairs. Part of the bundle caught the back of the chair before the rest flopped onto the sand. Corrie picked them up and tossed the bunch onto the top of the mound of their other rag-like clothing at the foot of the bedstead.

Their mother, Cornelia, wore a dress far too large for her. She sat in the other chair, peeling a potato.

"We have potatoes?" Pietje yelled excitedly as he placed the cigarettes and chocolate on the table in front of his mother. His mother looked over, smiled, and looked up at Pietje.

"The Canadian soldiers. A present from Canada they said," Pietje smiled.

Corrie stepped up to the table and looked at the few peeled potatoes. "Potatoes!" she smiled.

Cornelia brushed aside some peels. "Yes, but the rations are barely enough to eat. We have a half a potato each. At least we are eating." She pushed the skins even further along the table. "Here, what do you think? Should we be brave and throw these peels away, or should we keep them to eat later?"

Corrie made a face. "Please, Mama. No."

Cornelia looked at the peels, deep in thought. Corrie saw she had brushed her hair but still looked dangerously anemic and thin. Her mother scraped the pile of potato skins together in a heap with the paring knife. "We'll keep them," she said. "Maybe we'll melt chocolate over them," she joked.

Corrie smiled and looked over to the stove. A pot of water was boiling and steaming. In the far corner, away from the oven, was their father's rose accordion. Out of its case, it sat balanced and slightly open.

She got up and trudged through the sand. She stood on her tiptoes and gently wiped the top of the accordion, making sure no sand or dust was covering the surface. They had fashioned a make-shift shrine. It represented their heartfelt prayers for their father's return. They had seen and heard of men returning from slavery, but they also understood many men had died and were never coming back.

Corrie cried with angst and fear when she heard someone's father wasn't coming back. Pietje had to calm her down. That's why they put the accordion up on display—a symbol of hope. To remind them no matter how difficult things were, how desperate they were, they had kept the accordion safe and never bartered it, never sold it for much-needed food. Their diligence and sacrifices must guarantee his return!

Suddenly, Corrie's thoughts were interrupted by running footsteps ringing through the alley. She quickly turned to look through the open door.

Beppie exploded into the house. "*Oom* Frans is back! He's at *Opa*'s!"

Corrie wanted to yelp. If *Oom* Frans was back, where's Pappa?

Corrie looked at her mother, who sat staring at Beppie. She saw her mother's shoulders shaking. Cornelia clutched at her dress and looked here and there. "I can't go. I can't."

"Mama, you don't have to go," cried Corrie.

"I can't. Not like this. I can't even walk as far as the door. How can I go to *Opa*'s? How will I see Frans?" Cornelia fretted, and Corrie felt at a loss.

"Maybe *Oom* Frans can come here, mama," suggested Corrie.

Cornelia shook her head. She looked at Corrie and Pietje. "Pietje, Corrie. Go back with Beppie and see if *Oom* Frans has any news about your father."

Beppie, Corrie, and Pietje ran out of the house. Corrie tried to keep up with them, but their long legs took them further faster. Her eyes darted around the streets as she huffed and puffed. Corrie looked back behind her. She thought maybe she would see her father appear. Though many more people were out and about, no one looked like her father. She began to cry but kept running as her soul and heart expanded with silent prayer.

"They say that over 500,000 people, almost all men, were taken as slaves from Holland alone," said *Meneer* Gelauf. He had lost a tremendous amount of weight and looked older than his seventy years. He sat, his cheeks vermillion red with excitement, at the end of the long dining room table looking at *Oom* Frans, where he was slumped.

Oom Frans was not well, Corrie could tell. She eyed the hollow look in his eyes. He had lost much weight, and his skin was grey. He had lost two front teeth and smoked continually, his hand shook each time he took out another cigarette. Someone had to light the cigarette for him; he shook too much. Though he was finally home, he didn't seem to be happy to be back.

To her surprise, suddenly, he broke down and cried. Heavy sobs. Heaving.

Tante Antonia went to him and held his head. He turned and cried into her frayed and faded work shift. Corrie's three cousins, Rieky, Sientje, and Philip, got up from the table and stood quietly beside their mother and father. Concern etched their faces.

"So far, they estimate that 30,000 may have died. About a third of that from The Hague alone" said their *Opa* to *Tante* Antonia.

Corrie blinked at her *Opa*. *What did he just say?* She turned to look at her *Oom* Frans. She turned back again to her *Opa*. "Where's Pappa?"

Her *Opa* looked at her blankly. He sighed and looked at Frans.

"One shouldn't talk about these things. Not with the children here," whispered *Tante* Antonia.

Corrie looked frantically from her *Opa* and back to *Oom* Frans.

Frans slowly pulled away from his wife. His downcast eyes showed grief. He covered his face. Then he looked up and shrugged. He grimaced and broke into a sob. "I'm sorry. I'm so sorry," he said, shaking his head at Corrie.

Tante Antonia gently patted him on his back. "Shhh," she said softly.

"What exactly happened, Frans?" asked *Meneer* Gelauf. Corrie saw his eyes tear up and turn red. His bottom lip quivered.

"Pap, maybe we shouldn't—" started *Tante* Antonia.

"No!" shouted her *Opa*. He pounded the table and stared at *Oom* Frans.

Corrie fought back the tears. She stood up at her chair and looked from her *Opa* to her *Oom*. Her chin quivered.

Oom Frans shifted in his chair. "I, uh," he wiped his brow with a quivering hand. "I was pulled out of this building, a crematorium—"

"What's a crematorium?" tearfully asked Corrie.

"Shhh," said Pietje.

"And it was on fire. I was pulled out by," Frans paused and motioned around the table at everyone, "people who were a sort of underground at this camp."

"Was Pappa there?" asked Pietje.

Oom Frans nodded slowly. Tears ran and dripped off his cheeks. He wiped them away. "I was with your father, with Henk," he said, looking at his father-in-law. "I was taken away in a truck, and as they went around this camp, they picked up as many people as they could and then drove out of the camp before the Russians came. I became very sick. After I was well enough, they took me to a half-way house. I was in a big house. Where I slept and washed. They gave me clothes. I didn't know who was in charge. I couldn't think straight. After a while, someone put me on a train to Belgium, and after a day or two waiting for trains for Holland that didn't come, I decided to walk the rest of the way home."

"And Pappa?" asked Corrie.

"I have not seen your Pappa since that fire," he sobbed. "He was still in there. And it was completely in flames."

Corrie gasped. "No," she said, shaking her head slowly. The tears overwhelmed her. She couldn't see him anymore. "No!" she cried.

*Tante Anton*ia went over to comfort Corrie. Corrie heard Beppie and Pietje cry as well. For a moment, she burrowed her head into *Tante* Antonia's skirt. *Tante* Antonia patted her back and pulled Pietje and Beppie toward Corrie. The three of them huddled with their *Tante*.

Corrie stopped crying and, as she allowed herself to be swayed back and forth in the loving arms of her aunt, she thought of the accordion. She pulled away. "But we still have Pappa's accordion," she said, looking around the table.

Pietje put his hand on her shoulder.

She looked up at him. "But we still have Pappa's accordion, I said!"

Pietje tried to hug her. She pushed him away.

"No!" she yelled. "No, Pappa's not dead. He can't be!" She pulled at Pietje. "He can't be, Pietje. We still have his accordion, and we were so careful."

"I know," he cried.

She scrambled past the chairs to *Oom* Frans. "*Oom* Frans, are you sure he's not alive?" Her eyes begged him for something positive. "How do you know?"

Oom Frans, torn by grief, gently put a hand on her face. "*Meisje*, he did not come out of that fire. I'm so sorry."

Corrie stood, shaking. She didn't want to give in to the truth. But, as she stood there, hearing everyone else's cries around the table, she surrendered to the very thing she feared the most.

She was never going to see her father again.

Chapter 25
September 1945

Corrie stared at the wash. She stood beside her mother, sadly pulling and yanking at clothes as her mother fed them through the hand-cranked wringer. They had fallen into a zombie-like routine existence. Slowly, life shifted. No more bombs or air raids. No more sirens. The Queen had returned and the government was once again put in place, replacing the NSBers and the Nazi rule. The new *Regeering* provided new food ration tickets, but it still represented far too little. At least, there were more soup kitchens spread throughout the city to feed the hungry survivors.

Corrie and her family were some of the lucky ones, as many had no homes and had to board with friends, relatives, and strangers. Although they were still living in their flea-infested sandbox, the *Regeering* promised them, and everyone else, to help rebuild their homes into sturdy shelters.

Their main concern, however, was the coming winter. Somehow repairs had to be made to the roof, and wood trim was needed around the windows and doors to prevent the coming snow and wind from entering.

Corrie could hear children playing in the streets. Her two cousins, Sientje and Rieky, were out front playing with Hennie. She listened to a distant *draaiorgel*. The sun shone, the birds sang, and school had started. Again, she was the oldest and tallest in the class. She had asked her mother if she could go and work at a job and make some needed cash instead. Eleven years old was still too young, her mother said.

Pietje, in his undershirt and loose corduroy pants, suddenly appeared in the small back court. He was barefoot, as was Corrie. They still had to find shoes and clothes but, like everything else, these things came slowly. Pietje had suggested they consider selling the accordion in exchange for the new currency The Netherlands minted to replace pre-war and Nazi money. But Corrie and their mother couldn't bear the thought of selling it.

Whenever they could, they put flowers in front of the accordion on the corner shelf. Corrie's mother put a framed photograph of her and Henk taken just before they married; he in his army uniform and she in a flapper's cloche hat and dropped-down waistcoat. In the photo, they were both smiling as they walked along a street. Her mother kissed the picture every night before going to bed.

"What were you looking for?" asked her mother.

Pietje flicked the hair from his eyes. At 15, he was as tall as a man and starting to build up arm muscles he said he would so long ago. "I'm looking for a hammer," he said, looking around pails and pots stored against the back fence.

"What for?" asked Cornelia.

"I'm going to see if I can use some of that scrap wood we got yesterday, and maybe I can go ahead and cover the cracks around the door and windows."

"Don't you dare, right now. I just finished washing those front windows," said their mother. "You'll just get sawdust and finger marks all over them."

Corrie looked up at Pietje. "Maybe you could go and see if *Oom* Frans needs any help with those stairs of theirs."

"But I would still need a hammer."

"Go ask Beppie. Where is she?" asked their mother, focusing on the wash.

"In the water closet as usual," said Pietje.

"Did you look in the sand?" suggested Corrie. Things got lost in that sandbox.

Pietje went into the house.

Cornelia went back to feeding the wringer and turning the handle, and Corrie continued to pull gently and steadily. Sometimes, if you weren't careful, the clothes double backed on themselves and jammed the wringer.

Pietje came back. "No, can't find it."

"Well, maybe *Oom* Frans has an extra hammer," their mother suggested.

Pietje looked around, then at Corrie who eyed him carefully. He smiled at her sadly, and she smiled sadly back.

Tante Antonia and *Oom* Frans were still in the same house on Van Ostadestraat about eight blocks away. *Oom* Frans was not the same person he used to be and spent much time down in the pub. There was no work available but, somehow, Frans was always able to get a drink or two. Many like him went there to share their experiences and their horrific memories, but to his own family, he didn't say a word.

Nothing.

Corrie contemplated on this, as she looked at her mother's polka dot dress. Her mother grew stronger every day, though she never smiled. She did not laugh or cry ever since she and Pietje had to tell her that their father was dead.

Strangely, hearing the news of their father's death became the reason their mother chose to live. Before too long, though far from being well enough, she took over her role as mother to her three children. With Corrie's help, the day to day running of the house fell into a rhythm. Cornelia washed the windows every week, and Corrie helped Cornelia with the wash twice a week. They changed what bed sheets they had and continuously freshened up the mattresses. They still had to live with bugs and fleas, but even the sand was swept of debris and sifted for lost objects every night. When, again, there wasn't enough to eat, or rain came through the roof and down to the sand below, Cornelia would always say, "We survived the war so we can survive anything."

"Cornelia!"

Cornelia kept turning the handle on the wringer. Corrie looked over her shoulder to where she heard the woman's voice.

"Cornelia!"

The call had a desperate tone to it. Corrie turned to her mother and touched her on her arm. "Mama, someone's calling you. I think it's *Tante* Antonia."

Cornelia kept turning the handle and looked up briefly. "Oh *ja*? Check Corrie. I don't have time to listen to gossip if it's that woman in the Aaronson's house. Can you go see if it's her? I'll keep at the wash here."

"Okay," said Corrie. The woman who lived in the Aaronson's house with her little family was talkative, and that annoyed her mother. She had more important things to worry about than to know whose husband ran off with whom and whose daughter was a *moffen hoer*.

Corrie was about to drop the wet garment she was holding and walk to the back door when they heard the woman calling again but this time from inside their home.

"Cornelia! Where are you? Come quick! I think it's Henk!"

It was definitely *Tante* Antonia.

Cornelia looked over at Corrie, who stared back with wide eyes. She felt the blood drain from her face to her chest.

Tante Antonia is mistaken, thought Corrie.

"I'll go see, Mama." She stepped away from the laundry tub.

Suddenly, her mother let go of the wringer and headed for the back door. Her mother's hip caught on the handle of the wringer, pulling the laundry bin over the edge of the kitchen table. The whole tub of soapy water and wet clothes spilled onto the dirt in the little courtyard. The water rushed and slapped against the threshold of the back door and over Cornelia's bare feet. Corrie watched her mother run past her, but not before she caught sight of her face. Corrie's breath suddenly escaped her as she hurried after her mother to the back door. She could tell her mother felt something she didn't. Then she watched her mother jump through the back door down into the sandpit and fly through the sand to the front door.

Corrie did the same. When she got to the front door, she clung to its sides. She looked down at Rieky and Sientje, still sitting on the warm, dry cobblestones playing with Hennie. Sientje looked up. "When's Beppie coming back out from the washroom?"

Corrie shook her head distractedly. She looked over at the gate into the alley. There, Corrie saw her mother standing beside *Tante* Antonia, both frozen on the pavement. She saw Pietje appear from behind her mother, breathless. He also stopped and froze, staring off in the distance.

"Beppie," Corrie called over her shoulder.

"What?" Beppie answered from the water closet.

"Something funny is happening."

The door to the water closet opened, and Corrie turned to see Beppie come out holding a comic book. "What?"

Corrie silently motioned for her to come. Beppie walked to her and squeezed into the doorway.

Corrie stepped down from the threshold and jogged to her mother on the street. She stood beside Pietje and also looked toward the bridge and canal. Off in the distance, a skeleton in rags was walking beside a battered bike. It used to be a common sight seeing bedraggled people coming back from their own personal hell, but in the last few months, there were fewer of them. She squinted and could see the bike had no tires. The man's head was shaven, and he was gaunt-looking.

"That's not Pappa," said Pietje.

Corrie agreed. "*Ja*, Mama, that's not Pappa. Come on." She pulled at her mother's polka-dot dress.

Beppie caught up to them. "What are you looking at?"

Suddenly, their neighbor from the Aaronson's house caught up to them. "Did I hear your husband is back?" she asked, looking from Cornelia to Pietje, to Corrie and Beppie. The neighbor turned and looked in the distance. "Do you think it is your father?"

Corrie turned to step back through the gate, and Pietje followed. "That's not Pappa. He's dead," Pietje said to Beppie.

Beppie looked at him and shrugged. "Maybe. Maybe not."

Pietje stood and stared at her.

Suddenly, their mother screamed.

Corrie, Beppie and Pietje looked back and saw their mother biting her fist. Then she broke out into a run.

Corrie hurried back to the gate and watched as her mother struggled to keep running, staggering and grabbing at her dress.

Then she saw the pallid man stop and drop the bicycle. He slowly walked forward. He was barefoot and limped. Corrie stepped forward a little to get a better look, and her heart did a flip against her ribs.

"It's Pappa!" hollered Pietje. He bolted toward his mother and the man.

Corrie still wasn't sure. She looked back at Beppie. She could tell she wasn't sure either.

She decided to look for herself. As she walked toward them, she saw Pietje almost jump on the man. The man stopped to hug Pietje.

"No," she whispered. She walked a little faster until she could see the man's eyebrows and brilliant aqua eyes. "Pappa!" She turned back to Beppie and screamed without realizing it. Then she turned back and raced, crying to her father. When she finally got close enough, she ran to him with arms wide.

Henk grunted as his daughter grabbed him. "Is this Beppie? Or is this Corrie?" he said weakly.

She pulled away, "It's Corrie, Pappa." She beamed at him, but her smile disappeared when she saw that he had no teeth. Toothless, he looked sick and much older than he was. His face was covered in sores and she could see lice on his tattered and sun-bleached top. But even so, he looked beautiful. He was alive! She grinned again.

Beppie caught up to them. As they huddled all together, they could hear their mother crying. For the first time since before the entire length of the war, Cornelia was finally overwhelmed with tears. Slowly, the small group continued up Spinozastraat toward the gate to their alley.

Tante Antonia and the neighbor ran to them. *Tante* Antonia clasped her hands together, beaming. "I knew it had to be you!" she said as they approached. She turned to Rieky and Sientje, who stood at the gate watching. "Quick. Go home and get your father. Your *Oom* Henk is alive!" she called loudly. Corrie saw her cousins bolt across the street diagonally to the corner of Oranjeplain, a short cut to their house.

Corrie's father grabbed *Tante* Antonia and held her. Then he looked at the new neighbor quizzically.

"Oh, you don't know me." She grabbed his hand and shook it. "My husband worked with your brother Frans, and I remember you once when we visited your father. And you were there playing the accordion."

Corrie looked over at *Tante* Antonia. "How did you recognize Pappa from so far away?"

"I didn't. I saw this poor man far, far away coming down the street as I was walking home from *Opa*'s. I didn't think much of it, but when I turned back to look at him again, I saw that he was turning into this street. Then as I got to your place to get Sientje and Rieky, it suddenly dawned on me." She turned to face Henk. "It was you!" she said, smiling with watery eyes. "I don't know how but I felt it in my bones!"

It took a long while to get their father into the alley. He was slow and weak, but they laughed, and they cried, and they touched his head, his hands, and they read his eyes. They saw him also cry, and laugh showing his gums. He looked so old, so frail, so weak, so wonderful.

As they finally reached their alley, they guided him over to the house, and Pietje ran in to get one of the chairs. He set it out against the front wall. They slowly helped their father sit down on the chair. Corrie ran in to get the other chair and brought it out for her mother. She placed it beside her father. Her mother sat and grabbed her husband's hands.

For a moment, no one said a word. Just sniffled, giggled, and sobbed.

Suddenly, Hennie poked her head over the threshold from inside the house. Everyone looked over. Corrie went over, lifted her up and took her to their father. Hennie looked at Henk and wailed, shaking her head.

"I just look pretty bad," said Henk.

A bike came through the gate. It was young Philip riding with his father on the back of the bike. They stopped, and Philip immediately helped his father off the bike. Frans' eyes did not leave Henk's face.

Slowly, their *Oom* Frans stumbled toward them at the wall. Just as he reached them, he was suddenly weak in the legs and almost fell. Cornelia stood up and let Frans settle into the chair next to her husband's chair. Henk turned to face Frans. Frans' face slowly collapsed as he gave way to tears grasping both sides of Henk's wrinkled, grey face.

Henk's heavy brows knitted above his eyes as he searched Frans' face. "Frans," Henk whispered. He squinted his eyes and nodded.

Corrie suddenly turned and ran into their house. She jumped down into the sand and struggled to get to the corner as fast as she could. She couldn't reach the accordion, and there were no chairs inside to stand on, but Pietje appeared behind her and quickly lifted the accordion off its perch. They looked at each other and grinned. They rushed out together.

As they approached their father, Henk looked up and eyed his son holding the accordion. He reached out with shaking hands and slowly took the beautiful instrument by the straps and immediately looked at the top. He fingered the indent made by Pietje so very long ago. Henk squinted up at Pietje and smiled tearfully.

"Play, *Meneer* Gelauf. I hear you play so beautifully," said the neighbor.

Henk looked around at his wife, at Frans, Pietje, Beppie, Corrie, Hennie, Philip, Rieky, Sientje, *Tante* Antonia, and the neighbor.

The neighbor grabbed Pietje. "You can take whatever chairs I have in the house. Corrie, you might have to help him."

Corrie rushed with Pietje into the Aaronson's house. As Pietje grabbed two kitchen chairs, Corrie stopped and stared at the inside of the house. It didn't look the same, and yet it did. She saw the table and remembered that last night with Rebecca and her family.

Pietje also looked around. Then he held a chair up to her. "Here, take this. I'll take the other one in the corner."

Corrie silently took the chair from Pietje and took one more look around. She stepped out of the little house, walked across where she could still see burn marks, and stopped. Then she raised her eyes and looked over at the group in front of her home. Pietje passed her with two chairs. She slowly followed him.

Pietje put the chairs on the cobblestones, and his mother and *Tante* Antonia sat down. As Corrie put her chair down, she saw her father reaching for Pietje.

"Son," he said, "thank you." Their father shakily stood up, and his long thin arms pulled Pietje to him. For a few moments, their father cried into Pietje's neck. Pietje was now as tall as their father. Corrie's eyes brimmed with tears, and she cried as she stared at the two men in her life. Slowly, her father pulled away from Pietje.

"Pietje, thank you for being the man of the family while I was gone. Your mother just told me a few things." He shook his head. "And I know I could not have done any better." He patted Pietje's shoulders and stared at him with such gratitude that everyone cried.

Pietje stood and stared. Pietje hung his head, covered his face, and let his blonde locks fall over his face to hide his emotions.

Corrie went over and hugged him, as did Beppie. After a few moments, they all sat down and watched their father's gnarled, filthy hands caress the piano keys and buttons. Slowly, Henk lowered his head and rested his bony cheek against the dent in the polished surface and began to play as the bellows stretched and revealed the beautiful rose pattern. Corrie's heart burst with joy. Then her father began to play the most beautiful music they had ever heard. At least, not since they heard him play last before the terrible days of the great war had begun.

EPILOGUE

November 2019

Corrie stared unseeing at the salt shaker she inadvertently played with while her thoughts lingered over the memory of that group sitting in a cobblestone alleyway. She remembered they listened and cried to the beautiful music her weary father played. She remembered more people from the alley and along Spinozastraat slowly joined them, helping to celebrate the return of a loved one thought lost. They danced, they laughed, they cried.

Her thoughts raced through the years.

Oom Frans finally couldn't take the pain and guilt of the horrific memories that drove him mad. He took his own life years later, but not until he shared some of the horrors he and Henk witnessed before he died.

Opa *de heer* Gelauf, the patriarch of the family, died a happy old man with an army of grandchildren sometime in the 1960's.

Henk, the father she doted on, died with cancer in the 1990's, maintaining his proud and handsome, quiet demeanor. He rarely spoke of the war but he went through years of drinking, waking in the night with nightmares.

Her mother, Cornelia, died at a healthy age of 87 in the new millennium after decades of smoking. This time the angels finally took her home.

Older sister, Beppie, died prematurely with Parkinsons Disease, leaving a husband and two sons.

Her youngest brother, Herman, was the last to be born after the war. He was a happy Downs Syndrome child and lived longer than expected well into his fifties.

Tears came to her eyes when she thought of Hennie, her little sister. She grew to be a beautiful woman, had married and gave birth to a son. She was widowed far too young and died of cancer while barely out of her sixties.

Corrie's young brother, Gerard, born nine months after her father's return, died young with early on-set Alzheimers, leaving a wife and two daughters.

Corrie's older brother Piet, the hero of the family, was a widower and still lived. Almost 90, he was still strong and full of vigor, residing in a retirement home in The Hague. He had two beautiful daughters.

The rooms of her memories were hollow, most of the long-gone voices echoing in the rafters of that little house in the alley off Spinozastraat which also was no more. All the hovels in the alley kitty-corner from Oranjeplein were replaced by a modern apartment building. The entrance to the alley is still there, but now it was access to the rear of the apartment flats.

Suddenly lights switched on, and the banquet room burst into life. Corrie was torn away from her deep thoughts. She blinked. She looked around at all the people pushing back their chairs to turn and look in her direction. For a moment, she'd forgotten where she was and wondered if she should also stand when she realized they all started clapping.

She turned to look at her husband, Rudy, who was stunned and looked back at her. She touched his face to see if it was real. She looked at the crowd in front of them again. *Oh, yes. They were in the Brighton Legion Hall.*

"Should we be standing, too?" asked Rudy, her husband.

"I don't know," she shrugged. She leaned into her husband's ear. "I don't think so. I've never had people clapping for me like this."

Her eldest daughter appeared behind them and bent down. "You're getting a standing ovation!"

Corrie fought back the tears. "*Ja?*" she said, surprised. "A standing ovation for us?"

"*Ja*. And everyone's crying, Mam."

Corrie looked around. Indeed, even the men had tears in their eyes. Their clapping continued for what seemed like an excessive amount of time. Finally, people eventually stopped and sat down, their chairs scraping back into position. Their daughter handed them a microphone.

One of the women of the Legion stepped up and addressed the crowd. "I know we are all feeling overwhelmed with this incredibly brave presentation. I'm sure some of you have questions, and we've arranged a little time for that." She stepped away as people sat, staring at her and Rudy. There was silence. The images were still too raw, and people needed time to digest the incredible range of emotions they were all feeling. Eventually, individuals raised their hands, looking for answers to their questions.

Corrie felt panic rise in her chest. She didn't have the emotional strength or know English well enough to express herself adequately. She didn't think she could answer any questions directed at her.

Her daughter bent down again and whispered into her ear.

"Mam, you wanted to say something that was the most important message you wanted to give tonight?"

Corrie's heart jumped. *Yes!* Even though she was frightened.

"Mam, you said yourself that now was the only time you could probably ever share it."

Corrie, stunned, knew she was right. She remembered back to the overwhelming love the beautiful Canadian soldiers shared with such a bedraggled looking people so long ago. She remembered that they had sacrificed through their sweat, tears, fear and, for far too many, death. But she hesitated. She remembered going up to the blackboard, knowing the answer, but giving the wrong one. Because she didn't think she was good enough.

She wasn't good enough to stand and tell these people anything at all. Who was she but a nothing? A nothing.

But the Canadian soldiers. They saved their lives.

Then she heard her mother say so very long ago: *We survived the war, so we can survive anything.*

She mustered up the courage to say the one thing she so needed everyone to hear. She looked at the microphone her daughter was holding, and took it with shaking hands. She held it close to her lips. She had never spoken into a microphone her entire life. But she intuitively knew how to hold it. She stayed sitting down, for her legs were too weak to stand. But she was able to muster up the courage to speak.

"When we went on the big ship in Holland to come and live in Canada," she began haltingly in her thick Dutch accent, "I went the day before to the graves of the Canadian soldiers who died fighting for us. I always went every year, with flowers, to thank them. And now I came with flowers to tell them something else. Something very special. I said to them, in their graves, 'Hey you wonderful guys, because of you I am alive. And because of you, we love your country Canada, and now, tomorrow, my husband and I, and our two little girls are going on a big boat to go to your beautiful home, Canada. I want to thank you so much for everything you have done for me. I don't think I will ever be back to see you. So, goodbye, and thank you."

Corrie gave the microphone back to her daughter, sat back, and sighed, shaking. She was that little girl seventy-four years later, and for the first time in her life, she felt the door close on a nightmare which had always strangled her heart and mind.

Corrie understood that the world must never forget, for the sake of all who suffered so much grief and loss. They must always remember the bravery shown by young men and women who willingly fought against an enemy that was brutal, ugly, and horrific. She knew that the atrocities, starvation, and death that one sick, powerful man had unleashed on millions of people must remain at the forefront of every person's awareness. Corrie Gelauf, a little girl they did not know, survived Hitler's hellish war. Because of them, seventy-four-years later, she can sit in the Brighton Legion Hall and speak of them and their bravery.

She also realized there may not be many left such as her and Rudy, who could still speak first hand of what they had gone through during the war. She was relieved she fought through her pain enough so that she—a little Dutch girl in Hitler's war—could remind the world that they should never repeat such unnecessary, costly, and horrific atrocities to their fellow man.

The world must never, ever, forget.

GLOSSARY OF DUTCH, GERMAN AND RUSSIAN TERMS

Abspielen: Play, (German) 'abshpeelen'
Ach, mijn medeleven mevrouw: Oh dear, my condolences, madame. 'agh, mine maydaylayfen mufrow'
Bedankt: Thanks, 'bedunked'
Bedankt voor de koffie: Thanks for the coffee, 'bedunked for de cohfee'
Biertje: A little beer, 'beertye' Dag: Hi and/or bye, different inflections make the difference between the two, 'daagh'
Borreltje: A shot of gin or hard liquor, 'boareltye'
Brievenbus: A postal box on the street, 'breefenbeus'
Brood: Bread, 'broht'
Chocolat: Chocolate, 'shocolah'
Commandant: Commander, 'comandahnt'
Dag: Hello or goodbye. 'dahgh'
Dames en Heeren: Ladies and gentlemen, 'dahmes en hearen'
De Heer: Formal way of saying Mister
De mazl: Slang for Good Luck/derived from Yiddish 'zol zayn mit mazl', 'de muzzle'
Draaiorgel: A hand-cranked musical street organ, 'drheyeorghel'
Du sollst mich nicht ansehen: You are not to look at me! (German) 'dtu zoits migcht nigcht unzaiyn'
Engeland: England
Ersatz: Replacement, (German), 'airzahts'
Entshuldigen Sie mich: Excuse me, (German), 'entshuldigin zi mich'

Fiets: Bike 'feets'
Fuhrer: Tyrannical leader (German), 'feeuurar'
Geld: Money, 'ghelt'
Geh raus: Get out (German), 'Geh rouws'
Godverdomme: God damn it. 'ghotveradomme'
Graag gedaan: You're welcome, 'ghraagh ghedaan'
Guilders: A Dutch currency (In 1938, 1.28 guilders was the equivalent of 1 US dollar), 'gilder'
Haagenaars: People who live in Den Haag, 'haaghenaarhs'
Haagsche Courant: A newspaper in The Hague
Haagsche Bosch: Today called Haagse Bos, Forest of The Hague, 'haachgse boes'
Halt: Stop, (German), 'halt'
Heel erg bedankt, dokter: Thank you so much, doctor. 'hail ehrgh bedunked deuktar'
Heel graag gedaan: You're very welcome, 'hail graagh ghedaahn'
Herr: Mister, Sir (German), 'hair'
Honger's Noot, Honger's Dood: Hunger's Need, Hunger's Dead, 'hohng-ar's note, hong-ar's dodte'
Hou je mond: Shut up, 'how yeh mohnt'
Ja: Yes, 'yaah'
Ja, Pietje, Pappa's terug: Yes, (young) Peter, Pappa's back, 'yaah, peetye, pappa's treugh'
Jenever: Dutch gin, 'Yanayver'
Jezus Christus: Jesus Christ, 'yaysuz kreestos'
Jij blijft hier: You stay here, 'yeye blifdt heer'
Joden niet gewenst: Jews not wanted, Yoden neet ghevenst
Jongen: Boy, (Dutch and German) 'yoangen'
Kadish: A Jewish prayer, 'kadish'
Kerstmis: Christmas, 'kechstmis'
Kijk: Look, 'kike'
Kind: Child, 'kint'
Kinderen: Children, 'kinderen'
Kleine: Small, 'klineh'
Klompen: Wooden shoes, clogs 'kloompen'
Kom Schatje, Come, sweetheart, 'kome, schratye'

Koningin: Queen, 'koningin'
Lekker: Delicious, 'lekkahr'
Liefje: Sweetheart, 'leefye'
Loempias: Spring rolls, 'loompeeyas'
Markt: Market, 'mahrkt'
Meer: More, 'mier'
Meester: Master, another name for male teacher, 'maystair'
Meisjes: Girls, 'myshyes'
Meneer: Mister or sir, 'm'near'
Mevrouw: Mrs., 'mufrow'
Mezuzah: An oblong receptacle nailed to the doorframe holding a small document with the written word of God, Rabbinic Judaism
Moffen: Huns, Nazis, 'mofen'
Moffen hoer: Hun/Nazi whore, 'mofen hoer'
Moffen meiden: Hun/Nazi girls, collaborators, 'mofen myden'
Natuurlijk: Of course, 'nateurlick'
Nau: Now, 'now'
Nederlanders: Netherlanders, 'naydairlundahrs'
Nee: No, 'nay'
Nein: No (German), 'nine'
Nein. Das bleibt: No. That stays. (German) 'Nine. Das blipt.'
Nou zeg: slang for Oh my gosh, or Oh dear. 'now segh'
Nyet: No (Russian), 'nyet'
Nyet obezbolivayushchikh: No painkillers. (Russian) 'nyet abizbollevishigch'
Ome: Uncle, 'ohme'
Ach, onze liefe heertje: Oh, our baby Jesus (slang for our little gentleman), 'agch onseh liefeh hearyeh'
Op Bezoek: For a visit, 'Op bazook'
Opa: Grandfather
Opyat' taki?: Again? (Russian) 'upyet tohkee'
Ouwe loren: Old used things to take for resale, which can include clothing. 'owe loren'
Pannenkoeken: Dutch crepes, punninkookin'
Paraplu: Umbrella, 'parapleeu'. Similar to the French, *parapluie*

Patates frites: French fries, 'pahtaht freet'
Pietje: Little Peter, 'Peetye'
Prikkeldraad: Barbed wire. 'prickledraht'
Prins: Prince, 'prints'
Prost: Cheers, 'proast'
Radio Oranje: Radio Orange, 'rahdio orahnyeh'
Regeering: Governing body, 'raygheering'
Regeeringsgebouwen: Government Buildings
Reichskommissar: Reich Commissioner, 'riegh commissioner'
Schatje: Little darling, 'srgruhtye'
Scheisse: Shit (German), ‚scheyeseh'
Schnell: Quickly, (German) 'shnel'
Schon: Beautiful (German) 'sheun'
Ses en een kwart: Six and a quarter, 'sess en ain kvaardt'
Sinterklaas: Santa Clause, 'sintarklaas'
S'jonge: Of boy, a figure of speech, 'shyongeh'
Sonderbauten: Special buildings, German referring to the brothels in Auschwitz, 'sohnarbowtin'
Spekulaasjes: Little cinnamon/ginger/ clove cookies, 'speckyoulaashyes'
Spinozastraat: Spinoza Street, a street in the center of The Hague
Sta nu op: Stand up now, 'stah neu ohp'
Stom: Dumb, 'stohm'
Stront: Shit, 'strohnd'
Tante: Aunt, 'tunteh'
Tomatensoep: tomato soup, 'toemahtensoop'
Tom poesjes: Tom kittens, custard-filled phyllo pastry with black and white icing on top, 'tohm pooshyes'
Tram: Trolley car, 'trem'
Vader Jacob: Father Jacob, a Dutch rendition of Frere Jacque, 'faadahr yahkup'
Van der Heem: A manufacturer of radios until 1966, when it was sold to Philips.
Vies: Dirty, 'fees'
Volgetje: Little bird, 'foeghehtye'
Voorzichtig: Careful, 'forsightigh'

W.C.: Slang for washroom, literally w.c., 'way say'
Wat: What, 'wot'
Wehrmacht: The unified army of Nazi Germany, 'vermacht'
Willem de Zwijger: William the Silent, 'willem de sweigher'
Worst: Sausage, 'worhst'
Zes en een kwart: Six and a quarter, 'zes en ain quart' (Nickname for Arthur Seyss-Urquart because of his limp)
Zuster: Sister, 'zeuhstar'

BOOKS FORTHCOMING BY LIESJE WAGNER

TENANT WOES, TENANTS' WOES

A LANDLORD'S EAST COAST EVERYDAY HEROES

FOR MORE INFORMATION, CONTACT:
Publisher, Tina Assanti Books: tinaassantibooks@gmail.com
Author, Liesje Wagner: dollivertwist2014@gmail.com
www.TinaAssantiBooks.com
1 844 244-4822

www.ingramcontent.com/pod-product-compliance
Lightning Source LLC
Chambersburg PA
CBHW072142100526
44589CB00015B/2054